THE LONG SHADOW
OF WATERLOO

Myths, Memories and Debates

TIMOTHY FITZPATRICK

CASEMATE

Oxford & Philadelphia

Published in Great Britain and the United States of America in 2019 by
CASEMATE PUBLISHERS
The Old Music Hall, 106–108 Cowley Road, Oxford OX4 1JE, UK
and
1950 Lawrence Road, Havertown, PA 19083, USA

Hardcover Edition: ISBN 978-1-61200-761-8
Digital Edition: ISBN 978-1-61200-762-5 (ePub)

A CIP record for this book is available from the British Library

Printed and bound in the UK by TJ International

Typeset in India for Casemate Publishing Services. www.casematepublishingservices.com

For a complete list of Casemate titles, please contact:

CASEMATE PUBLISHERS (UK)
Telephone (01865) 241249
Email: casemate-uk@casematepublishers.co.uk
www.casematepublishers.co.uk

CASEMATE PUBLISHERS (US)
Telephone (610) 853-9131
Fax (610) 853-9146
Email: casemate@casematepublishers.com
www.casematepublishers.com

Front cover: Top image: Orlando Norie, 'Ces terribles chevaux gris as Napoléon designated the
Royal Scots Greys … at Waterloo' (1880) (*Prints, Drawings and Watercolors from the
Anne S. K. Brown Military Collection.* Brown Digital Repository. Brown University
Library).
Bottom image: Tourists visiting the battlefield by Waterloo, 1835 (unknown artist,
Creative Commons License).

Contents

Introduction

The battle of Waterloo changed the world. The world changed Waterloo. Few battles in history can be described as so decisive and complete in their geo-political consequences. It marked the end of nearly a century of war between France and Great Britain and ushered in an era of peace. Waterloo was significant because, for some countries involved, the story of Waterloo became a part of their national identity. This work attempts to understand how the battle of Waterloo was interpreted and how it served the political needs of various factions within the countries involved during the 19th century. Historians have focused on the military operations of the campaign and how the battle unfolded. This book does something else: it looks at the battle over the memory and meaning of Waterloo.

The purpose of this book is to provide a clearer understanding of how the history of the battle was made and its impact on Waterloo. This approach to Waterloo is multinational and thematic. It was refought many times in books and in art during the 19th century for various political purposes. This work hopes to shed light on why it mattered so much to refight the battle so many times. Waterloo became a prism through which nations could construct their own national myths and identities. Each of the nationalities or political factions within those nations had the same problem regarding their national identity. How could the interpretation of the battle of Waterloo be made to serve their political needs? Each country came up with different solutions on how to fit the battle within their national community's identity. To some nations, the battle was extremely important, while for others, less so.

For Great Britain, Waterloo was the culmination of nearly 100 years of warfare against France. Waterloo became a symbol of British hegemony.

The victory at Waterloo has often been called the furnace in which forged the bond of the English, Scots, Welsh and Irish into one people called the Britons.[1] Under the leadership of the British upper class, Britain had prevailed against the self-made man, Napoléon. To magnify the victory, the Duke of Wellington propagated the myth of the battle as a 'near-run thing', the British were outnumbered by a huge French army bent on the annihilation of Great Britain. It was the spirit, determination, efficiency, character and will of both Wellington and his men that secured victory from the jaws of defeat. British moral character was tested – and emerged triumphant. France had the most problems dealing with the defeat at Waterloo. After nearly conquering all of Europe, France was prostrate at the hands of the allies. France was occupied and made to pay for both occupation and war reparations. Waterloo was known in France for most of the 19th century as the 'catastrophe' by men like Victor Hugo. After Waterloo, they blamed each other for the loss not the British or the Germans. Waterloo was a divisive topic for French national identity. Waterloo marked the end of the dream of uniting Europe under France's leadership. It became the 'lost cause'.

The battle of Waterloo was not used as a symbol of unity in Germany. The German states of the 19th century saw the battle of Leipzig as the most important victory of the Napoléonic Wars. It became a symbol of German military virtue. The battle of Leipzig was called the 'Battle of Nations'. It was the largest battle of the Napoléonic Wars, and the Germans viewed Leipzig as the most significant victory to the end of Napoléon's empire. The Germans celebrated Napoléon's defeat and many Germans called it the birthplace of modern Germany. The Germans sought national unity in the memory of Leipzig, through the Leipzig memorial, called the *Völkerschlachtdenkmal*. The monument was started in 1863 and completed in 1913 for the 100th anniversary of the battle.[2] The monument was paid for by donations from across Germany and was dedicated to the spirit of the German people. Guarding the 300-foot monument at its entrance is a massive statue of the Archangel Michael that unites all Germans under God.[3] The most critical element that made Leipzig more important than Waterloo was because Leipzig was in Germany. Waterloo, even for the

Germans of the 19th century, became a British, not a German, victory.[4] Leipzig was more important to the Germans than Waterloo.

The problem for the Belgians was the opposite one faced by the Germans. The battlefield was in its territory and yet it was not a unifying force for the Kingdom of the United Netherlands. Belgium was part of the newly formed country and it was only united tenuously. The kingdom was divided in two parts – Belgium and the Netherlands. The Netherlands was protestant and spoke Dutch; Belgium was Catholic and spoke mostly French. Belgium had been part of Napoléon's France and had divided loyalties during the 1815 campaign. Many of the troops in the Dutch-Belgian army had served in Napoléon's army. For 15 years, the King of the United Netherlands, William I, tried to use the battle to unify his nation, but to no avail.

William wanted to make a monument to reflect his new kingdom. He transformed the battlefield by erecting an earthen mound and placing a huge statue of a lion on the top of it. It was called the Lion's Mound. The monument was dedicated to the Prince of Orange, the king's son, to commemorate the place where he was wounded in the battle. William I thought it would please his new country's ally, Great Britain, by using a lion to symbolise the victory. It, and the memory of Waterloo, failed to bring Belgium and the Netherlands together. Indeed, constant bickering between the Walloons, Flemings and Dutch over their respective conduct during the Waterloo campaign led to disagreements and eventually led to the revolution of 1830. William I alienated the people of Belgium with the Lion's Mound monument and annoyed the French. Waterloo is in the Walloon region of Belgium and it has cultural and linguistic ties to France. William I underestimated how the people of Belgium would react to a monument that celebrated France's defeat.

Brussels was a leading destination of those exiled after Napoléon's abdication in 1815. Revolutionaries like Jacques-Louis David and Napoléonic generals like Étienne Gérard settled in the large exile community in Brussels. These exiles detested the monument and fomented a revolution against the government. By 1830, the Kingdom of the United Netherlands had split into two separate nations over various internal divisions, one of which was the Lion's Mound Monument at Waterloo.

This work will focus in greater detail on Great Britain's and France's struggles with their national identity regarding Waterloo. For those two countries, how did the battle of Waterloo help form their national identities? The battle between Wellington's and Napoléon's myths and legends never really ended in 1815. Both men struggled until their respective deaths to control the information, interpretation and history of the battle. The two men viewed themselves as mythical heroes who needed to write their own versions of events for posterity. Both men were legends to their followers, and those followers fiercely defended their idols' respective version of events. Even today, those myths and legends are important to understanding the national identities of both Great Britain and France.

However, both countries' versions were challenged by others and by their own countrymen. For instance, the British army was not British but an allied force of Germans, British and Dutch Belgians. The British myth and legend also had to account for the Prussians' role in the victory. Were they or were they not essential for victory? Wellington's interpretation was directly challenged by the man who was supposed to aid the understanding of the battle by building a model – William Siborne. Napoléon's version of the battle had even greater challenges to overcome; Napoléon's account of who was responsible and how the battle was lost was directly contradicted by one of his most loyal and able lieutenants – Marshal Emmanuel de Grouchy.

Waterloo was celebrated by Britain in the 19th century. Britain's commemoration of the battle was more triumphant than solemn. Waterloo became a symbol of British greatness that during the 19th century spread across the world. Waterloo became synonymous with British victory and hegemony. Wherever the British went in the 19th century a new town or city was called either Wellington or Waterloo.[5]

However, France's way of commemorating the battle was very different and much more solemn in tone. They chose to commemorate the heroism of the day with poetry, painting and novels. There is not a French monument to Napoléon at Waterloo.[6] It was not until the 20th century that a French monument was dedicated on the battlefield.[7] For the French, the battle was a place where heroes died while defying the world.

In this work, I will demonstrate how different perspectives are useful in understanding the battle of Waterloo. By combining several historians' methodologies, I will explore the myths and legends of the battle and the people who made them. It will examine the challenges people faced in fighting the myths, legends and national identities.

In the first chapter, I will focus on the myth of Waterloo from the allied and Bourbon perspectives. Starting with Wellington's account of the battle that was famously called the 'Waterloo Dispatch', Wellington tried to control the memory of the battle by writing it himself. In contrast to Wellington's account were the accounts of Marshal Gebhard Blücher and his chief of staff General August Gneisenau. They simply praised the Prussian army for winning the battle, while Wellington barely mentioned their efforts. The Bourbons also created a version of Waterloo. The Bourbons viewed themselves as paternalistically protecting the people. Waterloo, according to the Royalists, was an act of treason against them and the people. Those responsible for treason had to be held accountable. They used trials as an act of retribution to purge the army of the Bonapartists and regain control of the army. Through the trials of Marshal Michel Ney and General Charles de la Bédoyère, the Bourbons unintentionally ended up making martyrs of the two men.

In Chapter 2, I will examine the reasons why Napoléon chose to blame his subordinates for losing the battle. Critical to the myth of Napoléon was the work of his biographers who accompanied him to the island of Saint Helena. It was at Saint Helena where one of the most enduring legends of the battle of Waterloo was woven: Marshal Emmanuel de Grouchy was responsible for losing the battle of Waterloo.

The third chapter deals with Grouchy's response to the Napoléonic myth and legend; Marshal Grouchy fought a lifelong battle to defend himself from criticism for the loss of the battle. The problem for Napoléon was that Grouchy was one of the most decorated officers in the entire French army and a veteran of almost every campaign of the Napoléonic Wars. Indeed, until Waterloo, Napoléon considered Grouchy one of his most loyal and best generals.

In the fourth chapter, the views of two military theorists are examined, underscoring how not all approached Waterloo from the 'myth and legend' perspective. The military theorists Antoine-Henri Jomini and Carl von Clausewitz wanted to discover what was the objective 'truth' of Waterloo. They did so by using two different methods. Jomini tried explaining the battle of Waterloo along scientific lines, while Carl von Clausewitz's conclusion was the outcome of war was based on chance. Clausewitz introduced the idea of the fog and friction of war. His simple analysis was the French made more mistakes than the allies or Prussians and thus lost the campaign.

In the fifth chapter, I examine the life and works of Victor Hugo to demonstrate how the myth and legend of Napoléon affected the French before and after Waterloo. For men of Hugo's generation, Waterloo became a source of shame and pride. Hugo's family was directly tied to the Napoléonic legend and found a way to admire Napoléon but not be trapped by his Bonapartist legacy. Victor Hugo was able, through writing of perhaps his greatest novel, *Les Misérables,* to win the battle of Waterloo for France by transforming the defeat into a crucible from which a republic would ultimately emerge. The soldiers of Waterloo were the martyrs of France. They were the paragons of the republic. Sacrifice was a national virtue – they were essence of *Le Peuple.*

Chapter 6 explores how the legends and myths of the battle were visualised. The British myth of Waterloo was scripted by Wellington. Three men were instrumental in establishing Wellington's heroic vision. The bard of the legend of Waterloo for the British was Sir Walter Scott. Scott wanted his readers to be able to imagine they were actually at Waterloo, either through his poetry or in his prose. William Siborne created models of the battle. But in his pursuit of historical accuracy, they did not conform to Wellington's version of the battle. He ran afoul of Wellington and was nearly ruined. He was a victim of Waterloo; a rare British martyr of Waterloo. In contrast, Henry Barker chose to depict the battle in a panorama that conformed to Wellington's account and incorporated Scott's work. It made a fortune. However, there were other reasons to represent Waterloo visually.

For those visiting the battlefield, one cannot help but notice the Lion's Mound. This huge monument dedicated to Prince of Orange's wounded arm is the visual symbol of Waterloo today. It was hoped the monument would become a symbol of national unity for the Kingdom of the United

Netherlands. Instead, it was hated by Wellington and nearly torn down several times. Yet, it is still the most memorable monument of Waterloo.

The final chapter examines how Waterloo changed during the 20th and 21st centuries to accommodate its commemoration despite two world wars. The first of these 20th-century commemorations was the *Panorama of Waterloo*, painted by the French artist Louis Dumoulin in 1912, which depicted the grand French cavalry charge or, for the artist, the moment in which France might have won. The battle of Waterloo was as much a real event as it was an abstract idea. The battle of Waterloo was on the minds of people of the 19th and early 20th centuries, but especially in France and Britain. For the 2015 commemoration, there was an intense competition for the role of Napoléon between two passionate reenactors for the commemoration. This chapter underscores how the impressions of Waterloo developed and are maintained today.

All these visualisations of Waterloo, from Napoléon's version of the battle to Louis Dumoulin's panorama and the 21st-century reenactments, had one thing in common. They all tried to get people to believe in a particular version of the battle, even if it meant leaving things out, lying, making things up or forgetting key aspects of the campaign. Over the two centuries since the battle, these versions were changed, debated and some were forgotten. However, for what may be the most enduring monument to Waterloo, people were offered many choices of which version or visualisation to believe. Many histories of the battle of Waterloo have been written, but this work tells a different story. It highlights the battles over the history of Waterloo.

CHAPTER ONE

Nationalism and Waterloo

Soon after the battle of Waterloo ended, debates started to emerge on exactly what had just happened and why. The political ramification was clear; Napoléon's defeat ended his bid to re-establish his empire. Debates focused on who, what and why things happened during the 'Hundred Days' of Napoléon's return to power. In 1810, France was at its height of its power, but five years later, it had lost all it had fought for. There was a sense France had lost its honour and its place in the world. If Napoléon won, perhaps France could have regained at least its national honour.

After Waterloo, France was humiliated, the allies occupied Paris and France had to pay the allies for the wars in which they said France started. In 1814, Louis XVIII did not seek revenge for the revolution or Napoléonic era. However, after Waterloo, he was determined to control his own country. He ordered trials for those who rose against him. As for Napoléon, he was finished but not his son – he hoped Napoléon II would return to rule France. From 1815, there were debates, trials and books written to help France cope with what had just happened. The name of what the battle was to be known as became a matter of debate between the major combatants. The British called the battle 'Waterloo' after the location where Wellington wrote the dispatch announcing the victory to Britain. The Prussians called the battle 'La Belle Alliance' after the place where Blücher and Wellington met at the end of the battle. The French called the battle 'Mont Saint Jean' because the village of Mont-Saint-Jean was in the centre of Wellington's line. The battle became known as Waterloo because Wellington made the case the British won the battle before the Prussians effectively intervened.

Louis XVIII by François Gérard (unknown, public domain)

In the British version of events, the battle was a 'near-run thing', ultimately won by British determination, steadfastness and moral character. The battle was a defensive struggle, but it was not the British who bore the brunt of the fighting. The reality was that on 18 June 1815, the bulk of Wellington's army consisted of Germans and Dutch-Belgians. Less than half of the Anglo-Allied force consisted of British troops. However, as history proved out, the laurels of victory went to the British. The downfall of Napoléon was popularly portrayed as an act of supreme courage by the British – not of their allies or the Prussians.

Wellington depicted himself as being hopelessly outnumbered but was still able to defeat the French and managed to hold on long enough until the Prussians arrived. Nothing could be further from the truth. Wellington fought the battle of Waterloo in full knowledge the Prussians would arrive on Napoléon's right flank with at least two, and possibly three, corps. The only reason the battle was, according to Wellington, a 'near-run thing' was

Napoléon II, also known as Franz Duke of Reichstadt by the Austrian painter Leopold Bucher (1797–1858) (Malmaison, Musée national des châteaux de Malmaison et Bois-Préau, public domain)

because Blücher was late. However, even before Blücher's belated entrance, Wellington slightly outnumbered Napoléon. Wellington's 'Waterloo Dispatch' was a political report to his superiors in London, and he knew it would be the basis for the future interpretation of the battle. Wellington wanted his version to be first in London and the one remembered. It was to be a British victory.

The British were responsible for blunting Napoléon's attacks, but it was the Prussians who aggressively attacked and ultimately overwhelmed the French. The Prussian accounts credited Marshal Blücher's decision to unite with Wellington after his own defeat at Ligny on 17 June as the decisive decision of the campaign. The Prussians credited the arrival of Bülow's men early in the afternoon on 18 June with preventing the French from launching an all-out assault on the British early in the battle. It was Blücher's appearance on the battlefield later in the afternoon with two more corps that turned the battle into a stunning victory. Even though Blücher was late, Bülow was early and saved the British from being attacked by the whole of the French army.

The British got the credit for winning the battle and moreover the war; they imprisoned Napoléon on Saint Helena and their version of events spread around the world. The world would call the battle Waterloo. It was now up to the men who fought it – or did not fight in it, as the case may be – to relate how the British and Prussians won the battle and how the French lost it. Judging from the divergent accounts, those causes varied by nationality and personality. When the battle at the village of Mont Saint Jean,[1] near the town of Waterloo, was over early in the morning of 19 June 1815, the exhausted Arthur Wellesley, Duke of Wellington, headed to the Brabant Inn in the town of Waterloo, some miles north of the battle site. His purpose: to write to the British Secretary of State for War and the Colonies, Henry Bathurst, the 3rd Earl of Bathurst, on the victory and present his own version of the battle. When *The Times* published the contents of Wellington's dispatch on Thursday 22 June, the British populace burst into celebration.[2] The dispatch was read and re-read in *The Times* and the excitement of the victory was palpable in Britain. The famous moment was captured in David Wilkie's painting – *Chelsea Pensioners Reading the Waterloo Dispatch*. The nation was united in relief that Napoléon was defeated.

Wellington's 'Waterloo Dispatch' started with Napoléon's movements on 15 June at Charleroi, his subsequent crossing of the Sambre River and the action forcing Dutch troops back to Quatre Bras on the same day. On 16 June, Wellington praised the Prussians for holding out against the French, despite being outnumbered.[3] He also claimed not to be able to help his allies on 16 June because his men were being attacked and they had too far to march to assist the Prussians under Marshal Gebhard Blücher.[4]

In his dispatch, Wellington expressed surprise that Napoléon made no attempt to pursue the defeated Prussians on the night of 16 June. He noted the French in his own sector were timid in the face of his patrols and he was able to retire towards Waterloo unmolested on 17 June. Wellington confirmed Blücher's promise to him of at least one or more corps via the Ohain and Wavre road to aid him against the French. Wellington admitted he made a mistake of believing only the French III Corps (Vandamme's) followed Blücher towards Wavre.

Wellington's account in *The Times* naturally praised his troops. He singled out the defence of Hougoumont as critical to the success of the battle. He wrote that his generals conducted themselves in the most steadfast and distinguished manner. He lauded Major General Sir William Ponsonby for capturing an eagle (a French flag standard) and taking many prisoners. He also praised Generals Cooke, Maitland and Byng of the Grenadier Guards for their handling of their troops.

The dispatch noted Wellington's army suffered many casualties in the action. He reported with deep regret to the king the loss of his most able generals, Lieutenant General Thomas Picton. Wellington reported the arm wound of His Royal Highness the Prince of Orange and thanked him for his services on the day. Henry Paget, the Earl of Uxbridge, lost his leg at the end of the battle. Wellington reported that Colonel De Lancey was killed in the action by a cannon ball but was mistaken the ball had only wounded the Colonel.

Wellington described the battle during the afternoon as being a piecemeal affair. The cavalry and infantry took turns attacking. According to Wellington, the affair went along like this 'till seven in the evening, when the enemy made a desperate effort with the cavalry and infantry, supported by the fire of artillery, to force our left centre near the farm of La Haye Sainte, which after a severe contest was defeated'.[5] He added the Prussians' arrival on his left near Ohain was fortunate and General Friedrich von Bülow's arrival at Plancenoit helped Wellington make up his mind to order a general attack on the French army. The attack by British troops, proved successful and crucial. He met Blücher at La Belle Alliance and let the Prussians continue the pursuit of the enemy because of the extreme fatigue of his own troops. The Prussians captured nearly 60 additional cannons to add to his 150 captured French guns. In symbolic celebration, Wellington sent Sir Henry Percy with the dispatch and two of Napoléon's eagles and laid them at the Prince Regent's feet. Wellington's report finished with two postscript notes: first, General Ponsonby had been killed; and, second, Colonel De Lancey was wounded but still alive.[6]

In the same edition of *The Times*, the official report of the British government appeared. This account offered a much harsher interpretation of the battle. It acknowledged the fine abilities of the 'rebel' Frenchmen, but they were met on the field of battle by their 'betters'. Like the battles in the Peninsular campaign, superior British arms once again won the day over the Frenchmen.

Also, on 22 June, Wellington wrote another epistle, this time addressed to the King of the Netherlands. He begged the king's pardon for not presenting himself in person but explained he was busy following Napoléon. Wellington was careful to stress to the king that the Prince of Orange acted in the best possible manner.[7]

The British government loathed Napoléon and called him 'Buonaparte' in disparagement. They wrote he was a cowardly 'calculating kind' of man who chose to run rather than fight. They argued his abdication at Fontainebleau the year before was simply a ploy to fight again and save himself. They wanted to see Napoléon's officers brought to justice: Marshals Michael Ney and Emmanuel Grouchy, Generals Charles Desnouettes, Bertrand Clausel, Charles and Henri Lallemand, and Charles de la Bédoyère.[8] The British government accused these men of helping Napoléon before 20 March 1815, of committing high treason and deserving of the death penalty. Not surprisingly, Louis XVIII's government followed the advice of the British.

Waterloo resulted in immediate financial gains for many British subjects. The London stock market gained six per cent upon receiving news of the victory. Apparently, a 'Mr. Sutton' procured a faster route back to England from Brussels than did Major Percy and conveyed the news to certain businessmen who were able to capitalise on the news.[9]

The British government rejoiced at the news of the victory; however, it was tempered by the loss of many good men. Two much-admired British Generals, Sir Thomas Picton and the Duke of Brunswick, died in the battle. For the Duke of Wellington, he had nothing but praise for their bravery and skill.

In another letter to Earl Bathurst, Wellington wrote he was continuing into France on 22 June. He mentioned the Prussians took the fortress of Avesnes and the French retreated to Laon in a terrible state. The French forces occupied Wavre until 20 June and then escaped via Namur and Dinant. At the time, Wellington thought this French force was comprised only of III Corps and thus of minor importance.[10] Wellington did point out the French state of affairs was so bad following his victory that the French cavalry and artillery drivers were selling their horses to the French peasants and deserting.[11] He added Colonel De Lancey was not dead and predicted (incorrectly) that he would recover from his wounds.

News broke on 22 June in London of rumours of an uprising in Paris against Napoléon. By 22 June, Napoléon had abdicated for the second time, but the news had not reached London. The British government knew support for Napoléon would not last long if he was defeated on the battlefield. The victory of Waterloo was welcome news to a nation at war with France for roughly 20 years. The British government and people hoped for a lasting peace that affirmed their place as masters of Europe and the world.

The Times articles and the 'Waterloo Dispatch' on 22 June 1815 were critical for constructing the British official history of the battle. Wellington's dispatch and the government's public statements established the tone and approach through which the battle would be interpreted by the British for nearly 200 years. The British account took credit for the victory, while downplaying the multinational contribution to the battle. The battle was both real and symbolic for Britain. Waterloo became a symbol of British hegemony both over France and other European nations. The effect of defeating Napoléonic France allowed Britain to establish and control a global empire. The British official history contrasted with the Prussian account in several areas, most notably, what to call the battle.

The Prussians thought the battle should be called La Belle Alliance to reflect the multinational character of the fighting. La Belle Alliance inn was the meeting place between Blücher and Wellington on the night of 18 June. It represented the meeting of two of the two allies and their relationship; it was a beautiful alliance between Britain and Prussia. The Prussians thought this battle was won by teamwork and it took both powers to defeat France. The other reason was it reflected the entire alliance of Austria, Russia, Spain, Prussia and Britain to defeat France.

On the morning of 19 June, Marshal Gebhard Blücher wrote a proclamation to his men to be read to battalion of the *Armée du Rhin* for their role in the campaign's final battle. He commended them on their courage for having fought two battles in three days. He extolled the men's virtue, despite losing a difficult battle, they had marched hard to fight another. He thanked the men for believing both in God and in the commanders of

Marshal Ney by François Gérard (Christie's, public domain)

their army. Blücher recognised the importance of his men's contribution to the successful outcome of the battle: they had marched to the aid of the brave English and, in so doing, won a great victory. Blücher put the contest in these terms: 'The hour which was to decide this great struggle has struck, and has shown who was to give law, whether an adventurer or governments who are the friends of order.'[12]

Blücher praised his men for storming out of the woods at Plancenoit and into the rear of the enemy. He cited revenge as the motivation for the Prussian efforts, stressing only a few more days remained to finish off the enemy. Blücher ended with a final commendation: 'Never will Prussia cease to exist, while your sons and grandsons resemble you.'[13]

On the same day, Blücher wrote to his Excellency the Governor of Berlin, General Kalkreuth. He stated, in conjunction with the Duke of Wellington,

Charles de la Bédoyère (public domain)

he had won the most complete victory over Napoléon to be obtained. He wanted the battle to be called La Belle Alliance. He thought it fitting since he met Wellington during the battle.[14] He added a great quantity of artillery was taken and he would send news as soon as he could.

In a letter to his wife, written on 19 June 1815, he stated he was unwounded, but that two horses were shot from under him. He captured Napoléon's carriage and took his personal decorations. Blücher's son added that the embrace at La Belle Alliance between Wellington and his father was extremely touching and everyone present was affected. Blücher consoled his wife that the entire affair with Bonaparte would be soon over.[15]

Blücher seemed thrilled for his troops who profited from Napoléon's defeat. The Prussian 15th Infantry Regiment seized Napoléon's baggage train and his personal carriage, forcing him to flee on horseback.[16] Blücher noted several soldiers got between 500–600 gold coins each out of the carriage. As a trophy, Blücher sent Napoléon's hat and sword to the King of Prussia.[17] Besides Napoléon's personal carriage, the Prussians captured his state carriage and its eight cream-colored horses. The bounty did not stop there: 80 Arabian horses, numerous diamonds, Napoléon's baggage and his travelling 80-volume personal library were also taken.[18]

The official battle report of the *Armée du Rhin* under Marshal Gebhard Blücher's command for Waterloo was written by his chief of staff, General August Gneisenau.

According to the report, Blücher had four corps available to engage the French. On 15 June, these corps were located at Fleurus, Aucy, Namur and Hannut. Thus dispersed, they would be able to unite the entire army at any of these points within 24 hours.[19] Blücher had dispersed his corps like Napoléon's *bataillon carré*.[20] Blücher learned much from fighting Napoléon for nearly ten years. It was a tough education having often been defeated by Napoléon, but each time Blücher learned something new about Napoléon's way of war. During the Waterloo campaign, those lessons would pay off. The fighting began in the middle of June 1815. Blücher was ready.

General Hans Zieten's I Corps was attacked on 15 June near Fleurus: Blücher ordered his other three corps to Fleurus to support Zieten. Blücher was under the impression Wellington had concentrated his forces between Ath and Nivelles and he could count on support from Wellington on 16 June if a major action developed.

On 16 June, Blücher fought Napoléon at the battle of Ligny with the assumption Wellington would support him with at least a division and the better part of his reserves.

However, Blücher chose to give battle without one of his corps; Friedrich von Bülow's IV Corps. The report states the 80,000 Prussians faced 130,000 enemy troops. He thought the support would arrive soon and tip the balance in the Prussians' favour. However, news reached Blücher that the English division, who intended to support him, had been violently attacked by a French corps. Bülow's corps was delayed on the way to Ligny, and Blücher lamented it not arriving on 16 June. Blücher thought the battle of Ligny could have been won if those troops arrived.[21] Neither Bülow nor Wellington's men arrived.[22]

Blücher contended the decisive moment at Ligny occurred near the end of the battle when a French division surprised the Prussians and broke through their lines. The battle was lost, and the Prussians retreated northwards towards Tilly. Blücher ordered the Prussian cavalry to cover their retreat. He took personal command, almost being killed several times in the battle. The French did not pursue them, allowing an orderly retreat. The Prussians still held on to the villages of Sombreffe and Brie on the night of 16 June and allowed the rest of the army to slip away from the French. During the night of 16 June, the Prussian IV Corps arrived in Gembloux where the Prussian army was rallying to fight again.

According to Blücher, on 17 June, Wellington wrote to him for the support of two of his corps. Blücher replied he would bring his whole army. If Napoléon did not attack on 18 June, the two armies would attack in unison on 19 June. The IV and II Corps marched to Mont Saint Jean via Saint Lambert at daybreak with the II Corps proceeding via Ohain.

Blücher specified the battle at Mont Saint Jean started at 10a.m.

Gneisenau's report likewise estimated the French force facing Wellington at 130,000, compared to Wellington's force of 80,000. Gneisenau guessed Napoléon was trying to widen the gap between the Prussian and allied army by attacking the centre left of the allied army. He added the march from Saint Lambert was exceedingly difficult and it was only at 4.30p.m. that Bülow's men were able to enter onto the battlefield. At 6p.m., Blücher learned the Prussians under General Johann Thielmann were under attack at Wavre. Blücher decided to attack Napoléon's forces rather than try to save Thielmann.[23] Gneisenau credited General Zieten with the decisive attack that carried the battle. He reported Zieten's men charged the flank of the French troops near Papelotte, catching them in the middle of an attack on allied troops, 'This movement decided the defeat of the enemy.'[24] The French right was shattered. The general advance by Wellington's men, combined with the storming of Plancenoit, doomed the French army; the French were attacked from their front and their rear. At 9:30p.m., Blücher met with his senior commanders and ordered a general pursuit during the night. As there was a waxing gibbous moon that night, there was plenty of moonlight to chase down the fleeing French soldiers.[25] The Prussians claimed to have captured 40,000 men and nearly 300 cannons.

The French perspective took longer to develop than the British or Prussian one. To the French, it seemed the unimaginable had happened. The shock of losing so badly led to a search for answers and the apportioning of blame. The first report from the battlefield to reach Paris was the battle of Mont Saint Jean was a resounding victory, and Napoléon was on his way to Brussels.[26] Napoléon sent a message to Paris at 3p.m. on 18 June declaring, '*Veni, Vidi, Vici.*'[27] Marshal Louis Davout posted public placards in Paris confirming the victory:

> The Emperor has just obtained a complete victory over the Prussian and English armies united under the command of Lord Wellington and Marshal Blücher. The enemy experienced a dreadful overthrow. Wellington and Blücher saved themselves with difficulty. They were routed in all directions. We have already several thousand prisoners and 40 pieces of cannon. Prisoners every instant are announced. –Prince of Eckmühl, Minister of War.[28]

From 19 June to the morning of 21 June, the people of Paris believed Napoléon had won a great victory and all was well. The people of Paris did not suspect the defeated army and Napoléon were on their way to Paris from the battlefield. Rumours then began to spread a great calamity had beset Napoléon. Things were happening so quickly few people in Paris even knew Napoléon was back in Paris on 21 June.

On 21 June, the official news reached Paris of the defeat. The *Le Moniteur Universal's*[29] account of the battle tried to soften the defeat by calling it a glorious defeat. At 9a.m., the rain began to lessen, and preparations were made to start the battle. At about 11a.m., Napoléon's forces were ready to commence their attack. The I Corps was on the left and II Corps on the right, with the cuirassiers in reserve. The forces were nearly equal, with a slight advantage for the French, and the battle started well. The battle started at noon with an artillery duel. Prince Jerome's division led the attack on the left. At 1p.m., he held the woods on the left and attacked the chateau of Hougoumont. The affair went back and forth until the Prussians arrived. Georges Mouton Comte de Lobau's VI Corps held off a Prussian corps, which had escaped Marshal Grouchy. The French account estimated a total of 80,000 English and 15,000 Prussians were on the battlefield by 3p.m., with more Prussians arriving every moment. As the day progressed, the French became outnumbered nearly two to one.[30]

Things were going well, despite the odds being against the French army, until 8.30p.m., when the French efforts began to falter. The French cavalry had been badly deployed and decisive action could not be achieved, except by Marshal Grouchy who marched on the rear of the Prussians.[31] All that was left to do was to send in the guard and finish off the English troops who were exhausted. Four battalions of middle guard were deployed to carry the plateau of Mont Saint Jean. As they arrived, they took a fierce barrage by English troops and then were attacked by several squadrons of English cavalry on their flanks. The middle guard fell into disorder and retreated. Other French soldiers who witnessed this thought these men were the old guard. They called out to retreat, signalling a general panic. This panic lost the battle. The men cried 'All is lost! The guard is retreating! Save yourself!' The army panicked and melted away. It was a defeat but a glorious one.[32] Napoléon had been defeated and now was in Paris! Some Parisians wished him to assume command once again after establishing martial law in Paris. They wanted another campaign like 1814 but hoped for a different result.

When the news of defeat reached the Chambers (Peers and Representatives), in response and out of fear of their own position they declared themselves to be in permanent session. They feared Napoléon would make himself dictator and Napoléon could have taken the field again with the forces of Marshal Grouchy and the remnants of the men from Waterloo who were being rallied by Marshal Soult to continue the struggle. However, the defeat sealed Napoléon's political fate. The Chambers would not allow Napoléon to continue to fight the allies; he had had his chance to defeat the allies and he had failed.

Politics took over before Napoléon knew what to do. The Chambers would not follow Napoléon into another 1814 campaign, fearing it would only inflict hardship on the nation and devastate the north-eastern part of the country. Instead, they hoped to reinstall the king as soon as possible and make peace. Support for a military campaign evaporated. Napoléon remarked he doubted the outcome of another fight before Paris. He lamented, 'Grouchy is an honest man, but weak. Soult has been given his money.'[33] Louis-Joseph Marchand, Napoléon's valet, claimed Napoléon sent letters of reprimand on 21 June to both Marshals Ney and Grouchy for failing to comply with orders he sent to them.[34]

Napoléon chose to abdicate rather than fight. In his abdication, he expressed belief he could make France independent but admitted too many things were against him. He came back full of hope but circumstances had changed. Napoléon abdicated on 22 June in favour of his son. He would sacrifice himself for the nation. 'My political life is finished, and I proclaim my son, under the title of Napoléon II, Emperor of the French.'[35] It was a forlorn hope; the allies wanted to restore Louis XVIII to power. Minister of Police, Joseph Fouché took over the reins of the provisional government and tried to get the best possible deal for France – and himself – he could.

Napoléon decided to voluntarily go into exile, with the express purpose of writing a memoir and preserving his son's chances of succeeding him.[36] He took with him into exile numerous books to write his tale. He wanted books on Egypt, America and all the books written on his campaigns. He also wanted a complete copy of the *Moniteur*, as well as the most thorough and reliable encyclopedia and dictionary.[37] He wanted to write his own history.

On 25 June, Napoléon, Jerome, Lucien and Joseph Bonaparte gathered in Paris where they agreed to go to America. Napoléon went to Malmaison to arrange for passage to the United States via Rochefort. A ship was waiting for him and he could have easily boarded and set sail for America, but he hesitated and dithered on what to do. Lucien had already backed out of the plan and Jérôme went to his wife. Joseph convinced Napoléon to join him in Rochefort. Napoléon arrived at Rochefort on 3 July and could have set sail on a ship Joseph had chartered called the *Commerce*. Joseph even offered to act as a decoy for Napoléon while he made his escape since the two looked so much alike. Napoléon brushed aside his brother's request saying to one of Joseph's aides:

> Tell King Joseph that I have given his proposal careful consideration. I cannot accept. It would be flight. I could not leave without my staff, all of whom are devoted to me. My brother my do so; he is not in my position. I cannot. Tell him to leave immediately. He will make a safe landing. Goodbye.[38]

Napoléon took a calculated risk the British would let him go into exile in England.[39] Napoléon was invited by British Captain Frederick Maitland to board HMS *Bellerophon*. Napoléon accepted and voluntarily became a prisoner on 15 July 1815. However, Napoléon was offered no deal to go to England or America. He was offered his life, nothing more, and to avoid arrest by Louis XVIII's agents. He was heading not to England but to Saint Helena in the middle of the Atlantic. There, he would write his official account of what happened at Waterloo.

The issue facing France and Great Britain was the legitimacy of the French government. Napoléon's rapid return and the utter collapse of the Bourbon government made it clear without allied, and British, support the Bourbon government could fall. When the allies installed the Bourbons in 1814, they thought Louis XVIII could handle France. The second time around, they made sure Napoléon could not return. Louis returned to Paris on 8 July 1815 accompanied by the allies. Napoléon and some in the provisional government hoped a deal could be made to make Napoléon's son the next ruler of France, but Britain refused and insisted Louis XVIII be restored to power. The Second Treaty of Paris (1815) was harsh and France would have to pay for its own occupation for up to five years and make reparations to the victorious powers. Louis' first task was how to find the vast sum of money. Remarkably, he was able to find the money and pay the allies to leave France by 1818. However, the fact remained the Bourbons were a relatively unpopular government imposed on France by the allies after Waterloo. There was a brief period in which the Royalists sought revenge on the Bonapartists in what was called the 'White Terror'.[40] Support for the Bourbons was lukewarm at best, but they did keep the peace. Bonapartists were quick to point out the fact the Bourbons were not the true choice of the people and Republicans and Bonapartists could agree the Bourbons were not the legitimate rulers of France. By losing at Waterloo, France was humiliated, but the real disgrace, according to the Bonapartists, was Louis XVIII being restored as the King of France. Many in Britain agreed with that point of view, but they also did not want to see a Bonaparte, Napoléon or his son, ruling France. The allies would maintain the peace at any price. Louis' second task was how to deal with the men who betrayed him in 1815.

The Bourbon's version of Waterloo was that it was illegal and an unnecessary waste of soldiers' lives. According to the Bourbons, the military adventurer Bonaparte had caused severe harm to France with the battle of Waterloo. The military was responsible for harming the people and Waterloo was an

Nicolas Soult by George Peter Alexander Healy (15 July 1813–24 June 1894) (public domain)

act of treason against the king and the people. The Bourbons had to protect the people from the leaders of the military who allowed Napoléon to regain power in 1815. A purge of Bonapartists from the military was ordered to regain control of it. The Bourbons would punish those leaders and would protect the people from further acts of violence.

Marshals Michael Ney, Nicolas Soult, and Emmanuel Grouchy were wanted men in July 1815. On 24 July, Louis XVIII issued an order for the arrest of several leading men who had joined Napoléon. Other men included on the list were Henri Bertrand, Jean-Baptiste Drouet, Régis Mouton-Duvernet, Antoine Drouot, Charles de la Bédoyère, Pierre Cambronne, and Charles and Henri Lallemand. Most of the condemned men or leading Bonapartists escaped by going into hiding or went into exile. Gérard and Exelmans went to Brussels. Grouchy and Vandamme went to the United States. However, some remained, La Bédoyère and Ney were arrested and put on trial.

Napoléon on the Bellerophon *at Plymouth* by Sir Charles Lock Eastlake (1815). Eastlake was rowed out to the *Bellerophon* to make sketches, from which he later painted this portrait (National Maritime Museum, public domain)

Colonel Charles de la Bédoyère was one of the first to feel the wrath of Louis XVIII and his ministers. The king had a problem: the French army had willingly sided with Napoléon during the Hundred Days. How was he to control the army? He had to make examples of some of those who, according to the Royalists, had betrayed the king, the army and the people. He chose La Bédoyère, a minor but promising young officer who helped Napoléon on his march to Paris. La Bédoyère defended himself at his trial by arguing that since the king fled to the Netherlands and abandoned France, he no longer had to honour any oath he swore to serve him. Further, since Louis had not granted a free constitution, his allegiance was only to Napoléon. La Bédoyère was found guilty of treason and sentenced to be shot on the plain of Grenelle. He rejected the blindfold offered to him and advanced on the firing squad, declaring: 'Above all, do not miss me.'[41] The king wanted to show he was just, but instead he demonstrated he was petty. La Bédoyère died because of Waterloo.

Marshal Ney likewise paid the ultimate penalty for rallying to Napoléon. Soon after the 'usurper's' fall, Ney tried to plead his case to Minister Joseph Fouché; however, the king's ultra-royalist ministers wanted him arrested. Fouché gave him a passport to get out of the country, but he bungled his escape and was arrested on 8 August 1815. Ney faced court martial; however, the council of war would not try him. The king tried to get several marshals to sit in judgment of Ney. Marshal Bon-Adrien Moncey refused to be president of the court martial.[42] Once the court was assembled under Marshal Jean Jordan, the court martial could begin. The officers of the court martial were Marshals André Masséna, Pierre Augereau and Édouard Mortier and Generals Honoré Gazan, Michel Claparède and Eugène Vilatte. They debated the merits of the case and, before a judgment could be rendered, voted to recuse themselves and forwarded the matter to the Chamber of Peers.[43]

Ney's supporters circulated a pamphlet in Paris to defend the marshal's defection to Napoléon. The pamphlet claimed Ney remained loyal to Louis XVIII until the night of 13 March when he was told that England had engineered Napoléon's escape and Austria welcomed Napoléon's return to the throne of France. He received news of the King of Naples, Marshal Joachim Murat, and he was marching to Napoléon's aid; only Prussia objected to Napoléon's return. According to the pamphlet, Ney joined Napoléon only to prevent a civil war.[44]

In the Chamber of Peers, Ney was put on trial for treason from 21 November–7 December 1815. The Duke of Richelieu presided over the trial. Marshal Laurent de Gouvion Saint Cyr, the new Minister of War, pleaded with the king for clemency. In the Chamber of Peers, only Achille Victor, Duke of Broglie, spoke on Ney's behalf. The key to Ney's defence was the 12th article of the surrender of Paris, the formal negotiation to end hostilities between the Provisional Government and the Allies was signed 3 July 1815. The 12th article states:

> Shall be equally respected, persons and private property: the inhabitants, and in general, all the individuals who are in the capital, shall continue to enjoy their rights and liberty, without being disturbed, or sought after for anything relating to the functions they occupy, or shall have occupied, *their conduct and their political opinions.*

Ney argued the convention had been ratified by each of the allied sovereigns and as being the work of the two powers, the first delegated *de facto* to the second.[45] It acquired all the force that the sacred right of nations, the rights of nature and of persons could impart to it. It became the unalterable safeguard of all Frenchmen whom the misfortune of the trouble may have exposed to the legitimate resentment of their prince.[46]

However, the royal government argued the provisional government had no right to enter into agreements with anyone. The attorney general objected to the use of the treaty to defend Ney and the President of the Chamber sustained the objection.[47]

General Louis Bourmont was called as a witness for the prosecution. His version of events differed from Neys. He told the Chamber of Peers on the night of 13 March he was informed that the king left Paris and General Claude Lecourbe had protested the proclamation of 14 March.[48] Lecourbe opposed ordering Ney's troops to join Napoléon. Ney brushed his protests aside, insisting he too, had honour and, 'therefore, I will join him. I will not have my wife come back to every night with tears in her eyes, on account of ill treatment.'[49] According to Bourmont, Ney then signed the proclamation.

Ney was astonished at Bourmont's testimony. He told the Chamber of Peers, 'Bourmont has got his part.'[50] When he implored Bourmont to tell the truth that he agreed with the proclamation at the time, Bourmont shook his head no.[51]

General Étienne Heudelet was called as a witness for Ney. He confirmed that troops had already mutinied before 13 March in Dijon and the king had few supporters in the army. The defence also asked if Ney had enough men to successfully oppose Napoléon. Heudelet maintained that he did not.[52]

Soon the Chamber of Peers retired to deliberate. The verdict was 131 for death and 29 for banishment.[53] Bourmont had perjured himself but it did not matter; Ney was found guilty of treason. Bourmont's treachery was complete.

On the night of 7 December 1815, the marshal smoked a fine cigar, said his goodbyes to his wife and prepared to meet the firing squad. At 9a.m., near the Luxembourg gardens, at the wall of the observatory, the sentence was carried out.[54] Marshal Ney told the firing squad, 'My comrades, fire at me.'[55] Three bullets entered his head. What the British and Prussians could not accomplish at Waterloo, the French did themselves. Marshal Michael

General Bourmont (public domain)

Ney was dead.[56] He wrote no memoirs of his conduct of the battle of Waterloo. His family would release his papers in a book in 1834 entitled *Memoirs of Marshal Ney*, but it did not cover Waterloo.

In a final insult to La Bédoyère and Ney, their widows had to pay for the costs of their dead husband's trials and the executioners' bill – each of the men in the firing squads was paid three francs each by the widows.[57]

Marshal Nicolas Soult was in a perilous legal position in 1815. He had rallied to Napoléon and acted as his second in command. He had been Louis' Minster of War at the beginning of 1815. On 24 July, a royal ordinance proscribed many officers and charged him of revolt and treason.[58] In August of 1815, Soult immediately published a pamphlet to defend himself from accusations of revolt and treason against Louis XVIII. Far from being condemned for his actions, he expected the king to pardon him for them since he acted in good faith for France. In it, he claimed he was able to stop the bloodshed before Paris after Napoléon's abdication. He contended if it was a crime to fight the Prussians and the English at Ligny and Waterloo, then he was guilty.[59] As for his actions during the campaign, he remained silent, but on politics, he was more than willing to give his opinion. He argued he acted in the best interest of France and was not a political figure but an apolitical military one at the hands of politicians. He blamed Marshal Grouchy for wanting to continue the struggle, and he argued the honour of France depended on prompt submission to the King.[60]

However, Soult did have a problem with his appeal to Louis XVIII. Soult had vigorously prosecuted Rémi Exelmans for treason for acting with Marshal Joachim Murat, King of Naples, in January of 1815. Exelmans was found not guilty, but Soult made a strong case for those who were traitors to be punished severely. He stated his case was unlike Exelmans and his involvement with Napoléon during the Waterloo campaign was an entirely different matter.[61] He claimed to be more a victim than active participant in Napoléon's return to power.[62] The pamphlet explained his actions up to the battle and after the battle but completely avoided addressing his role in the battle.

Soult reminded the king he had tried to stop Napoléon before he arrived in Paris. He issued orders on 8 March 1815, to stop Napoléon at Lyon, calling him an adventurer and usurper.[63] Soult argued it was Ney who let Napoléon proceed to Lyon. He also sent a letter to Marshal Édouard Mortier to arrest Generals Charles Lallemand and Jean-Baptiste Drouet Comte d'Erlon.[64] In addition to these actions, he reminded the king he had left Paris to retire to the country with his family, devoid of any offices. He only accepted a position in the new government a month and a half after Napoléon was already running the government on 11 May 1815.[65] Soult insisted he was loyal to the king all the time and, despite the political hurricane, his conscience was clear.[66] He was able to make his legalistic argument stick and the Bourbons forgave him by 1819. He eventually was returned to his rank of marshal and made a peer by the Bourbons.

When Soult died in 1851, his son, Hector Soult, took on the task of publishing his memoirs, intending a five-volume series.[67] He published three volumes but never completed the fourth and fifth volumes. These volumes covered the Waterloo campaign and his father's political career after 1830. Hector left clues as to why the other volumes were not published.

Marshal Soult's memoirs revealed he had been to both Fleurus (Ligny) and Waterloo in 1794.[68] Nicolas Soult was present during the conquest of Belgium; Napoléon certainly knew this when he chose Soult to be his chief of staff for the Waterloo campaign in 1815. However, Soult's time in Belgium and relative familiarity with the area never seemed to benefit him during the Waterloo campaign of 1815. Neither Hector nor his father wrote publicly again on the topic of Waterloo. Ever the politician, Soult found it better to remain silent than to explain his actions.

Soult escaped the wrath of the Bourbons, but the Bourbons had given the Bonapartists unintentionally what they needed to claim the Bourbons were unjust and illegitimate by making martyrs of La Bédoyère and Ney. The Bonapartists insisted these trials were orchestrated by the British and Louis was just their puppet. Bourmont lied and few could see the justice in punishing La Bédoyère with death. The other trials quickly ended with acquittals for most of the men who were arrested in 1815. The Bourbon version of Waterloo failed at demonstrating the king as the protector of the people. He had accomplished his mission of purging the military of the Bonapartists but at a cost of his own legitimacy. Louis XVIII allowed most of the men of 1815 to come back home in 1819 after France had paid its war reparations to the allies and the occupation was over.

Wellington wanted to establish a history for his country that could be celebrated as a British victory. The British version of events commemorated and honoured Wellington and the British men who fought there. The Prussians wanted to document and honour the heroism of the men who fought against Napoléon and for the Fatherland. Louis XVIII's objective in ordering trials for those who collaborated with Napoléon was to restore order in his army. He also wanted to punish those responsible for Napoléon's return and discredit Bonapartism. Instead, the Royalists gave the Bonapartists martyrs to a 'lost cause'.

CHAPTER TWO

Napoléon's Myth and Legend of Waterloo

Napoléon could not remain silent, nor did he want to after Waterloo. He admitted his defeat at Waterloo ended his bid to re-establish his military and political career. What he hoped for was to create a history in which he could be shown to be a friend of the people and the army. He wanted a narrative that allowed his son to be able to regain the throne of France. As for Waterloo, this defeat was not his but his lieutenants'. If only his vision had been executed, then liberty and glory would have been restored to France. He hoped one day his followers would install his son to the throne.

The French account of Waterloo mirrored the British point of view in that it glorified Napoléon and supported Wellington's view that the battle was a 'near-run thing'. The foremost proponent of this view, besides Wellington, was Napoléon himself. It was close and should have been a French victory if not for the failings of his marshals. French authors tended to take a more negative view of their own countrymen, placing blame not on Napoléon but on Soult, Grouchy and Ney. The accounts coming from Saint Helena were consistent: Napoléon repeatedly blamed others, rather than taking responsibility for the defeat himself. He had six years on Saint Helena to ponder how he lost.

Napoléon's accounts on the island served to augment his military acumen at the expense of his marshals. As his servants took dictation, Napoléon knew he was shaping his place in history and how he would be perceived, despite of his defeat at Waterloo.

In 1815, Napoléon was head of state and head of the army. As both, he failed at Waterloo. Napoléon had run out of both armies and excuses. In 1812, he said the weather was against him. In 1813, he blamed his marshals for failing to properly execute his plans. In 1814, treason caused his downfall. In 1815, he used all three excuses to shift blame from himself. The pivotal battle and campaign were refought in public. The reaction by the men who were publicly blamed varied. Ney was dead by the time these accusatory accounts were released. Soult stayed silent about Waterloo. However, Grouchy and his descendants launched a public relations counter-offensive, spanning the next 60 years, to defend his honour. They fought an uphill battle against both the myth of Napoléon and his legend.

Napoléon started his narrative about Waterloo with a journey of glory, when he was welcomed back to France as a liberator from Bourbon tyranny. The road to Waterloo for Napoléon started with a bold plan. He escaped the isle of Elba, where he had been exiled for the last ten months, and invaded France with 600 men from his Old Guard. Napoléon landed on 1 March 1815 at the Gulf of Juan in the south of France. He marched to Gap, then to Grenoble on to Lyon and, finally, to Paris all the time counting on the popular support of the people.[1]

Along the way to Paris, several divisions of troops were sent against him. According to Joseph Fouché, Marshal Ney promised Louis XVIII to bring Napoléon back in an iron cage. Napoléon had to be both bold and careful. On 5 March, the 5th and 7th Regiments of Line were sent to arrest him near Grenoble. On 7 March, near Laffey, the 5th Regiment met Napoléon and his Old Guard. In a dramatic gesture, Napoléon stood between his Old Guard and the 6th Regiment and declared, 'Soldiers, you have been told that your Emperor fears death; the first man who pleases is at liberty to plunge his bayonet into this bosom.'[2] The response of the 6th was unanimous and immediate 'Vive l'Empereur!' The men joined Napoléon's ranks and marched on Paris. Soon the 7th Regiment would meet Napoléon.[3]

Colonel Charles de la Bédoyère[4] marched his 7th Regiment of the Line to meet Napoléon at Grenoble. He and his regiment defected to Napoléon on 8 March.[5] Every detachment sent out to stop Napoléon's march met a similar fate. By 11 March, Napoléon was in Lyon. At Auxerre on 17 March, Marshal Ney, instead of putting Napoléon in an iron cage, joined him. On

20 March, Napoléon entered Fontainebleau. On 21 March, commanding an army of nearly 100,000 national guardsmen, Marshal Soult could have opposed Napoléon outside of Paris near Melun. Again, Napoléon awed the men into submission without firing a shot. Marshal Soult, who now had no army, resigned as Minister of War. He was replaced by Henri Clarke Duke of Feltre. Upon hearing the news that Napoléon was once again in control of the French government, Britain and her allies set out to destroy Napoléon's new regime.

Napoléon assembled a new army in 1815, but on Saint Helena he declared that this new army lacked enthusiasm and its generals character. The 1814 campaign had dulled their abilities; both the soldiers and the generals had lost the audacity, resolution and confidence that had characterised the campaign.[6] Napoléon attributed the decline in no small measure to the betrayal by many of the marshals at the end of the 1814 campaign, particularly that of Marshal Auguste Marmont Duke of Ragusa.

In 1815, the troops were skeptical of their officers, and it was an army afraid of itself. Napoléon asserted in his correspondence, 'The treasons of 1814 were always present in their minds ... they were anxious ... they believed there was treason.'[7] They had reasons to be wary of their leaders. On 15 June 1815, General Louis Bourmont, along with some of his staff, Colonel Clouet and Major Villoutreys, went over to the allies as soon as they neared the Prussian army. After that, Marshal Soult, who was Napoléon's chief of staff during the 1815 campaign, ordered anyone caught deserting to be shot on sight. However, Napoléon noted this did not change the general mood of the army, which was in relatively good spirits, but it did make some soldiers anxious.[8]

One example of the level of anxiety about their officers was evident on the night of the battle of Waterloo when many of men of the 4th Division resorted to cries of 'Save yourself!' After fighting for hours to take La Haie Sainte from the British, the French soldiers were abandoned by their officers after the repulse of the Imperial Guard, and the Prussians easily retook the farmhouse. The French soldiers guarding La Haie Sainte were left with no orders or leadership; it was no wonder they felt betrayed.[9]

According to Napoléon, he had devised a brilliant plan to defeat the Prussians and British. Ultimately, the mistakes of his generals were to blame for the campaign's failure. First was Vandamme's delay. On 15 June,

Vandamme's III Corps was late, upsetting Napoléon's timetable. Napoléon had planned to have his entire army across the Sambre River on the morning of 16 June, but Vandamme's tardiness disrupted this move.

Napoléon also blamed Marshal Ney for two key mistakes. He should have taken Quatre Bras sooner.[10] Napoléon claims Ney was the one who had pointed out its importance; yet Ney had failed to take it as soon as he could have. Secondly,, Napoléon found fault with the way Ney deployed his men during the battle of Quatre Bras.

As for Grouchy, his 34,000 men should have been on the battlefield on 18 June. As Napoléon saw it, Grouchy was at fault for stopping at Gembloux on the night of 17 June. Napoléon blamed Grouchy for losing sight of Blücher's forces for 24 hours, between 17 and 18 June. In ordering the march to Wavre, Blücher broke an essential rule of war: when defeated, a general should retreat on his supply base.[11] Though the move proved strategically successful, Napoléon criticised Blücher for taking such a risk. If Blücher and Wellington had not won at Waterloo, Blücher would have been cut off from his supply base and lines of communication. His army could have been destroyed. This could have been achieved had Marshal Grouchy encamped at Wavre on the night of 17 June. From there, he could have blocked the Prussian Army from arriving, thus thwarting the allies' strategy.[12]

Napoléon thought Mont-Saint-Jean was a weak position; the English should not have chosen to fight there. The English fought with woods at their back, were separated from Bülow's Prussians and had few escape routes. The problem for the French was not strategy; it was a failure of Napoléon's subordinate leadership.[13]

When Napoléon died, he did not forget those who fought at the battle. To demonstrate his friendship towards the army, he made provision for the veterans of Waterloo. In his will, the tenth article left 50,000 francs to Dr Percy, the chief surgeon at Waterloo.[14] He thanked him for his kind service to the wounded. In the 22nd article, for the amputees and seriously wounded at Ligny and Waterloo, he left 200,000 francs. The guards got double compensation, and if they were on Elba, quadruple.[15] Though Napoléon made up stories on Saint Helena, he did take care of the men who were most loyal to him at Waterloo. He wanted to be remembered as a friend of the army and the people who served him.

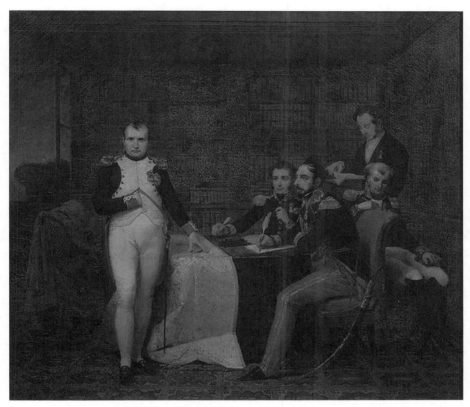

Napoléon dictating his memoirs to Generals Montholon and Gourgaud in the presence of Grand Marshal Bertrand and the Comte De Las Cases (French School, 19th century, Napoléonic Museum of the Island of Aix)

Count Emmanuel Las Cases accompanied Napoléon into exile with the purpose of assisting with the writing of Napoléon's memoirs. Upon completion of the book, Las Cases expected to become a rich man from its sale. Las Cases was happy to write the memoirs and was thankful to Napoléon for letting him write them.[16] However, on 16 December 1816, Count Emmanuel Las Cases was deported from the island by the governor because he was caught smuggling letters to Napoléon.

He spent the next eight months in prison at the Cape of Good Hope.[17] His record of Napoléon's last conversations on Saint Helena, *Mémorial de Ste Hélène*, was published in 1823. It has been called the 'Koran' of the Bonapartists.[18]

General Gourgaud (public domain)

In Las Cases' book, Napoléon lashed out at Marshal Grouchy for having 'lost his way'.[19] On the first anniversary of the battle in 1816, Napoléon called the battle an 'incomprehensible day … concurrence of unheard-of fatalities! … Grouchy! … Ney! … D'Erlon! … was there treachery or misfortune!'[20] Napoléon explained he should have won the campaign in the Hundred Days: 'Had it not been for the desertion of a traitor (Bourmont), I should have annihilated the enemy at the opening of the campaign. I should have destroyed him at Ligny had my left done its duty. I should have destroyed him again if my right had not failed me.'[21]
According to Las Cases, Grouchy lost Waterloo by not arriving on the battlefield and for failure to engage the enemy. Mention of the battle of Wavre was omitted.[22] He also claimed Grouchy got lost on his way to the battlefield of Waterloo. However, Las Cases did not explain why the army, which had been victorious until eight o'clock, was suddenly seized with panic and fell apart.[23] Napoléon seemed shocked to have lost the battle for a long time after it ended. He lamented that he should have turned

Wellington's left flank to keep the allies separated. He thought piercing the centre of Wellington's line was the better option at the time.[24]

Napoléon even argued he could have continued the fight the next day had he known where Grouchy was. He could have maneuvered the army towards Grouchy and fought again the next morning if only Grouchy had communicated with him. He even boasted if he had combined with Grouchy, he could have defeated both the British and the Prussians in the morning.[25]

British visitors to the island wanted to talk to Napoléon about Waterloo. Las Cases' account cited the example of Admiral Sir Pulteney Malcolm. In 1816, Sir Pulteney arrived on Saint Helena bringing news from London. He conversed with Napoléon at length about the battle and its outcome. Napoléon learned Sir Pulteney was responsible for transporting 4,000 crack troops from America directly to Ostend in record time to take part in the battle of Waterloo. According to British accounts, it was these soldiers' steadfast defence that won the day for the British.

Napoléon argued with the admiral that these troops were not the decisive element of the battle; rather, Grouchy's failure to arrive at the battle was to blame for the defeat.[26] Las Cases made it clear Napoléon resented Grouchy for not rescuing him at Waterloo. Grouchy's ineptitude might have cost him the war, but Napoléon would not allow it to cost him his reputation.

General Gaspard Gourgaud was an aide-de-camp of Napoléon and accompanied him to Saint Helena. Gourgaud was difficult to get along with on the island, constantly arguing with General Charles Montholon and Las Cases.[27] In fact, the feud between Gourgaud and Montholon grew so heated Gourgaud challenged him to a duel. Eventually, he would leave the island and travel to London to publish his account of the failed campaign.

Gaspard Gourgaud kept a daily journal of his contact with Napoléon at Saint Helena. Though his journal was not published until the end of the 19th century, it had formed the basis for his earlier works on Napoléon. In the journal, the subject of Waterloo comes up often. Napoléon refights the battle in his mind over and over at Saint Helena, unable to accept he had lost the campaign.

Consistent with Las Cases' account, Napoléon blamed his subordinates for his defeat. First, he blamed Marshal Joachim Murat, King of Naples, for attacking Austria when he learned of his escape from Elba. Napoléon had hoped he could have made Austria an ally, or at the least kept Austria neutral. Murat's attack on Austria put her firmly in the allied camp.[28]

Napoléon told Gourgaud, 'I assure you that Murat was the main cause of our being here at Saint Helena.'[29]

Napoléon was critical of Marshal Ney for having joined him at all. Napoléon noted that after Ney joined him most of Ney's troops deserted. He also denied Ney's claim that Marshal Henri Bertrand wrote to him; vowing Austria would support Napoléon. Napoléon insisted Ney was as an ambitious man who acted like a 'scoundrel'.[30] He openly criticised Ney's actions at Quatre Bras, questioning why he did not take the position. Napoléon never thought the English would support the Prussians at Ligny, and Ney should have taken advantage of the fact.[31]

Napoléon, however, did accept some fault for the outcome. He took the blame for not moving Drouet's corps on 16 June and blamed himself for not sleeping near Ligny on 15 June. According to Napoléon, fatigue played a large part in his own conduct. However, he left out his conduct on the night of 16 June or the morning of 17 June as a contributing factor in the loss of the campaign. However, he placed the blame on the leadership of the *Armée du Nord* for the defeat at Waterloo. Napoléon divided the French officer corps and caused a rift between Bonapartists with these accusations. Napoléon implied that his officers in 1815 were a mixed bag of Bonapartists, opportunists, incompetents and traitors.

Napoléon reserved his harshest criticism of his leadership for losing the battle on his choices for the leadership of the *Armée du Nord*. He implied he had a second-rate team, while better men were chosen for more difficult assignments. He blamed himself for giving command to Vandamme because he was crude and rash. He made a mistake in giving the command to the aristocrat, Grouchy. Marshal Louis Suchet would have been a better choice in commanding a wing of the army. In Napoléon's view, Suchet knew his method of war; Grouchy could only be counted on in a cavalry charge.[32] Napoléon admitted to picking an aide-de-camp who was too young and Marshal Soult was a poor chief of staff. Soult's administrative leadership was hampered during the campaign in part because he could not grasp Napoléon's strategy for defeating Wellington.[33] Soult had foolishly chosen orderly officers who were too young for the job as well. Soult became easily discouraged and alarmed in the face of setbacks. Napoléon regretted not having appointed Antoine Andréossi as his second in command.[34] Soult would have been a better wing commander than Grouchy or Ney. He accepted blame for his appointments but not their actions.

Napoléon blamed Soult for his lack of communication with Grouchy. Napoléon stated he sent three letters to Grouchy on the night of 17 June. Napoléon maintained Grouchy should have left General Claude Pajol's cavalry corps and General François Teste's infantry division to pursue the Prussians and taken the rest of his men to Waterloo.[35] Napoléon admitted sending such a large force away from the main force was a mistake but then redirected blame back on Grouchy for not exercising his own initiative.[36]

Napoléon did find a moment to praise the English for their steadfastness, order and discipline. In contrast, he points out French General Claude Guyot charged the heavy cavalry of the guard without orders.[37] Napoléon argued such insubordination helped sow the seed for the defeat of his army.

Gourgaud's account made it clear Napoléon also missed the troops he sent to pacify La Vendée. If he had waited until it was pacified, the 12,000 troops under General Jean Lamarque would have been available for Napoléon's field army, but he overestimated the time it would take Lamarque to subdue La Vendée.[38]

Napoléon insisted the rain on 17 June had more to do with the defeat at Waterloo than he first thought. He was so exhausted, he did not have the energy he had at Eckmühl and was unable to stay in the field as long as he would have preferred in the morning.[39]

Gourgaud's stay on Saint Helena ended in January 1818. Gourgaud fought too much with Montholon; Napoléon even had to admonish Gourgaud for challenging Montholon to a duel. Gourgaud was hot blooded and did not shy away from duelling to back up his words.[40] He travelled to London and published a work specifically about Waterloo. *Campagne de dix-huit cent quinze, ou, Relation des operations militaires qui ont lieu en France et en Belgique pendant les cent jours* was published in 1818 in Paris and London.

In *Campagne de dix-huit cent quinze*, Gourgaud reproduced Napoléon's account of the battle of Waterloo. While remaining true to Napoléon's words, the book contains several factual errors. One such example is General Pierre Cambronne's response to the British to surrender the last square. He was put on trial in 1816 for treason but he was acquitted. Gourgaud records the response as '*La garde meurt et se ne rend pas.*'[41] Cambronne was already a Bonapartist legend when Gourgaud published his work and the quote was made up by a journalist. Cambronne's quote was fictitious and Gourgaud probably knew it. The lie was better than the truth and what mattered to Gourgaud was giving the French a hero for Waterloo. Cambronne became famous and he and his act of defiance became the subject of many paintings.

However, the factual errors did not stop with Cambronne. Gourgaud asserted Napoléon planned to march on Brussels in two columns, one via Waterloo and the other via Wavre.[42] According to Gourgaud, Napoléon sent a messenger to Grouchy at 10p.m. and told him there would be a battle on 18 June against the British and to move to Saint Lambert. Grouchy was to attack the British left flank and link up with the rest of the army. Gourgaud claimed Grouchy reported he was at Gembloux on the night of 17 June and had no idea where Blücher had gone.[43] Officers sent out to Grouchy could not find him.[44] The entire battle's outcome rested on Grouchy and his men arriving on the battlefield, but they did not come.

The French were astounded to find the Prussians arriving on the battlefield. Not only had Grouchy failed to arrive, but he also failed to stop the Prussians. Where was Grouchy?[45] At 7.30p.m., Napoléon heard cannon fire coming from the direction of Wavre. He interpreted the cannon fire as signaling Grouchy's arrival. Now was the time to finish the British.[46] Napoléon sent La Bédoyère to tell the troops Grouchy had arrived. Napoléon attacked the British with four battalions of the Middle Guard. However, they were taken by surprise and retreated.[47] The troops arriving on the battlefield were not French, but they were Prussians. Then the traitors and villains of the army took over, spreading terror and panic.[48] Even heroes could not stem the tide of the allies and treachery.[49] The legend of Waterloo blamed everyone but Napoléon.

According to Gourgaud, the defeat of Waterloo could have been avoided had Marshal Grouchy marched on Saint Lambert instead of going to Wavre. Generals Exelmans and Gérard implored Marshal Grouchy to 'march to the sound of the guns'. According to Gourgaud, Grouchy did not want to take responsibility for, and was afraid of, disobeying Napoléon's orders to march to Wavre.[50]

Gourgaud's book had the blessing of Napoléon. It deliberately shifted blame for the loss of the campaign from Napoléon to Ney and Grouchy. Ney was dead and thus unable to defend his actions. Grouchy, however, was alive and well – and committed to protecting his name. The book started a debate about the battle of Waterloo that has yet to be resolved: the battle between Gourgaud and Grouchy and which version of history was true.

CHAPTER THREE

Grouchy and Waterloo

'Had I had Suchet at Waterloo instead of Grouchy, I would have won the battle!'[1] Napoléon argued Marshal Emmanuel de Grouchy was responsible for losing the battle of Waterloo and the Belgian campaign during the Hundred Days.[2] Why did Napoléon make the decision to put Grouchy in command? Some historians argued Napoléon deliberately fielded second-rate leaders during the Hundred Days to underscore Napoléon's own genius.[3] They attributed this plan to Napoléon's political need to be solely responsible for the victories of the campaign. Grouchy was a competent, if not brilliant, general who proved himself over 20 years of campaigning. His conduct during the Belgian campaign of 1815 has been a source of conflict about the memory of Waterloo and how his participation, or lack thereof, contributed to the French defeat at Waterloo. While in exile at Saint Helena, Napoléon blamed Grouchy for losing the battle of Waterloo by not coming to his aid and following orders to the letter to attack the Prussians holding the town of Wavre.

Despite Napoléon's analysis on Saint Helena, Grouchy earned his place among the marshals of the empire through the merits of his deeds. To illustrate why Napoléon made Grouchy a marshal, a closer examination of Grouchy's military career needs to be made.

Napoléon did not create a second-rate team on purpose.[4] The ablest and best leaders led the *Armée du Nord*. Napoléon hoped to re-establish his empire and consolidate his power. He needed victories and men who could follow his commands.

Emmanuel de Grouchy by Jean Sébastien Rouillard (public domain)

Emmanuel de Grouchy was destined to be a soldier from his birth on 23 October 1766. He grew up in his family's palatial home Chateau de Villette, an estate north of Paris, which was often called 'le petite Versailles'.[5] His ancestors rode with William the Conqueror in 1066 and went on the first crusade in 1099. His family epitomised the nobility of the sword.[6] He was a member of the upper nobility and had high prospects for advancement within the Royal Army.

His family was considered a part of the provincial nobility but had connections like a courtier. The Grouchy family served France in the army and navy. Emmanuel's parents wanted the best education for their son. The Grouchy's choice of schools for Emmanuel reflected the growing importance for sons of the upper nobility to become true military professionals.[7] Grouchy went to the Strasbourg Artillery School from 1780 to 1781 where he was a brilliant student. He earned a commission in the artillery as a lieutenant in 1781. Though a trained artillery officer, Grouchy transferred to the more prestigious cavalry arm of the army in 1784. In 1785, he was presented to King Louis XVI. He made a favourable impression and in 1786, at the age of 20, became lieutenant colonel of the Scottish Company of the Guard du Corps.[8] He came to know Louis XVI and was given two prized horses by the king through the Duke de Coigny.[9] His rise in the ranks came more from privilege than merit, but he was a talented young man. He left the army in 1787.[10] Like Napoléon Bonaparte, Grouchy's artillery training served him well in his future career. He became a master of how to use horse-drawn artillery in concert with infantry and cavalry.

When the Revolution broke out in 1789, the 23-year-old Grouchy and his brother-in-law Marie Jean de Caritat, Marquis de Condorcet supported the revolutionary cause. His family had exposed him to numerous ideas of the enlightenment. Along with his brother-in-law, he supported the revolutionaries in 1789.[11] Grouchy's early retirement (at the age of 21) in 1787 was in part because of his enthusiasm for reform and the ideas of the Enlightenment. He hoped to help reform the French military.[12] He joined the revolutionary army, as a private soldier.

However, the young marquis had a checkered military career under the Revolution and Consulate because of his noble birth. While most of the nobles emigrated from France, Grouchy stayed and remained faithful to the cause of the Revolution.[13] Grouchy's talents and pre-revolutionary formal training allowed him to become, by 1791, the lieutenant colonel of the 12th Chasseurs.[14] During the campaign in Savoy in 1792, he served as colonel of two separate cavalry regiments.

In January 1793, Louis XVI was executed. Most of the remaining nobles left France but Grouchy remained loyal to the revolution. Soon, the Royalists in the Vendée region of France revolted. The Vendée rebellion[15] served as an early proving ground for Grouchy's republican sentiments in 1793.[16] He needed to prove his commitment to the Revolution by serving against the Royalists in the Vendée. He served under General Louis Lazare Hoche, was wounded and on all accounts served meritoriously.

The republican government Grouchy supported soon turned its back on him. His noble background became suspect, despite ably serving in the army that defeated the Vendean rebels.[17] The crisis that gripped France during the Terror of 1793 led to him being removed from command on

30 September 1793.[18] A warrant for his arrest was issued by the Committee of Public Safety.[19] He was suspended from the army but not put in jail.

After the French Republican victories in the spring of 1794 helped bring the Terror to an end, the Thermidorian Reaction that ensued saved Grouchy and his career. He was returned to active service with promotion to the rank of general of division.[20] Hoche asked for Grouchy to remain in service with the *Armée de L'Ouest* since he was an effective commander of counter-insurgent operations.[21] He became second in command under his friend General Hoche in Vendée.[22] During July 1795, he and Hoche suppressed the British supported rebellion on the Quiberon Peninsula.[23]

In December of 1796, General Hoche and Grouchy set off in a fleet bound for Bantry Bay to invade Ireland. The invasion was aborted and was an utter failure. Once both men were back in port, , Hoche dismissed Grouchy as his second in command, calling Grouchy, 'a scribbler of no consequence'.[24] The friendship with Hoche was over.

The Irish fiasco of 1796 set Grouchy's career back, but France still needed his services as a trained cavalry officer. During the rest of 1796 and part of 1797, Grouchy was at Nantes and tried to defend himself from the Irish fiasco. During his posting to Italy in 1797 with a heavy cavalry unit, he met General Napoléon Bonaparte for the first time.[25] The meeting was uneventful but still Grouchy remembered the young Corsican.

Grouchy was employed once again conducting counter-insurgency operations in Italy from 1798 to 1799. On 20 June 1799, he fought the second battle of Marengo. Grouchy held on despite being outnumbered and lacking cavalry or artillery support. Like a year later during Napoléon's battle of Marengo,[26] the arrival of fresh French reinforcements carried the day for the French.[27] On 15 August 1799, at the battle of Novi, Grouchy successfully commanded the left wing of Joubert's army and took nearly 2,000 prisoners. However, the commander of the army was killed, and the battle was lost. Grouchy's men were cut off and he was wounded in the action. He tried to get his men to safety, but after fierce resistance, he and his men were taken as prisoners of war at Pasturana Pass.[28] His wounds were so serious, he thought he was going to die.[29]

Grouchy was a prisoner of war during Napoléon's *coup d'état* of 18 Brumaire.[30] While in prison, Grouchy penned a letter condemning the coup and the subsequent establishment of the Consulate.[31] Even with Grouchy's less than positive attitude toward the new government after his exchange in 1800, France required his services as an experienced officer. General André Masséna, General Moreau and his family convinced Grouchy to support the new regime.[32]

Moreau commanded the *Armée du Rhin*[33] and Grouchy took an assignment in Moreau's army as an infantry division commander.[34] During his assignment with Moreau, Grouchy met General Michael Ney. Both men eventually became marshals of France, Ney first then Grouchy. They worked well with each other and under Moreau.

Archduke Charles of Austria tried to reverse Napoléon's victory at Marengo by invading Bavaria.[35] Moreau's army met Archduke Charles' army at Hohenlinden on 3 December 1800. Ney and Grouchy attacked with such élan, the army of Archduke Charles broke.[36] The victory led to the Treaty of Lunéville. Grouchy's loyalty to General Moreau alienated him from Napoléon's inner circle and prevented him from being promoted to marshal after the establishment of the empire in 1804.[37] He would have to wait another 11 years for the distinction.

Napoléon did make Grouchy inspector of the cavalry. From 1801–5, Marshal Joachim Murat and Grouchy worked to perfect the French cavalry. Soon it became the finest of Europe. Building this force of cavalry required active administration of both men and horses. Grouchy was an expert in the command of cavalry.

Grouchy accepted command of a division in General Auguste Marmont's[38] II Corps and participated in the march to Ulm in 1805.[39] Napoléon believed Marmont could keep a close watch on this newly won-over general who had talent but lacked political sense. Grouchy did not participate in the victory at Austerlitz and returned home to recover from one of his old wounds and contemplated resigning. Grouchy felt that he deserved a promotion, yet he did not get one. However, Napoléon asked him to reconsider and rejoin the army. As an enticement, Napoléon offered a spot in the Imperial Cadet School to Grouchy's son, Alphonse.[40] Grouchy agreed to return to active service in September 1806 to participate in an upcoming war with Prussia.[41] Grouchy did not participate in the battles of Jena or Auerstädt. His division remained in reserve and his fresh cavalry division allowed

Marshal Murat to follow up both victories with a sustained pursuit to smash the Prussians.

Grouchy won several minor engagements while leading his cavalry division of dragoons. Dragoons were horse-mounted infantry that could be used as light infantry or as cavalry. The flexibility of dragoons aided Grouchy in catching detachments and stragglers of the main Prussian army. Grouchy's leadership helped win the battles of Zhendick on 26 October and Prenzlau on 28 October 1806.[42] At Prenzlau, Prussian General Friedrich-Ludwig Erbprinz zü Höhenlohe surrendered his forces and the Prussian Queen, Louisa, lost her personal flag to Grouchy's men.[43] The French rout of the Prussians was so thorough, Murat wrote to Napoléon, 'Sire, the combat ends for lack of combatants.'[44] Grouchy knew how to pursue an enemy and demonstrated his talent for it at Prenzlau. In the next campaign in Poland against the Russians in 1807, Grouchy acted heroically.

At the battle of Eylau, on 7 February 1807, Napoléon called upon Murat's Reserve Cavalry Corps to make a desperate charge. Napoléon ordered Murat to take personal command of the charge. The main assault force consisted of two dragoon divisions under Murat, Grouchy's dragoons, Général Comte Jean Joseph Ange d'Hautpoul's cuirassiers and the Cavalry of the Guard under Bessières. Murat's first attack forced the Russian infantry into the square formation to protect themselves from the attacking cavalry. Then, General Grouchy's division smashed the right flank of the Russian cavalry and drove them from the field. However, Grouchy's horse was killed and he was pinned underneath the horse. Meanwhile, the Russian cavalry regrouped and charged again. Grouchy's aide-de-camp and family friend Georges Washington de Lafayette galloped to his rescue.[45] Lafayette wrapped his hand around the horse's tail and both escaped, despite Russian cavalry.[46] Grouchy returned to his second brigade of dragoons and continued the charge. Artillery damage done to the Russian squares resulted in holes in the Russian infantry squares, which Grouchy exploited. Converging in the rear of the Russian lines, Murat ordered his troops to turn around and ride back through the stunned Russians.[47] This was a pivotal moment in the battle. The use of dragoons and cuirassiers stabilised the French position, which allowed Napoléon to bring up reinforcements to bolster his lines.

The cavalry had saved Napoléon's army. There was a price the French cavalry had to pay for their charge into the Russian lines. Although they were successful, the French cavalry suffered terrible losses. The morale of French cavalry sunk. Grouchy wrote to his father:

> This is a terrible battle that we have won at Eylau, all day I was occupied with charging the enemy, exposed to fire from muskets from the infantry. In three weeks, my division is reduced in half. I lost three hundred horses at Eylau, two of my colonels, Fontenilles [one of Grouchy's aide-de-camps] was wounded in the wrist, and many officers died. The Army lost many generals but the enemy also suffered a lot …this day reminded me of what Frederick the Great said about defeating the Russians 'Three or four more victories like that and I will no longer have an army'…the battle was not as decisive as they write.[48]

Unlike the successful pursuit of the Prussians, there would be no pursuit of the Russians after the battle of Eylau.[49]

Later in June of 1807, Grouchy played an important part in Napoléon's victory over the Russians at the battle of Friedland. Napoléon offered him an independent cavalry command, while Murat's cavalry marched on the city of Königsberg. Napoléon wrote to Marshal Jean Lannes, 'I cannot yet tell if the enemy is at Friedland, or only part of them. In any case, Grouchy's dragoons are on the march and (he) will command your cavalry.'[50] Grouchy commanded the Saxon Light Cavalry, two brigades of French light cavalry, and a division of cuirassiers under General Étienne Nansouty.[51] This was a major promotion for Grouchy and Napoléon trusted him with an important command.[52]

At the battle of Friedland, Marshal Lannes trusted Grouchy and Nicholas Oudinot for delaying the Russians long enough to allow all of Napoléon's army to march to the battlefield. The victory resulted in the Treaties of Tilsit, which made Napoléon the master of continental Europe. Napoléon generously rewarded the cavalry and its leaders for their efforts during the campaign. Grouchy received the Grand Eagle of the Legion of Honour, an estate in Poland and the Grand Sash of the Legion of Honour on July 13 1807.[53] Grouchy wrote to his father, 'It surpassed all that he hoped for and that it completely compensated for having to wait a while.'[54] The French cavalry deserved to be rewarded, the dragoons and cuirassiers stood out for their service against the Russians. Grouchy thought he was on his way to becoming a marshal.

When Napoléon invaded Spain in 1808, Grouchy was appointed as the governor of Madrid under Marshal Murat. Things went well for Grouchy at first, but on 1 April, an uprising against the French occurred in Madrid; thanks to Grouchy's decisive action, he put it down without much difficulty.[55] While a disaster for Murat, Grouchy fared better in the eyes of the emperor because he had taken the initiative to protect and defend his men. Napoléon made Grouchy a count of the empire in January 1809.[56] Grouchy was one of the few officers whose service in Spain enhanced his reputation.

Grouchy left Spain for an assignment in Italy with Eugéne de Beauharnais, Napoléon's adoptive son and Viceroy of the Kingdom of Italy. While in Italy, Austria declared war on the French Empire in 1809. The Austrians sent Archduke Johann and his 50,000 men to invade Italy. Near Paive, Eugéne attacked Archduke Johann. The battle of the Paive on 8 May 1809 earned more glory for Grouchy; Eugéne's army defeated Archduke Johann. Eugéne's careful placement of artillery, along with Grouchy's use of cavalry, carried the day for the French.[57] On 12 May, Grouchy pursued the defeated Austrians as far as beyond the Isonzo.[58]

After pursuing the Austrians out of Italy, Eugene and Grouchy were ordered to join Napoléon's main army near Vienna. They arrived in time to participate in the battle of Wagram on 5–6 July 1809. Grouchy commanded cavalry on the extreme right of the line, covering Marshal Nicolas Davout's corps. Grouchy's cavalry was able to strike the rear of the Austrian army, and the commander of the Austrian army, Archduke Charles, withdrew his army. Again, Grouchy had helped to win another great victory for Napoléon. Grouchy's reward for his service did not include a marshal's baton, but it did include Napoléon awarding him the Cross of the Iron Crown and making him Colonel-General of the Chasseurs, replacing one of Napoléon's closest friends Auguste Marmont.[59] This rank was just below marshal and Grouchy was now recognised as being one of Napoléon's elite officers.

Grouchy did not return to Italy after his campaign in Austria. His already numerous wounds and active campaigning left him in need of rest. For part of 1809 and to 1811, he remained in France.[60] He would need the rest for his greatest adventure laid ahead of him. Grouchy came out of semi-retirement in 1812 to take command of theIII Reserve Cavalry Corps for the invasion of Russia.[61] He was placed under the direction of his old army commander Eugène de Beauharnais. During the advance into Russia, he was with Eugène's 75,000 Italian and Bavarian troops, Grouchy served with distinction.[62]

As the campaign progressed, Grouchy performed successfully. He was often in the lead of the *Grande Armée* in its relentless pursuit of the Russians. Seventy miles west of Moscow, the Russian army, under Marshal Mikhail Illarionovich Kutuzov, turned to fight the French at Borodino on 7 September 1812. The bloody battle almost cost Grouchy his life. All day, the French attacked this heavily defended position. It took a massive cavalry and infantry attack led by General Auguste Caulaincourt to take the Great Redoubt.[63] Grouchy's cavalry corps was sent to exploit the hole made by Caulaincourt. However, Russian General Kutuzov released the last remaining Russian reserve of cavalry to check Grouchy.[64] Grouchy's cavalry could not advance without additional support. Though he swept the plain between the Great Redoubt, beyond it, there were a series of ravines and more entrenchments that blocked Grouchy's path.[65] Russian artillery fire killed Grouchy's horse, wounding him in the chest and injuring his son Alphonse during the fighting.[66] Many of Napoléon's marshals requested Napoléon use the Imperial Guard to force the final rupture of the Russian line. Napoléon refused saying, 'I will not demolish my Guard.'[67] Napoléon's decision at Borodino not to use the guard to follow Grouchy's attack allowed the Russians to escape from the battlefield.

With the pyrrhic victory of Borodino, the French took Moscow on 15 September 1812. After 35 days in Moscow, Napoléon realised the Russians never intended to surrender so he decided to retreat. The horrors of the retreat reduced the cavalry of the army to only a few mounted officers. Napoléon gathered around him the remnants of the cavalry and formed the *Le Bataillon Sacré* or the Sacred Squadron. Officers made up the Sacred Squadron and Napoléon viewed it as the best of the best and needed to be saved for the future. Napoléon entrusted Grouchy with the command.[68] Command of the Sacred Squadron was perhaps Napoléon's greatest reward for the wounded general.

The general's fragile health gave out while returning from Russia. His wounds and utter exhaustion from the retreat made him unfit for command. Grouchy requested he be relieved of command and retired. Napoléon granted his request and retired him on 1 April 1813.[69] He returned home to France and did not participate in the German campaign of 1813.

Napoléon would miss his able leadership during the 1813 campaign. The disastrous battle of Leipzig drove the French out of central Germany and to the frontiers of France. Napoléon recalled his most experienced cavalry general[70] and Grouchy was sufficiently recovered from his wounds in Russia to answer Napoléon's call to arms.[71]

His return could hardly have turned the tide of fortune against Napoléon at this point, but Napoléon appreciated his loyalty nevertheless. Grouchy commanded the shattered remains of the finest cavalry in Europe. He showed his old brilliance at Vauchamps on 14 February 1814 by charging Blücher's disorganised forces and inflicting 5,000–7,000 Prussian casualties.[72] After this action, Napoléon promised to make Grouchy a marshal. At Troyes on 23 February, he was lightly wounded, and at Craonne on 7 March, he was seriously wounded in the leg.[73] Grouchy returned to his home but remained loyal to Napoléon. Napoléon's abdication prevented him from being promoted and he was lucky to have survived with his life during the political tempest followed Napoléon's downfall.

Grouchy only accepted Louis XVIII's restoration as king after Napoléon had formally abdicated. He applied to the government on the behalf of his four children to be reinstated into the army.[74] He still was recovering from his wounds from the battle of Craonne when he received the news of his demotion from Louis XVIII. He was surprised and shocked that his titles under Napoléon were not recognised by Louis, even though he had publicly proclaimed that he would uphold all titles and dignities conferred under Napoléon.[75] He reasoned many marshals and generals retained their position, why should he not be accorded the same respect? Louis' brother, Charles the Comte d'Artois, did not forget Grouchy was a true noble[76] and had supported the Revolution against the king, his brother. Grouchy presented himself at court to protest the demotion to Charles Ferdinand Duke de Berry.[77] During the meeting with the duke, Marshal Marmont entered the room and started to make comments about the situation.

Grouchy became agitated in the presence of Marshal Marmont saying he would not speak with Marmont in the room.[78] Marmont continued talking when Grouchy interrupted him saying 'I have told you already it is not you I am addressing myself – you have the contempt of the whole Army.'[79] For his outburst, the king forced him to leave Paris. Grouchy's income was sharply reduced, according to Grouchy by over 89,000 francs. Grouchy was deeply troubled, not only for[80] himself but for his four children.[81]

Marie Therese Duchess of Angoulême[82] intervened on Grouchy's behalf. Soon, Louis nominated him as commander of the Order of Saint Louis with a modest pension.[83] Unfortunately, even this decoration did not cover his expenses. The general was still in negotiations with the king over his back pay and military honours when the unthinkable happened. Napoléon escaped from Elba.

Upon Napoléon's eventual return from exile on Elba in March 1815, Grouchy looked to restore his fortune. Grouchy took command of the *Armée du Midi* on 31 March 1815.[84] The Duke de Angoulême raised an army of Royalists to fight Napoléon. Louis XVIII's nephew did not realise Grouchy and his forces surrounded him. Angoulême surrendered to Grouchy after a brief period of manoeuvring. Grouchy dealt fairly with the men who rallied to Angoulême. He let the civilians go home, while the troops took an oath of allegiance to Napoléon. Napoléon allowed Angoulême to go free and Grouchy provided him safe escort to Spain.[85]

The foundation of loyalty and merit developed over a period of ten years convinced Napoléon that Emmanuel Grouchy should be the 26th and last marshal of the empire.

On 15 April 1815, Grouchy received his official promotion to the rank of marshal. The relationship Grouchy nurtured through his own deeds made Napoléon's choice a logical one. Grouchy, with years of training and leadership experience in the Napoléonic Wars, had a reputation for being a winner. Napoléon's choice for leading the right wing of the *Armèe du Nord* made sense to him at the time. After all, Ney and Grouchy had fought together several times since their first meeting at Hohenlinden in 1800. They were a proven and winning team. Napoléon was confident the army he had assembled could defeat the Anglo-Prussian armies in Belgium.

The Belgian campaign, culminating in the battle of Waterloo, started when Napoléon sealed the borders of France on 7 June 1815. He concentrated his forces near the town of Beaumont and by 14 June was ready to start the campaign.[86] Napoléon noticed the allied/British army under Arthur Wellesley, Duke of Wellington, and the Prussian army under Marshal Gebhard von Blücher had supply and communication lines going in opposite directions. He would attack where the two armies met and occupy the central position. Napoléon knew he could not face the combined armies of Wellington and Blücher. By using the central position, he could face each army separately, have numerical superiority and defeat each army. To do this he had to get between the armies and divide them from each other. This tactic had worked well in the past.[87] Napoléon hoped to use it one more time to defeat his enemies.

Napoléon seized the initiative and drove his forces between the two armies at Charleroi.

He divided his *Armée du Nord* into three parts. The left wing would be under the command of Marshal Michel Ney and the right wing under the command of Marshal Grouchy; Napoléon retained the Imperial Guard as a reserve for the army. The plan started well and the initial movements of the campaign favoured the French. On 15 June, he took the key city of Charleroi.

The inhabitants of the city were enthusiastic when Napoléon arrived.[88] However, on 15 June, General Louis Bourmont, who was a division leader of Étienne Gérard's corps, defected to the Prussians and informed them of Napoléon's intentions. This treachery in the face of the enemy made the rank and file soldiers distrustful of their generals.[89] The effect of this mistrust would haunt Grouchy for years.

On 16 June, there were two battles, one at Quatre Bras between Wellington and Marshal Ney, and another at Ligny between Marshal Blücher and Napoléon. The battle of Quatre Bras was a confusing affair. Napoléon's original intention was to support Ney, but as events unfolded, he switched his line of attack to defeat the Prussians at Ligny. Napoléon thought Ney could defeat the scant forces in front of him and take the crossroads at Quatre Bras. Ney did not act until after 2p.m. At the same time, Napoléon massed 71,000 men to attack the Prussians. Blücher reached

Étienne Gérard by Jacques-Louis David (Metropolitan Museum of Art, public domain)

the area at around 4p.m. but his 84,000 men were ready to meet the attack.[90] The battle of Ligny should have been one of Napoléon's greatest triumphs. He won the battle, but it was only a tactical victory, instead of a strategic one. Marshal Blücher assembled most of the Prussian army around the small town of Ligny, but he was missing Friedrich von Bülow's IV Corps, one of his largest. Napoléon hoped to be at either Fleurus (near Ligny) or Sombreffe (beyond Ligny) by nightfall. Perhaps, the French Army could be in Brussels by the next morning.[225]

At 2.30p.m., the battle of Ligny began. Napoléon's battle plan was to launch a frontal assault and pin the Prussians to his front. Dominique Vandamme's III Corps and Gérard's IV Corps were to lead the assault on the villages of Ligny and Saint-Amand. Marshal Grouchy commanded the cavalry on the far right. Napoléon thought at some point Ney would be able to send reinforcements from Quatre Bras. Napoléon sent for Jean-Baptiste Drouet Comte d'Erlon's I Corps to come in behind the

General Dominique Joseph Vandamme (public domain)

right flank the Prussian Army. With the Prussians pinned to their front and with D'Erlon attacking in the rear and on the flank of the Prussian army, Napoléon planned to launch his Imperial Guard in the centre of Prussian army to divide and destroy it. That was the plan. Execution was quite another matter.

Napoléon made two critical mistakes on the morning and afternoon of 16 June. In the morning, Napoléon made the mistake of not moving the 10,000 men of George Mouton Comte Lobau's VI Corps from Charleroi towards the front. They received no orders until the afternoon. Now, he could not use this corps either at Quatre Bras or at Ligny. In the afternoon, communication between Ney and Napoléon broke down when I Corps received conflicting orders from Ney and Napoléon, so it did not participate in either battle. They marched along the Nivelles–Namur road all day. Thus, Napoléon was robbed of two corps he desperately needed to destroy the Prussians.

Worse for Napoléon, D'Erlon's corps was not identified as friendly troops until 6.30p.m. This delayed Napoléon's attack with the 20,000 men of the Imperial Guard on the Prussian centre. It also allowed Marshal Blücher to regain enough strength to launch a counter-attack on Vandamme's exhausted troops who had just taken the village of Ligny. Blücher personally led this attack to retake the village. The village was soon retaken by the Young Guard[91] but the Prussians gained time with their lives.

This counter-attack delayed the attack of Imperial Guard until 7.30p.m. A sudden thunderstorm drenched the battlefield, but the Imperial Guard went forward towards the Prussian line anyway. The hats of the grenadiers of the guard were known throughout Europe and the mere sight of these men in their tall bearskin hats had struck fear in many men for 20 years. The Prussians were no different. Their line broke within half an hour. By 9p.m., the Prussians were broken and beaten, but the army was not destroyed.

With his lines ruptured, Marshal Blücher ordered a desperate counter-attack with his cavalry to cover the retreat of his army. Again, he personally took command. His bravery this time almost cost him his life. During the engagement, his horse was killed, and he was pinned under it. Only the heroism of a staff officer saved him.

Napoléon needed success to stay in power and now, even though there were mistakes at Ligny, it could be called a victory. The famous Prussian General Ludwig Lützow was taken prisoner.[92] They had taken many flags, cannons and wagons. Things seemed to be going well for the campaign, despite the mistakes. However, it was a hard-fought affair by both sides.

Vandamme's III Corps and Gérard's IV Corps took many casualties and needed rest. Indeed, Napoléon himself needed rest. He went to his tent and slept. Yet it was this rest that would become Napoléon's nightmare for many years to come.

The fighting at Ligny continued into the night of 16 June. At 11.00p.m., Marshal Grouchy asked for instructions for the pursuit of the Prussian army. He still had two fresh cavalry corps, of Exelmans and Pajol, to pursue the Prussians, and he could have used Lobau's VI Corps for infantry support. The opportunity came for Napoléon to pursue the Prussians after the battle of Ligny and turn the defeated and disorganised army into a mob of panic-stricken men. Grouchy came to Napoléon's headquarter thinking he would receive orders for the pursuit of the defeated Prussians. However, Napoléon did not see the immediate need to order a pursuit. After a heated exchange between Grouchy and Napoléon, Grouchy was told to come back in the morning and await orders from the emperor. Napoléon was indisposed and could not speak with Grouchy further, possibly because of an acute attack of hemorrhoids.[93] However, Napoléon did allow the cavalry at first light to go and seek where the Prussians went towards the east, but there was not to be a vigorous pursuit.[94] The following morning at 8a.m., Marshal Grouchy again arrived at the headquarters to ask for instructions on the pursuit. Napoléon waited on the battlefield of Ligny and decided to take a tour of the battlefield and discuss his political situation with his marshals and staff. The Prussians did not waste time like their adversaries.

While leading the last cavalry charge, Blücher turned operational control of the army over to his chief of staff, August Gneisenau. Even though the Prussians lost the battle, they maintained their commitment to support the allied forces under Wellington. While Blücher was incapacitated, General Gneisenau ordered a retreat towards the town of Wavre.[95] The nature of the attack on the centre and right wings of the Prussians made the men flee northwards, not eastwards from the battle. Units were already heading towards Wavre when they recovered their cohesion and received their orders to go to the north. Some elements did move towards the east to Gembloux, where Prussian reinforcements under General Bülow of IV Corps were waiting. Elements of Thielmann's III Corps covered the retreat of the Prussian I and II Corps during the night and stayed near Ligny until 3a.m. on 17 June. They waited, and expected, to be attacked but they never were.[96] This retreat put Blücher closer to Wellington than Napoléon would be to Grouchy on the night of 17/18 June.

By the time Napoléon issued orders to Grouchy at 11a.m. on 17 June, the main Prussian army was on its way to Wavre unmolested. The reprieve of 12 hours allowed the Prussians to escape. What was worse for the French was they did not know exactly in which direction the Prussians had retreated. Before leaving Napoléon, Grouchy pointed out the Prussians had already broken contact with them and he wanted to march with Napoléon to unite the army at Quatre Bras.[97] Napoléon declined the offer and sent Grouchy to find and attack the Prussian army. Napoléon made it clear to Grouchy his job was to first find and then attack the Prussians.

Reports from Grouchy's cavalry, under Pajol, located a detachment of retreating Prussians in the direction of Namur. Pajol reported numerous prisoners and capture of a Prussian horse artillery battery. Pajol thought the Prussians were heading towards Namur and Louvain.[98] It seemed to the marshal that Napoléon's initial guess, that the Prussians would retreat towards their supply base in Namur, was correct. Napoléon thought he had achieved the first part of the plan for destroying the Prussian and British/ allied armies. He thought he occupied the central position and was between the main Prussian army and the allied army. A force of roughly 8000 men had retreated towards Namur, fleeing the battle.[99] These men only confirmed in Napoléon's mind the Prussian army was heading towards Namur.

The rain engulfed the area on the night of 17 June and made the valley of the Dyle a quagmire. Mud, ankle deep, sucked the boots off soldiers. The artillery was virtually immobile. Without artillery support and wet powder, the Prussians would have been easily destroyed by pursuing cavalry. Neither Napoléon nor Grouchy knew exactly where the main Prussian army was on the morning of 17 June. However, Napoléon assumed he knew. The French cavalry was east, away from the Prussian army, where Napoléon thought the Prussians were heading.

The cavalry corps of Exelmans did little better than that of Pajol. Exelmans followed Pajol's route towards Namur. General Jean Baptiste Berton, who commanded Exelmans' dragoons, learned from some peasants in the town of Le Mazy that the Prussians had retreated towards Gembloux; north not east. Unfortunately for Pajol, General Berton sent word back to Exelmans, but neither Berton nor Exelmans told Pajol about locating the Prussians. Pajol continued onwards towards St Denis after finding nothing at Le Bouquet. The Cavalry of Exelmans found Thielmann's Prussian corps resting at Gembloux at 9a.m.[100] Once again, no one from Exelmans' command sent word to Pajol and, to make matters worse, Exelmans failed to report the discovery to Grouchy. Meanwhile, Grouchy had ordered the Vandamme and Gérard corps to Gembloux and ordered Gérard to push his cavalry eastwards by dawn.[101]

During the early morning of 18 June, Grouchy sent word from Gembloux that he had learned from a local Belgian that part of the Prussian army passed the town in the night and they were heading towards Wavre. Grouchy passed on this information to Napoléon who should have realised if he were to fight on 18 June at Mont St Jean[102] at least a part of the Prussian army could aid Wellington against him. Grouchy still did not know exactly where the main Prussian army was in the area. Napoléon ordered him to keep his infantry corps together, have avenues of escape and place cavalry pickets to be able to communicate with headquarters.[103] Grouchy kept his army together and had them at Gembloux on the night of 17 June. He planned to march his troops further to the north-east towards Sart-a-Walhain. Vandamme was to start at 5a.m.[104] and Gérard at 8a.m. He knew the troops were in a foul mood since it had rained, and he authorized giving the men a double ration of brandy for the night.[105] Grouchy for the time being was a popular commander.

During the day of 17 June, General Pajol's corps, along with his infantry support under General François Teste,[106] went from Balatre (near Ligny) to Le Mazy to Le Bouquet and on to close to St Denis and then back again. The Prussians had not retreated towards Namur.

Vandamme reported after talking to local inhabitants; the Prussians, who passed by Gembloux (Thielmann's corps), were asking for the marching distances to Wavre, Perwes and Hanut.[107] The Prussians were confirmed to be in the village of Tourinnes after a sharp cavalry skirmish.[108] At 9p.m. General Édouard Milhaud's cavalry reported to Napoléon's headquarters the Prussians were withdrawing from Tilly towards Wavre.

At 10p.m. on 17 June, Grouchy sent word to Napoléon on his intentions to move towards Sart-a-Walhain in the morning and the Prussians were in at least two columns. One was heading towards Wavre via Sart-a-Walhain and the other via Pervez-le-Marchez. Grouchy informed Napoléon that Gérard's and Vandamme's corps were in and around Gembloux and parts of his cavalry were at Sauvenieres.[109] The most telling message Grouchy sent to Napoléon was, 'Perhaps we can infer that some of the Prussian corps will go to join Wellington and that some others are retiring on Liège.'[110] Grouchy added Marshal Blücher was wounded but still retained command and he did not pass by Gembloux. Grouchy sent part of Exelmans's cavalry to Sart-a-Walhain and Pervez-le-Marchez to follow the Prussian columns.[111] Grouchy followed up with Napoléon at 3a.m. on 18 June by informing him that he discovered I, II and III Corps of the Prussian army marching towards Brussels.

He thought all indications were the Prussians were retiring on Brussels to join up with Wellington or give battle after linking up with them. Grouchy also informed Napoléon that Namur was empty of enemy troops and he was sending some National Guardsmen to occupy the town with some cannon from Charlemont.[112]

Grouchy also wrote at 6a.m. on 18 June that the Prussian I and II Corps were heading to Corbais and Chaumont. Also, he reported to Napoléon his command was moving towards Wavre via Corbais. Exelmans left Sauveniere at 6a.m., while Vandamme and Gérard broke camp and started moving about 7.30a.m. with the troops marching in one column towards Corbais.

Napoléon received the Grouchy's letter dated 10p.m. on 17 June at around 4a.m. on 18 June.[113] However, Napoléon did not respond to Grouchy's letter for six hours. He finally responded at 10a.m. on 18 June. Napoléon confirmed the Prussians were moving towards Wavre and he should follow them to Wavre with utmost speed.[114] Marshal Jean Soult, Napoléon's chief of staff, wished to recall Grouchy's wing before commencing the battle, but Napoléon refused to recall Grouchy. He must have reasoned the Prussians could not effectively intervene against him on 18 June. Napoléon followed up his 10a.m. communication with one sent out at 1p.m. again ordering Grouchy to Wavre.

General Thielmann planned to march his corps towards St Lambert and onto Waterloo, but his forces detected Grouchy's men advancing on Wavre. His force protected the rear of the main Prussian army marching on Waterloo. The Prussians dug in and waited for the French. They made the town a virtual fortress. The three bridges that crossed the Dyle were barricaded and defended by the Prussians.

At 11a.m. on 18 June, Grouchy made it to Sart-a-Walhain. He stopped to have lunch with a prominent local lawyer and write to Napoléon. He wrote that at least 30,000 men and 50 cannons had passed by Sart-a-Walhain. He also added another corps (Bülow's IV Corps) had come from Liège and joined the other corps. He also reported the terrain between Sart-a-Walhain and Brussels was difficult, and the Prussians were bragging while in town. They were not defeated but going to join Wellington. He thought Napoléon's forces were sufficient to force Wellington to retire north towards Brussels. There Wellington was willing to give battle once linking up with Blücher. Grouchy went on to communicate he was marching on Wavre and would be there by nightfall. Most of all, Grouchy requested instructions from Napoléon on how he wanted him to proceed tomorrow.[115]

Grouchy knew from his last communication with the emperor that Napoléon was pursuing Wellington towards Brussels. Soon after writing his 11a.m. letter to Napoléon from Sart-a-Walhain, a cannonade came from the west interrupting his lunch.[116] General Gérard upon hearing the firing coming from the west urged Grouchy to 'march to the sound of the guns' and towards the forest of Soignies. Besides, Grouchy had standing orders to keep both of his corps together, and he could not allow Gérard to go by himself. The cannonade began to grow louder and several officers put their ears to the ground to determine if, in fact, the gunfire was from the west. General Basile Baltus, who was Gérard's artillery commander, agreed with Grouchy. He had campaigned before in Belgium and knew the terrain. In his opinion, the distance to the sound of the gunfire was too great to arrive during the day. He noted there were no usable roads going to the west. The narrow lanes heading west would be extremely muddy and the artillery would have great difficulty following the troops. General Éléonor de Valazé, who was Gérard's commander of engineers, argued his men could cut a quick and easy way to the west.[117] Gérard became agitated and insisted that Grouchy allow him to leave with his corps to march towards the west. With the lessons of 16 June freshly in Grouchy's head, he firmly denied Gérard. He told Gérard he was not surprised. Grouchy knew Napoléon was going to engage Wellington near the forest of Soignies and he had himself wanted to remain with the main army to attack Wellington. He added to Gérard, he could not allow himself to divide his forces. The swollen Dyle River would have been between his two-infantry corps and they would not be able to support one another if attacked.[118]

Grouchy then rode forward with General Exelmans to reconnoiter the roads leading towards the north-west and the village of Limalette. The sound of a large battle increased to the west and Grouchy realized a major action was taking place and it was not a rearguard action.

Around 12.30p.m., a force of 300 cavalry was sent by Grouchy to maintain communications with Napoléon, but they were surprised near

Mont St Guibert. The Prussians were between Grouchy and Napoléon. Worse, they were astride the French lines of communication.[119] At 3.30p.m. on 18 June, Grouchy received Napoléon's letter of 10a.m. The letter instructed Grouchy to take the town of Wavre. Grouchy was happy he had not marched towards the west as General Gérard insisted. He recalled Pajol's cavalry corps and Teste's division from the south-west and ordered them towards Limal.

Near 4p.m., Vandamme's corps reached the hills outside Wavre, but Vandamme did not wait for Gérard's corps. He attacked without support the strongly emplaced Prussians of Thielmann's III Corps. Key for the town of Wavre was its bridges over the Dyle River. The assault did not go well. Vandamme wasted many men in a frontal assault without proper support or trying to outflank the position via the other bridges up or down stream. Grouchy was furious at Vandamme for not waiting for orders and tried to repair the situation.

Grouchy ordered Gérard's corps to support Vandamme by moving upsteam of Wavre to outflank Wavre via bridges in the hamlets of Bierges, Limal and Limalette. Grouchy then ordered Exelmans to go downstream of Wavre to try to cross the bridge at the hamlet of Basse Wavre.

Between 6p.m. and 7p.m. on 18 June, Grouchy received another order confirming Napoléon was engaged with Wellington and he was to continue and take the town of Wavre.[120] Napoléon also added he wished Grouchy to manoeuvre towards Napoléon's right and prevent any enemy corps getting between them.[121] The bridge at Basse-Wavre was blown up, but the bridge at Bierges proved to be too heavily defended. General Gérard was wounded in the chest while trying to storm over the bridge. After seeing Gérard was wounded, Grouchy assumed command of IV Corps and tried to take the bridge himself to no avail.

Pajol arrived at Limal around 7p.m. and charged with his cavalry across the bridge. This time the Prussians had not barricaded the bridge and Pajol was successful crossing the Dyle at Limal. Having secured a bridgehead over the Dyle, they secured another crossing point at Limalette. He pushed most of the IV Corps over onto the left bank of the Dyle at Limal and was set to outflank Biergres and Wavre. The fighting petered out around 11p.m. but intermittent exchanges of gunfire lasted the entire night. Grouchy slept that night in the front lines thinking he had done quite well and was set to take his objective in the morning. Grouchy wrote to Napoléon informing him of his position across the Dyle sometime between the night of 18 June and early morning of 19 June.[122] Grouchy did not know Napoléon had already lost the battle of Waterloo.

At 2a.m. on 19 June, Prussian General Thielmann learned of the great victory of Waterloo and that a corps was being dispatched to assist him against Grouchy. Around 3a.m., Grouchy sent cavalry to scout the area towards Waterloo to try to establish contact with the main French army. Grouchy did not know it but he was in grave danger. The victorious Prussians had sent General George Pirch's II Corps to come in behind Grouchy. Fortunately for Grouchy's men, the exhaustion of the Prussians returning from Waterloo meant they were not able to complete their mission of catching Grouchy.

At daybreak, the battle of Wavre started again. By 10.30a.m., Grouchy's troops had forced the river crossings at Bierges and Vandamme's III Corps had taken the town of Wavre. Thielmann pulled back thinking Grouchy would have to retreat at some point, and he could lure him further towards Brussels to trap him later.

Grouchy thought he had performed admirably on 18 June 1815 and during the campaign. He had followed Napoléon's orders. He had re-established contact with the Prussians after the battle of Ligny, followed them, and engaged and defeated the Prussian III Corps under Thielmann on 18 June at Wavre. On the morning of 19 June, his cavalry pushed into the suburbs of Brussels, where he thought he was going to reunite with Napoléon and Ney's forces. They would not want to be late for the victory parade. Grouchy's forces had taken the village of Bavette and his cavalry was on its way to Brussels, when a haggard and defeated-looking man approached Grouchy's headquarters. The man was an aide-de-camp sent by Marshal Soult informing him of the defeat of the French army.[123]

The shock of the news of Napoléon's defeat stopped the advance immediately. The officer had no written orders for Grouchy, only the news of the defeat. Grouchy and his wing were by themselves in a hostile country without any support. Grouchy informed Vandamme of the situation, and they thought first of proceeding towards Brussels or to advance on the rear of the Anglo-Prussian army to make them stop their pursuit of the main army.[124] However, Grouchy ruled out these options. His force was not able to take on the entire Anglo-Prussian army. Further, he did not have good news for Napoléon and many deserters from the battle had spread rumours among his troops.[125]

Grouchy decided not to march towards Charleroi but towards Namur. His main objective was to cross the Sambre River back into France. Grouchy retreated to the east, away from Paris, but he knew there were no enemy forces in the area. Namur offered a crossing point back into France.

Grouchy had already numerous problems with General Gérard and General Vandamme during the campaign. Neither one liked being under Grouchy's command and preferred to serve under the direct orders of Napoléon. Gérard wanted to be a marshal and Vandamme could have been if it was not for his rebellious and obstinate behavior. Grouchy had put up with them the best he could. Grouchy commanded Gérard's IV Corps during the retreat towards Paris.

Vandamme, though, finally exasperated Grouchy by travelling to Namur ahead of his troops on the night of 19 June to find a place to sleep and did not tell anyone where he was going. On the morning of 20 June, III Corps was leaderless.[126] The corps was almost cut off and destroyed by Prussian cavalry. Grouchy wrote that he needed news of what Napoléon wanted him to do, and he hoped that when he reached Givet, he would receive orders from him.[127]

Grouchy made it to Namur on 20 June with all his men, artillery, wounded and wagon train. General Teste's division was ordered to cover the retreat of the rest of Grouchy's men and he held the city against the pursuing Prussians until he was able to make his own escape. Grouchy arrived at Dinant and decided to go to Phillipville. He was looking for the debris of Napoléon's army to link up and make a stand against the Anglo-Allied army. At about 10a.m. on 19 June, an officer from Marshal Soult arrived at Wavre with the news that Napoléon and Ney's forces had been destroyed at Waterloo. Once Grouchy learned of the disaster, he skillfully manoeuvred his forces back to France. He had to get back to Paris with his portion of the army to give Napoléon the opportunity to continue fighting. Grouchy was cut off and further from Paris than both Blücher and

Wellington. He marched east away from Waterloo and detoured through Dinant and Namur. Soult ordered him to march on Laon as soon as possible to reunite with the fragments of the French army.[128] On 21 June, Grouchy wrote to Napoléon that he had won a victory over the Prussians at Wavre, which, along with the news of the heroic defence of Namur by General François Teste's division, gave Napoléon hope of continuing the war.[129] Meanwhile, Napoléon, for the second time, had abdicated. Grouchy collected the remains of the *Armée du Nord* and marched on Paris. On 25 June, the provisional French government put Grouchy in command of the *Armée du Nord*. Grouchy's forces entered Paris on 29 June and had beaten the Anglo-Prussian army to the capital. Grouchy had collected nearly 60,000 men in front of the capital for a fight if the provisional government wanted it.

They did not. Grouchy turned the army over to the Minster of War, Marshal Louis Davout on 29 June 1815 and ended his active military career.[130] Now, he had to fight for his life. He had to get out of France as soon as he could. He escaped via the island of Guernsey to escape to America. From there, maybe, he could wait for Napoléon's return one day. He was one of Napoléon's most faithful followers and now he would pay the price for his loyalty.

Like Marshal Ney, Marshal Grouchy was charged with treason against Louis XVIII; however, he had left France as soon as he could and escaped to Philadelphia in the United States. Ney's execution made him a martyr. Ney was at Waterloo and paid with his life. Grouchy was not at Waterloo and escaped with his life to live in exile in America.

Grouchy was an enigma. He was an ardent Bonapartist in 1815 but soon became the object of Bonapartist propaganda and an object of derision. The old regime aristocrat would be attacked as an incompetent, coward, and as a traitor by several officers and men who served with him during the campaign. Even before the myth was created, the Napoléonic legend began to question Grouchy's intentions and loyalty in 1815. He was an aristocrat who served in the *Armée du Rhin*, supported Moreau and became scapegoat for Waterloo. For Emmanuel Grouchy, the battle of Waterloo never ended. He fought a bitter battle with former colleagues and friends over his role in the campaign. Grouchy died a slow death; he watched his reputation and character be assassinated over the next 32 years.

In the peace negotiated between the provisional government and King Louis XVIII, Grouchy found out he was proscribed and wanted for treason. His promotion to marshal was nullified and he returned to a general's rank. Accompanied by his family, he went into hiding and waited, hoping for Napoléon's release from Saint Helena, possibly to return to England or come to America. Both Napoléon and Grouchy hoped for the return of Napoléon II and the fall of the Bourbons.[131] When it was apparent Napoléon was not going to be released by the British government, Grouchy plotted with Napoléon's brother, Joseph, to free the usurped leader. In 1816, there was a plan for Grouchy to lead an expedition to free Napoléon, but the plan failed because of an informant.[132] Another plan via Montevideo also failed in early 1817.[133] He had enough of intrigue and recognised the futility of rescuing Napoléon out of his island prison.

Grouchy wanted to go home after these failures. He worked to get a pardon and left the task of rescuing Napoléon to the Lallemands.[134] He and Vandamme laid low and started the process of applying to return home and petitioned for a pardon in late 1817. This created a rift between the Grouchys (father and sons) and the Lallemands. In 1818, Grouchy was forced to sell Chateau Villette to the former minister of police, Joseph Fouché, to raise money to further his efforts to secure a pardon.[135] While Grouchy was endeavouring to get pardoned, he heard the first reports of being blamed for losing Waterloo in American newspapers.[136] He rejected this accusation vigorously. He was accused by Napoléon's supporters as being a traitor. Were they more upset at Grouchy for not successfully rescuing Napoléon or for not being at Waterloo? Were his comrades upset he was abandoning not only Napoléon but Napoléon II?

Grouchy had a daunting task. After the numerous lies spread about him by Napoléon and his loyalists, Grouchy had no other choice but to defend himself publicly by writing his own accounts of the Waterloo campaign. The public fight was over Waterloo, but there may have been other reasons for such a smear campaign of Marshal Grouchy.

The first book in a long line of books written by Grouchy was Observations sur la relation de la campagne de 1815, publiée par le général Gourgaud: et réfutation de quelques-unes des assertions d'autres écrits rélatifs à la bataille de Waterloo (1818). He was being attacked to further officers' personal and self-serving interests.[137] Up until the emperor left Rochefort,

Napoléon had not said anything negative about Grouchy's conduct during the campaign.[138] According to Grouchy, everything coming out of Saint Helena was imaginary, intended to cover up Napoléon's own mistakes during the campaign. Grouchy was particularly disturbed by Napoléon's criticism of the deceased Marshal Ney, who could not respond to the allegations made against him. Grouchy recognised that people around the world searched for information from Saint Helena; he also understood news of Napoléon sold well. Gourgaud wanted to make money and further his career by telling his stories. Grouchy, on the other hand, wanted to protect his reputation and defend his conduct during the campaign.[139] Grouchy found fault with the *Moniteur's* and Napoléon's version of Waterloo that insisted it was the fault of the soldiers who panicked when they were attacked by the Prussians from the flank and the rear.[140] Grouchy thought it was unjust to blame the troops for losing the battle. As for himself, Grouchy was incensed that Napoléon sent an aide-de-camp to write the book in the first place; undoubtedly, it was composed with Napoléon's knowledge.[141] Grouchy rejected Gourgaud's assertion Grouchy should have been at Wavre on the night of 17 June; however, Grouchy did agree it was difficult to ascertain the direction of the Prussian retreat on that day since they had at least a 15-hour head start.[142]

The battle of Ligny ended around 9p.m. on 16 June. A cold weather front moved in and clouds blocked the moon, preventing effective pursuit of the Prussians that night. Grouchy knew that to destroy armies, one must pursue them vigorously. He asked Napoléon at 9.30p.m. for orders to pursue the Prussians but was told to wait for orders until the morning. The clouds obscured the moon making it impossible to ascertain in which direction the Prussians retreated.[143] On the morning of 17 June, Napoléon toured the battlefield of Ligny and conferred with General Gérard and Marshal Grouchy about political matters and the reaction of Paris to the victory.[144] While Napoléon was deliberating with his officers, the Prussian army had regrouped at Wavre. Grouchy also made the point he was not in command at Ligny on the morning of 17 June Napoléon was. Grouchy was only put in command of the pursuit force in the afternoon.

A disagreement broke out between Napoléon and Grouchy over the order to pursue the Prussians. Grouchy pointed out if Blücher had retreated on Namur, he would be out of his sphere of operations, splitting the army in two parts without knowing exactly where the Prussians were. He could find his forces isolated and destroyed. Grouchy asked Napoléon to go with him to fight the British. Napoléon's response was typical: he did not welcome Grouchy's observations and, instead, reiterated his orders to find and destroy the Prussians.[145]

Grouchy reminded Gourgaud the Prussians had two avenues of retreat: one eastward towards the Meuse River via Liège or Namur; the second north-westward to move closer to the British army. Thinking the Prussians were taking the first line of retreat, Napoléon ordered Grouchy to move towards the east, but verbally modified his orders to scout eastwards and move north-eastwards towards Gembloux, until the Prussian army had been located.[146] Grouchy could move either direction from Gembloux depending on which way the enemy retreated.

The order sent to Grouchy at 1p.m. from the battlefield of Waterloo by Marshal Soult proved controversial:

> Monsieur le Marechal,
>   You wrote this morning at two o'clock to the Emperor that you would march on Sartavalin. Therefore your plan was to take you to Corbaix or Wavres. This is in line with His Majesty's thoughts, of which you have been communicating. However, the Emperor ordered me to tell you that you must always operate in our direction; it is up to you to see where we are, you are to adjust accordingly, and link our communications and to be always able to fall on troops of the enemy which seek to disturb our right, and crush them. *At this time the battle is won on the line of Waterloo.* The center of the enemy is at Mont-St-Jean and manoeuver (towards us) to join our right.
>   The Duke of Dalmatia
>   P. S. A dispatch letter has been intercepted, General Bülow is to attack our flank: we believe we can see that body on the heights of Saint Lambert and do not waste a moment to get closer to us, and join us to crush Bülow, to catch him in the act.

The order was written in pencil; the line '*En ce moment la bataille est gagnée sur la ligne de Waterloo*'[147] would be, and still is, a source of controversy. If the battle at Waterloo was already won, he concluded he was to follow his orders to move towards Wavre. According to official documents, the word '*engagée*' (engaged) replaced '*gagnée*' (won). However, by the time Grouchy received this order, his forces were already fighting at Wavre.

He was already in the process of flanking Wavre at Limale and Limalette. Grouchy, without knowing it, had complied with this order by moving his forces closer to Napoléon's main force.

By the end of 18 June, Grouchy had crossed the Dyle River. He sent scouts towards Saint Lambert and Brussels in order to make contact with Napoléon's army. He was surprised the Prussians attacked him on the morning of 19 June. They received the news of Waterloo before Grouchy.[148]

Grouchy was not culpable for the failure of Waterloo; he would adamantly defend himself against anyone who tried to place the blame on him. He wanted Napoléon to be successful and, at the time, was considered a faithful servant of the emperor. He was exiled for this devotion; thus, it is of little surprise he took being blamed for losing Waterloo personally. He unwaveringly maintained the campaign was lost before 18 June.[149]

According to Grouchy, the idea Napoléon ordered him to Wavre on 17 June was absurd. It was Gourgaud's fantasy, Napoléon ordered Grouchy to cover his flank by marching parallel to the emperor's forces. Neither Napoléon nor Grouchy knew where the Prussians had retreated on the morning of 17 June. Napoléon ordered him to pursue the Prussians. He pursued the enemy to Wavre. He followed, found, and fought the Prussians on 18 June. He did not have orders to aid Napoléon's wing until the afternoon of 18 June. He had not acted indecisively, as Gourgaud claimed, but with energy and vigour.[150] He made up the lost time from 17 June by re-establishing contact with the Prussians.

Additionally, Napoléon did not order Grouchy towards Wavre until 18 June, as opposed to Gourgaud's contention it was the 17 June. How could Grouchy's forces intercept the Prussians, who were closer to the British than he was? Napoléon did not recall Grouchy until it was too late. Had Napoléon sent an order for Grouchy to join him on the night of 17 June or early morning of 18 June, he could have joined the main force at Waterloo in time to participate in the battle. Grouchy argued that by the time the crisis existed, it was too late. Napoléon did not think he needed Grouchy's men to defeat the British army at Waterloo. Grouchy added that not starting the battle at dawn on 18 June allowed the Prussians time to march to the battlefield.[151]

Generals Exelmans and Gérard argued Grouchy should have 'marched to the sound of the guns'. When Grouchy responded at the time with the decision to proceed towards Wavre, it was unclear where exactly the enemy was to west of their position. As they were discussing their options, a messenger reported the Prussians were strongly posted at Wavre. Grouchy had contacted the Prussians. He was determined to fight them according to his directives. At the three officers' meeting at Sart-a-Walhain, Grouchy declined the request of Gérard and Exelmans to go to Waterloo because he had orders to keep his forces together. Grouchy knew there were Prussians at Wavre, but he did not know how many of them were there. He could be facing the entire Prussian army. To send half of his forces towards Waterloo without orders, or knowing where the enemy was exactly, did not make sense. He also knew Napoléon would be fighting a battle on 18 June in the direction of Waterloo and had not recalled him. Grouchy did mistakenly think the cannon fire was a rear-guard action by the British whom he believed to be retreating. By continuing to Wavre, he could cut off the escape route for the Prussians back towards Liège and Namur. When he received Soult's orders at 4p.m. on 18 June, he thought Napoléon had already won the battle of Waterloo and, thus, he was in the perfect position to link up with Napoléon and march on Brussels.[152] It was plausible Grouchy thought he would fight another battle on 19 June against the Prussians with Napoléon's aide.

Finally, Gourgaud made the point in his book that Grouchy was ordered to do three things: he was to pursue the Prussians; he was to attack the left flank of the British army; and he was to cover the right flank of the army. Grouchy agrees the first order had been given but not the second or third. He argued when Napoléon detached him from the main army it was with the express order to pursue the Prussians, not to aid Napoléon's forces fighting the British.[153] Grouchy expressed a desire for events to have turned out differently, but in his view, he was not the cause of the defeat of Waterloo. The argument between Gourgaud and Grouchy would continue for years.

Marshal Grouchy was granted a pardon in 1819 but remained in America until after Napoléon's death in 1821. As soon as he returned, he began to write once more. A Paris edition of Grouchy's book, dated 1819, is a copy of the 1818 account; however, its publication in France had a slightly different purpose. Marshal Grouchy's son, Colonel Alphonse Grouchy, had been allowed to return to France in 1819; this edition was printed with the express intention to help his father be able to return to France. Alphonse worked on an English translation, but it was never published. He also took care not to directly insult Gourgaud, stating '[i]t was written under the eyes of Napoléon'[154] and he did not doubt its authenticity. Alphonse also added, 'I can prove that General Gourgaud, by an exaggerated honorable devotion without a doubt, has been led to commit some errors, and made to believe in orders that were not and could not have been given.'[155]

Soon after the publication of the Paris edition, Alphonse received a hot response from General Gérard. In the letter, Gérard was incensed by the assertion his corps was slow in getting to Wavre on 18 June. He complains, as well, about a newspaper article about the incident regarding the general's advice to march to the sound of the guns. It was only his friendship for Grouchy's brother-in-law, Louis Gustave le Doulcet, Comte de Pontécoulant, kept him from going public with his version of events.[156] The general was upset by the marshal's treatment of the IV Corps, which he commanded; he accused Grouchy of not telling the complete truth about the conduct of his corps.[157] He reminded the marshal that Vandamme's corps was bivouacked a mile and a half north of Gembloux and his was half a mile south. The 'slowness' was due to his men having to cover the extra two miles and march through the town.In addition, Gérard noted the marshal chose to use only one road to march in and in only one column.[158] Alphonse Grouchy wrote many times in 1820 trying to placate Gérard – but to no avail.[159] Gérard also insisted Alphonse retract statements made in the newspapers about orders his father received.[160]

By 1820, the matter seemed to be closed, but on 4 November 1829, a similar letter once again appeared in the military journal *Le Constitutionnel,* this time inserted by Marshal Grouchy. Gérard took the matter as an insult to both him and the men of IV Corps.[161] Gérard decided to publish the letters between himself and Alphonse in response to the insult. A new battle over Waterloo erupted.

The reaction was swift, and a new set of publications emerged from the debate. The marshal wrote a series of books defending himself from attacks, seemingly from all sides. The vicious attacks of the 1820s questioned the marshal's career, especially over his role in Waterloo. Grouchy seems bitter in these books and fed up with the criticism. The attacks were not just on him but on his family as well. The more he fought, the worse his critics attacked him. The legend and myth of Napoléon were too much for Grouchy to fight against, yet he persisted, much to the Bonapartists' dismay. The feud between Gérard and Grouchy grew over the years.

Grouchy's first book in the series, *Fragments historiques relatifs à la campagne de 1815 et à la bataille de Waterloo,* started by addressing the comments of Gérard's book.

Grouchy reiterated his explanation for why he chose not to 'march to the sound of the guns'. The marshal also reminded Gérard of the distances between Sart-a-Walhain and the site of the battle, calculating his forces could not have stopped the Prussians before the critical phase of the engagement.[162] Gérard's plan to cross the bridge at Moustier was rejected by Grouchy because he could not divide his force in the face of a superior enemy.[163]

Additionally, he rejected this plan because the last communication from Napoléon was to march towards the Prussians at Wavre not to Waterloo.[164]

The marshal took umbrage with Gérard's complaint about using only one column in approaching Wavre; the roads were in terrible shape from the rain and the countryside was much worse. The army could not traverse the rain-soaked landscape efficiently.[165] The Prussians were strongly posted behind the Dyle River at Wavre; to carry out Napoléon's orders, Grouchy would need all his forces to carry the town.[166] Gérard's chief of staff, Colonel Simon Lorière, could not have known at the time three Prussian corps had left Wavre for Waterloo and the corps at Wavre was only a rear guard.[167] If Marshal Grouchy had allowed Gérard's IV Corps to 'march to the sound of the guns' while Vandamme's III Corps was engaged with the Prussians at Wavre, Vandamme's force would have been placed in an extremely dangerous situation. Vandamme's men could have been isolated and destroyed by the Prussians. Grouchy's two corps likewise could be destroyed one by one if they could not support one another. As Grouchy did not know how many Prussian corps were at Wavre when the request was made to march to Waterloo, the best possible solution was to support Vandamme's corps with Gérard's corps. Therefore, Grouchy denied the request to 'march to the sound of the guns'.[168] Grouchy flatly rejected Gérard's claim Grouchy had misinterpreted his orders from Napoléon.[169]

Grouchy questioned how Gérard could believe such lies about him. He remarked if lies were often enough repeated, people would begin to believe them. Grouchy questioned why Napoléon tried to shift the blame onto both himself and Marshal Ney for losing the battle. Grouchy did not disguise his frustration in fighting these allegations of 'lies, false documents, and imaginary orders'.[170]

Grouchy wrote the next book in the series to defend his sense of honour. He was particularly offended by the satirical book *Waterloo: Au General Bourmont* by poets Auguste Méry and Joseph Barthélemy.[171] The authors dedicated their work to the treasonous General Bourmont. They described their poetry as being a combination of the politics of Charles François Lebrun and the poetic style of Victor Hugo.[172] In the text, they described the battle as the moment the English finally beat their arch enemy; the British would forever harken back to Waterloo and Wellington as their supreme triumph and hero.[173] However, their story included a version that insisted Wellington had the help of French traitors. Though Méry and Barthélemy do not call Grouchy a traitor outright – as they do Bourmont – they do question his loyalty to Napoléon.

In their poem on Waterloo, they address the right wing of the *Armée du Nord*. The authors questioned the loyalty of all the officers in the right wing of the army:

> What are you doing so far, Grouchy? Why do you delay, Exelmans, formerly always in the advance guard?
> And Gérard, never deaf to the call of the cannon?
> And Vandamme? And you so all powerful of reputation?
> No doubt that seeing your march deceived
> You broke in your hands your useless sword,
> And you covet, filled with a holy wrath
> The glittering plain which we fought without you.[174]

To have an argument in public was one thing, but to be mocked was quite another. In 1829, Grouchy responded to the poem by writing *Fragments historiques relatifs à la campagne de 1815 et a la bataille de Waterloo: lettre à messieurs Méry et Barthélemy*. In his response, Grouchy gave the two poets a detailed account of his movements on 17 June and 18 June, and he reminded them Napoléon ordered him to march on Wavre, where he fought a battle. The battle of Wavre was forgotten by the two poets. Grouchy denied starting late on 18 June so that his soldiers could make soup[175] and he did not communicate with Napoléon. He insisted the first assertion was absurd and the second false.[176]

The next issue Grouchy addressed was the poets' unjust blame of him for the loss at Waterloo. He explained to the authors, the documents and maps they were using from the 'official' record were made up after the battle to conform to Napoléon's version of events.[177] He asked his critics how Napoléon could have thought 30,000 men could contain 100,000 men. The enemy knew the plans of Napoléon to use the 'central position' strategy against them. Blücher had fought Napoléon many times and knew Napoléon was trying to separate the two armies.[178] Grouchy argued if Napoléon had moved at daybreak on 17 June towards Wellington with all his forces and attacked Wellington at sunrise on 18 June, then they would have defeated Wellington before Blücher could have intervened. Grouchy's point is clear: Napoléon chose to do many things in the campaign that led to his defeat at Waterloo.[179]

Grouchy had to respond to yet other attacks on his ability as a military commander. His friend, General Jean Lamarque, alerted him to an account by Anne Savary Duc de Rovigo; the former minister of police of the empire. Grouchy took Savary's book to be a direct attack on his actions in Waterloo.[180] His response was to compose *Refutation de quelques articles des mémoires de M. le Duc de Rovigo*.[181] In this 15-page booklet, he defended himself against charges that he was not loyal to France or Napoléon. Grouchy reminded Savary he was in the front lines throughout the period, while Savary was behind the lines. Grouchy was hurt by Savary's bitter attack against him. He also wondered why he would insert in his memoirs the writings of Gourgaud without consulting his refutation of the claims made in it. As for Savary's opinion on Waterloo, Grouchy disregarded Savary's 'proclamation of Napoléonic infallibility',[182] insisting there were many causes for the defeat at Waterloo that Savary refused to explore.[183]

From 1815 to 1830, the Bourbon kings, Louis XVIII and Charles X, did not suppress these public debates about Waterloo. The French military was divided into several camps, which was to the Bourbons' liking. Grouchy was a loyal follower of Napoléon; what could be better than an argument between Bonaparte's loyalists. Without the army's support, Napoléon could have never come back in 1815; they endeavoured to make sure Napoléon II would not either. Napoléon's old guard was disbanded and any officer

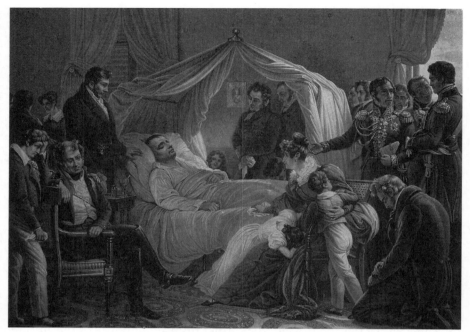

The death of Napoléon Bonaparte at St Helena in 1821 (Wellcome Images, Creative Commons license)

with Bonapartist leanings was retired and put on half-pay. The Bourbons also wanted the officers to atone for their sins by making it a requirement to receive their half-pay to attend church services once a week.[184] The army was for the most part was entirely remade between 1815 and 1820. Regiments were disbanded and renamed after departmental legions. The French army was destroyed and then pieced back together. In 1819, General Marie Latour-Maubourg was made minster of war and started the process of reassembling the army. Old veterans were allowed back in to the army and the new recruits were in awe of the men who fought for Napoléon. To the young recruits these men were the Napoléonic legend incarnate. In 1823, the army put down the Carlist revolt in Spain, but it only did so after bungling much of the invasion. It helped that the Carlist regime offered little resistance.[185] It was the old soldiers who had done most of the fighting.

In 1824, Louis XVIII died and Charles X became king of France. Charles X hated the army and tried to keep it at bay. He viewed the military as politically unreliable and he needed to boost his popularity and distract the military. On the pretext of protecting shipping and to collect old debts incurred during the Napoléonic era, Charles ordered the French Army to invade Algeria on 14 June 1830. The man chosen to lead the expedition was General Bourmont. It was nearly the 15th anniversary of Bourmont's betrayal of Napoléon before Waterloo. However, it was the anniversary of Napoléon's two greatest triumphs; Marengo and Friedland. Charles wanted to use the invasion as political cover for changing the charter of 1814. The invasion had the opposite effect; it only bolstered Charles' enemies when the new changes were announced in July 1830.

The Bonapartists flocked to overthrow the Bourbons once again, this time without Napoléon. They claimed the Bourbons were only the lap dogs of the allies. However, the revolution was in danger of going too far and the Bonapartists had to wait for events to unfold.

In three days of fighting, the revolution of 1830 overthrew Charles X. Politically, the allies would still not allow Napoléon II to rule France. The next best thing for the bourgeois minsters was to elect Louis-Philippe, Duke of Orleans, as king. Louis-Philippe took the title of king of the French; he was a constitutional monarch. He was a liberal at first who supported the cause of liberty. He wanted to aid revolutionaries in Brussels who were trying to form a new country, Belgium. Louis-Philippe decided to restore the *Grande Armée* and embrace Napoléon's officers. He chose Nicolas Soult to become Minster of War once more.[186] The King of the United Netherlands wanted Belgium to remain in the Netherlands. Louis-Philippe decided for the leader of the expedition to be the newly promoted Marshal Gérard.[187] Gérard, not Grouchy, would lead France's troops back into Belgium to redeem the French army's honour.

However, Louis-Philippe did find it politically expedient to keep their feud going. He reinstated Grouchy's promotion and granted him a peerage in the new government. Grouchy became once again Marshal Grouchy. For accepting the promotion and peerage, many of the Bonapartists labelled him a traitor.

Napoléon made Grouchy a marshal because he merited it. Indeed, over the years, Napoléon grew to like this outsider who once supported his rival Moreau. Napoléon came to rely on Grouchy's leadership and ability to execute his orders during the later years of the empire. He ably executed Napoléon's

Napoléon II, also known as Franz Duke of Reichstadt by the Austrian painter Leopold Bucher (1797–1858) (Malmaison, Musée national des châteaux de Malmaison et Bois-Préau, public domain)

plans on many occasions. Yet, he was blamed for losing Waterloo? Many historians have accepted Napoléon's account of what happened at Waterloo. By blaming Grouchy while imprisoned on Saint Helena, he was protecting his own historical legacy. Napoléon could have admitted his mistakes at Waterloo. He did not and blamed subordinates for his failures. Napoléon made a choice to sacrifice one of his most loyal men to maintain his place in history and for his son Napoléon II.

Napoléon's leadership during the Belgian campaign was sluggish. He did not communicate to his subordinates in a clear and concise manner, nor did he communicate with them often. His lack of communication with Grouchy became obvious only after the battle.

Napoléon should have never fought the battle of Waterloo. Napoléon should have pursued the Prussians on the night of Ligny but he did not. Napoléon followed his mistake by detaching Grouchy without knowing

Charles X of France in his coronation robes by Jean-Baptiste Paulin Guérin (public domain)

where the Prussians were located. Napoléon's entire plan required him to achieve the central position. Wellington and Blücher denied him the central position by retreating. Furthermore, the Prussians occupied the central position on 18 June 1815. Napoléon was caught in a trap of his own making. He sent Grouchy away from his army, thus separating his smaller force in the face of a superior enemy.

Hans Zieten's I Corps and Bülow's IV Corps did most of the fighting at Waterloo and 'marching to the sound of the guns' would not have saved Napoléon's army. The Prussians had two other corps and would have been able to delay Grouchy long enough and the outcome of Waterloo would have been the same. Napoléon had to come up with an explanation of how he lost. Napoléon blamed Grouchy for Waterloo but did not credit him for saving at least part of the army from the debacle Napoléon was responsible for. What mattered to Napoléon was his own version of events and his place in history. The scapegoat for Waterloo was Grouchy.

Louis-Philippe, King of the French by Franz Xaver Winterhalter (Royal Collection, public domain)

Napoléon's myth and legend would transcend Napoléon's death. Grouchy remained loyal to the emperor to the end and was even one of the few marshals who attended Napoléon's funeral in 1840, despite the bitter public debate surrounding Grouchy's role during the Hundred Days.[188] The battle of Waterloo never ended for Grouchy. He defended himself against the attack made by Napoléon for the rest of his life. He published many books defending his reputation and honour. His name was adopted by the English for a person who grumbles and complains. Grouchy's life became a never-ending defence against the legend of Napoléon. Grouchy died in 1847 and he is still defended by his family up to today.[189]

The debates about the battle of Waterloo kept the memory of the Napoléonic Empire and its glory alive during the restoration period in France and abroad. Interest in the topic during the 19th century only increased. Grouchy's honour required him to defend himself. Napoléon, through Baron Gourgaud, blamed Grouchy, and that was enough for the veterans of the French army. Napoléon and Ney were dead, Soult was silent and Grouchy defamed.

The next phase of debates would be waged between professional military historians, poets and the descendants of the men of the Waterloo campaign. The British continued to celebrate their 'near run thing', and the French continued in their attempts to understand what had happened to them at Waterloo. Grouchy could only defend why he was not responsible for the defeat. The Waterloo campaign became the 19th century's most refought debate. Was it Napoléon who lost or was it Wellington who won the battle? Which myth was correct? The militaries of Europe looked to the campaign to glean lessons of the campaign for the future. The debates on the theories that ensued still are being discussed today.

CHAPTER FOUR

Lessons from Waterloo:
Military Theorists

Grouchy's writings stirred the intellectual debate about military operations and his role at Waterloo. Antoine-Henri Jomini and Carl von Clausewitz tried to make sense of Waterloo. The two men tried to glean and distill Napoléon's military legacy for application in the future. Jomini was influential in military circles until World War I and Carl von Clausewitz's writings are still influential in the 21st century.

Jomini and Clausewitz were interested in the analysis of the battle of Waterloo and an accurate depiction of the battle. They called into question the accounts of both Napoléon and Wellington and tried to correct their attempts at controlling the memory of the battle. They were both veterans of the Napoléonic Wars and had real experience with war. After Waterloo, they had time to reflect on what had taken place.

People read their works to find out what to do and not do in war. From their writings on the battle of Waterloo, we have perhaps the greatest insight on war and how war is connected to political action. However, both men approached the topic differently.

Jomini tried to make sense of Waterloo by using maths and geometry to explain how the Napoléonic way of war worked. Jomini argued reason could explain the defeat at Waterloo. His interpretation of Waterloo celebrated the triumph of reason over emotion. Jomini exposed Napoléon's obfuscation of events and orders. In doing so, he exposed Napoléon's works on Saint Helena as a fabrication of memory.

Clausewitz, on the other hand, argued experience was the best method of explaining war. His experience rejected the idea that reason could explain

Antoine Jomini (public domain)

war and Waterloo. He argued Waterloo was a product of Napoléon's way of war. Napoléon's defeat was, in part, what he called the 'fog of war'. The Prussians had learned the lessons of Napoléon well. Their memory of their defeats at Jena and Aüerstadt in 1806 gave the Prussians, and especially Blücher, the desire for revenge pure reason could not explain.

The campaign in Belgium in 1815 influenced military thought and operations. The campaign served as a case study of operations and of the conduct of war. The theory of war was profoundly influenced by the campaign and the culminating battle of Waterloo. Jomini and Clausewitz looked for lessons that could help guide future generals and leaders on the nature and essence of war. They studied the campaign in Belgium in detail and produced detailed analyses and theories based on the campaign and the battle of Waterloo.

Antoine-Henri Jomini was Swiss by birth but was excited by the ideals of the French Revolution and joined the French army. He served under

Carl von Clausewitz by Karl Wilhelm Wach (public domain)

Marshal Michael Ney and wrote his first major theoretical work, *Treatise on Major Operations,* in 1805.[1] The book explained how Frederick the Great had managed to keep Prussia together during the War of Austrian Succession and during the Seven Years War. He outlined how to study warfare as a science. For Jomini, 'Strategy is the key to warfare; that strategy is controlled by invariable scientific principles; and that these principles prescribe offensive action to mass forces against weaker enemy forces at some decisive point if strategy is to lead to victory.'[2] He followed up his theoretical work in 1806 by publishing *Critical History of the Military Campaigns of the Revolution.*[3] Several editions of these two works were made during the Napoléonic Wars and were popular before Waterloo.

Jomini continued to serve Marshal Ney until 1808. He held a dual commission with the Russian army and resigned his French commission in August of 1813 to serve in the Russian army. He was not at Waterloo but did serve as a military advisor for Alexander I in 1815. After Waterloo, he wrote several books on military theory and the campaigns of Napoléon and the French Revolutionary wars.

In 1827, Jomini published a biography of Napoléon in four volumes. Chapter 22 of this work was dedicated to the campaign in Belgium in 1815. He examined the minutiae of the campaign. He wished to credit Napoléon for his genius but also wanted to rectify the reputation of the two men who Napoléon blamed most for the failure of the campaign, Marshals Grouchy and Ney.[4] In step-by-step fashion, Jomini described how the French lost the campaign and the battle of Waterloo.

The first major mistake of the campaign was made when Vandamme's III Corps did not receive orders to advance on Charleroi. This delay allowed the Prussians, who occupied the city, enough time to warn Blücher of the advancing French army. Blücher was able to issue orders for a concentration of his forces on Gembloux on 16 June.[5]

Napoléon's plan on 16 June was to occupy the crossroads of Quatre Bras on his left and Sombreffe on his right. This plan, according to Jomini, agreed with his own theory of interior lines. If either the British or Prussian army attacked Napoléon, he could have switched troops from either his left or his right via the road between Quatre Bras and Sombreffe.[6]

The French army made a series of mistakes on 16 June that led to the defeat at Waterloo. Napoléon blamed Ney for being tardy in taking the crossroads of Quatre Bras on 16 June but Jomini defended Ney. Jomini pointed out he had only been appointed to command the left wing of the army after travelling from Paris the previous day. He did not know where the men were positioned when he took command. Additionally, since he had arrived via stagecoach, he did not even have a horse.[7]

Ney received written orders from Napoléon via his aide-de-camp, Auguste Flahaut,[8] at 11a.m. on 16 June to take the crossroads of Quatre Bras. This written order was preceded by a verbal order by Napoléon on the evening of 15 June. Ney hesitated, according to Jomini, because D'Erlon's I Corps was in the rear of the army and needed time to march to the point of contact with Ney's other forces.[9]

Meanwhile, Wellington had collected enough forces to stop Ney's eventual advance.

However, it was the speed of the collection of the Prussian corps on the village of Ligny, south of the crossroads of Sombreffe, which alarmed Napoléon the most. Napoléon had to deal with the Prussians.

Jomini suggested Napoléon had the opportunity to completely defeat the Prussians at Ligny. The problem was the British occupied the crossroads of Quatre Bras. Jomini argued Napoléon had three options to defeat the Prussians at Ligny. The first option was to stop Ney's advance on Quatre Bras and move both I and II Corps on Mablais to turn Blücher's right flank and attack from the rear of the Prussian lines while Napoléon attacked the Prussians from the front. He could have then left Francois-Étienne Kellerman's III Cavalry Corps to cover Ney's flank from any British advance. The second option was to take D'Erlon's I Corps toward Ligny and leave General Honoré Reille's II Corps and Kellerman's III Cavalry Corps on the defensive in front of Quatre Bras. The third option was to have Ney attack Quatre Bras with his available forces (Reille's II Corps) as soon as possible and then, once in control of the crossroads, turn towards Ligny.[10]

Jomini argued the best option was the first option because it could have produced the victory Napoléon needed to destroy the Prussians. However, Napoléon rejected both option one and two in favour of option three. In attacking Quatre Bras, Napoléon hoped to pin the British there and not interfere at Ligny via the Namur Road that linked Quatre Bras and Sombreffe.[11]

Napoléon thought Ney had enough forces to take the crossroad if he moved immediately on the morning of 16 June. At 2p.m. on 16 June, Marshal Soult sent Ney the following order:

> In bivouac in front of Fleurus, 2p.m.
>
> Marshal: The Emperor instructs me to inform you, that the enemy has concentrated a corps of troops between Sombref and Bry, and that at half past two, Marshal Grouchy with the third and fourth corps will attack it. His majesty's intention is, that you also attack those in your front; that after having pressed them vigorously, you turn in this direction, and aid in enveloping the corps of which I have just spoken. If this corps is first routed, his majesty will then maneuver in your direction, to facilitate in a like manner your operations. You will immediately inform the Emperor of your dispositions, and of what is happening in your front.[12]

According to the order, Napoléon thought there was only one Prussian corps near Ligny. From the order, at some point Ney could also have expected troops to be sent his way if the Prussian corps was dealt with swiftly. However, the order also pinned Ney to Quatre Bras until it was taken.

Napoléon's attack on the Prussians at Ligny did not go as planned. During the afternoon, three Prussian corps arrived. Another mistake by the French was that on the morning of 16 June no orders were given to General Georges Mouton Comte de Lobau's VI Corps. Now Napoléon needed Lobau's men and he realised they were too far away to intervene at Ligny. However, D'Erlon's I Corps was marching towards Quatre Bras. Napoléon sent General La Bédoyère to D'Erlon with a copy of the orders Napoléon had sent to Ney. Soult wrote to Ney:

> In bivouac at Fleurus between 3¼ and 3½ o'clock.
>
> To Marshal Ney.
>
> I wrote you an hour ago, that the Emperor would attack the enemy in the position he has taken up, between the villages of St. Amand and Bry; at this moment the engagement is most decisive. His majesty instructs me to say, that you should at once maneuver in such a manner as to envelope the enemy's right, and fall with might and main on his rear; if you act with vigor this army is lost. The fate of France is in your hands; so do not hesitate in executing the movement ordered by the Emperor, and move forward upon the heights of Bry and St. Amand, to concur in perhaps a decisive victory; the enemy is taken en flagrant dèlit, at the moment he seeks to join the English.[13]

The order instructed Ney to assist Napoléon at the battle of Ligny; La Bédoyère told D'Erlon to start his men towards Bry and Saint-Amand, not towards Ney. Jomini noted this was one of the most important mistakes of the campaign. Ney did not know D'Erlon was already heading towards the battle of Ligny. Ney still needed D'Erlon's troops to defeat the enemy forces at Quatre Bras. Ney was furious D'Erlon was moving without D'Erlon being ordered to do so by Ney. At Ligny, D'Erlon's men were seen arriving on the French rear of their left flank. This movement pinned Napoléon's Imperial Guard, who were about to launch an attack on the Prussian centre, until they could confirm the men marching on their left flank were indeed friendly and not the British. Just as D'Erlon was spotted by Napoléon's men, he received an order from Ney to return to Quatre Bras.[14] Now, thoroughly confused, D'Erlon marched back to Quatre Bras.

D'Erlon's 20,000 men could have made the difference in either battle; however, they participated in neither battle, since his men were marching back and forth between the two battles.

Jomini argued it would have been better if Ney had not gone for Quatre Bras when he did. Jomini faults both Napoléon and Ney for the loss of time. Quatre Bras was not taken on 16 June, despite the efforts of Reille and Kellerman to do so. At Ligny, Jomini thought Napoléon got lucky.[15]

Roughly 60,000 French beat 90,000 Prussians. Jomini listed two reasons for the French victory. First, Marshal Grouchy had pinned Thielmann's Prussian corps in place. Thielmann protected the Namur Road. The Prussians needed to keep this road open because they expected Bülow's corps to arrive on that road via Namur. At the same time, Blücher took personal command of an attack on the Prussian right. At this time, Napoléon launched his Imperial Guard into the centre of the Prussian lines. Napoléon split the Prussian army in two.[16]

The victory at Ligny was mixed with the repulse of Quatre Bras. It was late when the battle of Ligny ended. Jomini was critical of Napoléon for not having launched his cavalry upon the Prussians while they were retreating. The delays of the day had compounded. It was late when the battle of Ligny ended and it was dark. Napoléon's cavalry could have caused the retreat to become a rout, but no pursuit was ordered by Napoléon.[17]

Jomini cited Ratisbonne in 1809, Dresden in 1813 and Montmirail in 1814, as instances where Napoléon acted vigorously to pursue an enemy after defeating them. After Ligny, he did nothing. Even if Napoléon had followed up Blücher at dawn on 17 June, the Prussians could have been defeated. Jomini argued Napoléon could have even marched all his men in the morning on Quatre Bras and finished Wellington. It was a mystery to Jomini why Napoléon did not vigorously pursue the Prussians on the morning of 17 June.[18]

Marshal Grouchy asked numerous times for orders to pursue the Prussians during the night and early morning of 17 June. Napoléon never sent orders to Grouchy but did issue orders to Grouchy's cavalry directly to find out where the Prussians were. Napoléon once again bypassed the chain of command of his junior commanders.[19] Reports from the French cavalry indicated the Prussians had fallen back towards Namur but also some units had retreated northwards.

Jomini came out on Marshal Grouchy's side of the debate on Grouchy's actions of 17 June. Jomini attacked Napoléon's narrative from Saint Helena that Grouchy was verbally told to pursue the Prussians, not to lose sight of them and hold Grouchy's forces between the Prussians and Napoléon's forces. Napoléon claimed on Saint Helena that the two forces could operate on interior lines to assist one another while separating the British and Prussian forces.[20] Jomini cited both statements from Grouchy and eyewitnesses were false. According to Grouchy:

> Nothing of the kind was said to him; that on the contrary, he received, without other comment, the order to direct his pursuit on Namur and the Meuse: finally, that having indicated the desire of not withdrawing to such a distance from the main body of the army, Napoléon humorously asked him, if he pretended to give him a lesson.[21]

Napoléon should have sent Grouchy to the north-east towards Liége. This action would still have put Grouchy between the British and the Prussians if Blücher had retreated towards Namur but also close enough to support Napoléon if he was needed. Jomini attacked Napoléon's narrative that Grouchy was supposed to protect his right flank from the Prussians.

The best order, if that was the case, was to order Grouchy to cross the Dyle River at Moustier to advance on Wavre via the left bank of the river.[22]

In Jomini's account, Napoléon claimed to have sent a courier to Wavre at 3a.m. to instruct Grouchy to occupy Saint Lambert, to the west of Wavre, on 18 June.[23] Grouchy denied the existence of the order and, additionally, it would have been impossible to carry out the order even if it was given. If an order was sent, the courier would have not reached Grouchy at Wavre on the morning of 18 June since the Prussians occupied it. Furthermore, Grouchy wrote to Napoléon he was at Gembloux on the night of 17 June. The vague orders given to Grouchy on 17 June had initially sent him east towards Namur. Napoléon then reversed the orders and sent him west towards Gembloux. Jomini was suspicious of Napoléon's account from Saint Helena that he had ordered him north.[24] Napoléon's supporters argued Grouchy should have been in Wavre on the evening of 17 June because Napoléon had ordered him to Wavre on 17 June. Jomini pointed out it would have been easy to have made such a march if he had been ordered northward to Wavre. The order to go to Wavre on 17 June was not executed or delivered and no such order was in the records of Napoléon's staff.[25] Was Napoléon lying about his orders to Grouchy?

Jomini did not completely exonerate Grouchy. He argued many mistakes could have been overcome if Grouchy had marched west towards Moustier in the morning of 18 June.[26] However, he also added this movement would not have affected the outcome of the battle of Waterloo. Blücher had enough troops to send to Waterloo and hold off Grouchy to affect the battle of Waterloo. This movement too had its risks since it would have put Grouchy up against a force nearly three times his size trying to cross a river.[27]

According to Jomini, the movement on Moustier would have done two things. First, it would have stopped the march of Bülow on Napoléon's right flank and rear. Second, it would have forced Blücher into a strategic dilemma of continuing on the Mont-Saint-Jean, meeting Grouchy and opposing his crossing of the Dyle or continue to retreat towards Brussels.[28] Even with a bold move on Moustier, Grouchy at best would have only lessened the scale of the defeat at Waterloo.[29]

Napoléon and his forces marched off towards Quatre Bras and Marshal Ney around noon on 17 June. It rained in torrents on 17 June and Napoléon chose not to give battle. Wellington retreated towards Mont-Saint-Jean on 17 June and made camp there that night. Napoléon's forces followed and rested in front of the British before starting another engagement. He wanted to rest his troops and horses while it was raining.[30]

Napoléon's plan of battle indicated he did not expect the Prussians to arrive on the battlefield. Jomini's ideas on interior lines dictated if Napoléon intended to link up with Grouchy; then his attacks on the British lines would have been directed towards the British left.

Napoléon launched a feint towards Hougoumont on the British right flank; then, he would attack the left of the British line. When both flanks were pinned or supported by moving troops from the centre, then Napoléon would send in his Imperial Guard to rupture the centre of the British lines.[31] For Jomini, this indicated he was trying to duplicate a similar battle plan against the British that he used against the Prussians.

Napoléon argued he waited four hours to let the ground dry before commencing the attack on the British. Napoléon also stated the weather began to clear in the morning. Jomini challenged both statements. First, it would have taken much longer than four hours to have dried out the waterlogged fields. Secondly, the sun did not appear to do any of the drying out and it was misty in the morning of 18 June.

Jomini concluded the delay on the morning of 18 June demonstrated Napoléon's belief that Blücher was nowhere near the battlefield. He wanted to rest his troops and thought he had the time to do it. Had he used those four hours to attack Wellington, the Prussians would have arrived on the battlefield after the battle had been won by the French.[32]

Jomini examined the great cavalry charge during the battle in which Marshal Ney took so much criticism from Napoléon. The charge was effective but not decisive. Napoléon claimed to have not wanted to use the heavy cavalry and guard cavalry in such a manner, but according to Jomini, the charge bought enough time for the Young Guard and Lobau's VI corps to retake Plancenoit. The cavalry did put the British army into square formation and pinned them in place, while the attack on Plancenoit was successfully carried out. Had Plancenoit not been needed to be retaken, the Young Guard and Lobau's VI corps would have been able to follow up the cavalry's charge. They would have caught the British infantry in square formation and destroyed them.[33] Therefore, in Jomini's opinion, the Prussians had affected the outcome of the Ney's great cavalry charge.

Napoléon hoped Wellington would weaken his centre to support his flanks.

However, Wellington did not and placed most of his forces in the centre of his lines.[34] However, Wellington was only allowed to shorten his left flank because of the timely arrival of the Prussians on the immediate British left.

According to Jomini, the battle of Waterloo was over once the Prussians arrived in force between eight and nine o'clock on 18 June. Hans Zieten's Prussian corps arrived to support the British left flank, which allowed Wellington to shift men from his left to the centre. Napoléon thought he still had time to win the contest and decided to attack the British centre with the Imperial Guard. The British repulsed the attack of the French Guard on its lines and followed up by counter-attacking the French. At roughly the same time, 60,000 Prussians finally overwhelmed the 15,000 French forces defending Plancenoit. Both the British and the Prussians advanced on the now outnumbered French forces. From 9p.m. on, the pressure on the French army was so great it collapsed into a rout.[35] Napoléon had lost the campaign in Belgium.

Jomini interviewed many of the participants of the Belgian campaign for his work and sought to refine his idea by examining how the Napoléonic Wars were fought. Jomini's books were popular and profitable. Readers enjoyed Jomini for his ability to consolidate Napoléon's way of war into universal maxims.[36] He put a collection of essays together on war called *The Synoptic Analysis of War* in 1830 that served a basis for his next book, *The Art of War.*[37]

In 1838, Jomini published *The Art of War* to try to explain how the Napoléonic Wars were fought. He sought to examine strategy in its component parts. He defined strategy as 'The art of war, independently of its political and moral relations, consists of five principalparts, viz.: Strategy, Grand Tactics, Logistics, Tactics of the different arms, and the art of the Engineer.'[38]

Jomini's main interest was in how one could repeat the Napoléonic way of warfare. He categorised the area in which an army was to fight as a 'theater of operations'.[39] Each operational area has a unique geography in which an army had to operate, and in the case of 1815, it was Flanders. Understanding the geography of Flanders was critical in the outcome of the battle. Rivers, roads, weather and topography were all important military factors that influenced the campaign of 1815.

According to Jomini, the dominant position in the Flanders was the Meuse River. Whoever controlled the river held the decisive strategic point. From the Meuse, the French could pick which direction to attack from and destroy an enemy. An enemy would be flanked by the river and could be pushed back into the North Sea. Jomini did make the exception for British forces since they could escape the fate of a continental army by using a base from either Antwerp or Ostend. In 1815, had the British lost at Waterloo, they could have easily retreated on either port to make their escape.[40]

Jomini explained the disaster of Waterloo because of the use of the theory of interior lines. Wellington was closer to Blücher than Napoléon was to Grouchy. Jomini was critical of Napoléon's decisions on how to take the initial objective of his campaign, the city of Brussels.

> Can the result of the march of Napoléon and Grouchy be forgotten?
>
> Leaving Sombref, they were to march concentrically on this city, – one by QuatreBras, the other by Wavre. Blücher and Wellington, taking an interior strategic line, effected a junction before them, and the terrible disaster of Waterloo proved to the world that in immutable principles of war cannot be violated with impunity.[41]

Jomini thought this strategic error was the reason Napoléon lost the campaign.

On the other hand, Wellington's choice of a battleground was also as important. Wellington's position at Waterloo followed what Jomini called a good tactical defensive position.

> The rules to be generally observed in selecting tactical positions are the following:
>
> To have the communication to the front such as to make it easier to fall upon the enemy at a favorable moment than for him to approach the line of battle.
>
> To give the artillery all its effect in the defense.
>
> To have the ground suitable for concealing the movements of troops between wings, that they may be massed upon any point deemed the proper one.
>
> To be able to have a good view of the enemy's movements.
>
> To have an unobstructed line of retreat.
>
> To have the flanks well protected, either by a natural of artificial obstacles, so as to render impossible an attack upon their extremities, and to oblige the enemy to attack the center or at least some point in the front.[42]

The position in front of Mont-Saint-Jean was similar to other places Wellington had fought and conformed to Jomini's rules. Wellington's defence at the lines of Torres Vedras in Portugal was one such example of a favourable defensive position. The flanks of the British lines were well protected by the Chateau of Hougoumont and by the rivulet of Papelotte.[43]

Jomini credited the Prussians with marching to the field of battle to destroy the French army. He insisted Blücher's march was a strategic rather than a tactical decision. Jomini maintained Blücher was lucky the battle had not ended before he arrived.[44] Had Napoléon started the battle earlier;

the British could have been defeated and the Prussians could have been defeated piecemeal as their corps arrived at Mont-Saint-Jean.

Jomini also wrote that the ability to use cavalry was diminished in the battle because of the terrain and the strong position on the flanks. He argued the position made Marshal Ney attack the centre of Wellington's lines with his cavalry. Papelotte and Hougoumont negated the ability of the French cavalry to conduct a flanking movement on the British.[45]

Another event that decided the battle, according to Jomini, was the formation the Middle Guard chose to adopt to attack the British lines at the end of the battle. The Middle Guard formed a column formation that was too deep and too tightly packed together. It limited mobility and was susceptible to small arms fire and artillery.[46]

Jomini continued his analysis in *Art of War* on Waterloo by adding appendices in subsequent editions to discuss troop formations at Waterloo. In a conversation with the Duke of Wellington at the Congress of Verona in 1823, he discussed the various formations of the French at Waterloo. Wellington stated the Hanoverian, Brunswick and Belgian troops were not as reliable as the British troops.[47] Wellington believed troops in line formation were superior to those in column formation depending on the circumstances and the spirit of those troops. The conclusion was if the British troops were not where they were, then the attack of the Middle Guard might have succeeded.[48]

Jomini argued this was not accurate. According to Jomini, the use of columns could have forced the centre. He discounted the British musket fire and their use of lines over columns. He cited four reasons for the loss as:

1. To the mud, which rendered the progress of the French in the attack painful and slow, and caused their first attackers to be less effective and prevented their being properly sustained by the artillery.
2. To the original formation of very deep columns on the part of the French, principally the right wing.
3. To the want of unity in the employment of the three arms: the infantry, and cavalry made a number of charges alternating with each other, but were in no case simultaneous.
4. Finally and chiefly, to the unexpected arrival of the whole Prussian army at the decisive moment on the French right flank, if not the rear.[49]

In Jomini's analysis, it was French mistakes and the arrival of the Prussians that determined the outcome of the battle, not the superiority of British firepower, formations or morale.

Jomini's works influenced both students and faculty at West Point, and he influenced the American way of war during the 19th century.[50] It was required of cadets to be familiar with the Napoléonic Wars and especially the battle of Waterloo. Jomini's writing and military theory influenced many of the leaders of the American Civil War. People read Jomini to understand how not to repeat the mistakes of Waterloo but also how to repeat the successes of Napoléon Bonaparte's way of war.

Jomini lived until 1869. He died the year before the next great debacle for the French – Sedan. His works were read until 1914, but the lessons of World War I exposed the weaknesses of Jomini's analysis for guiding military thought.[51] The military shifted from Jomini to the other great military theorist of the 19th century, Carl von Clausewitz.

Antoine-Henri Jomini and Carl von Clausewitz tried to understand the Napoléonic Wars and explain the genius of Napoléon Bonaparte. They both looked for lessons that could help guide future generals and leaders on the nature and essence of war. While Jomini concentrated on maxims and concerned himself with primarily military matters devoid of political matters, Clausewitz insisted the military could not act without its political connection. Furthermore, Clausewitz denied war could use universal principles for action. Clausewitz described war as a true art with risk and uncertainty, which could not be described solely using reason. War had to be experienced to be understood.

The Waterloo campaign was studied by both men in detail and both wrote books on the campaign. However, Carl von Clausewitz's major advantage over Jomini was that he took part in the campaign and thus had first-hand knowledge of the events of the campaign.

Colonel Carl von Clausewitz was the Chief-of-Staff of Johann von Thielmann's III Prussian Corps. Clausewitz was a veteran of many campaigns by 1815, having served in the army from 1793, when he was just 12.[52] Clausewitz attended the military academy in Berlin. In 1804, Clausewitz graduated first in his class and by 1805 had written his first major article on war.[53]

In 1806, he served in the Prussian army against Napoléon in the ill-fated Jena Aüerstadt campaign. He was captured at Aüerstadt and spent nearly a year in France as a prisoner of war.[54] Upon his release from France, he went to Königsberg and rejoined Gerhard von Scharnhorst. Scharnhorst was a capable military reformer who transformed the Prussian army. It was Scharnhorst's reforms that allowed the Prussians in 1813–15 to field an army capable of challenging the French.

Clausewitz took part in the reforms that the Prussian army underwent under Scharnhorst. During this time, he revised his thoughts on war and concluded theory must stand the test of reality. Jomini and others had used mathematics, including geometry, as foundations for forming military theory, but those assumptions did not work in practice.[55] War was not maths or geometry; it was emotional and unpredictable. Jomini's interior lines did not work in practice either because all war depended on actual engagement with the enemy.[56] War dealt with politics and uncertainty. The real purpose of war was to continue state policy by other means.[57] Perhaps the most important thing Clausewitz did in Königsberg was to attend the lectures of Johann Kiesewetter. His lectures emphasised logic and ethics. Kiesewetter was a student of Immanuel Kant and taught Clausewitz his method of analysis.[58]

In 1811, Clausewitz resigned his commission in the Prussian army in protest over the Prussian government's decision to allow Napoléon access to Prussia to serve as a staging area for the invasion of Russia in 1812. He was angry the Prussian government agreed to Napoléon's demand for 20,000 Prussian troops to serve in an auxiliary corps for the invasion. During the subsequent campaign, he served as a Russian colonel and at the end of 1812 was instrumental in concluding the Convention of Tauroggen, which allowed the Prussian auxiliary corps under General Ludwig Yorck to defect to the allies.[59] Even though he was acting in Prussia's best interest, he was not allowed to return to Prussian service for the 1813 campaign. He eventually returned to Prussian service, and by 1815, took up his post as the chief-of-staff of the corps under General Thielmann.

Clausewitz served admirably in the 1815 campaign. He fought at Ligny and at Wavre. At Ligny, III Corps covered the retreat of I and II Corps after they had been ordered to retreat at the end of the battle.[60] They held the Sombreffe crossroad until 3a.m. on the morning of 17 June. III Corps was directed to Wavre on 17 June with the mission to act as a rearguard for the main Prussian army, while Marshal Blücher took the rest of the army to Waterloo.[61] Thielmann had orders to follow the rest of the army to Waterloo if the French did not show up at Wavre.[62]

III Corps had a good defensive position at Wavre. The river was flooded on 18 June from the torrential rains of 17 June, while the buildings of Wavre were made of stone and masonry with only one major bridge in the middle of town. Thielmann and Clausewitz directed the defence of the town and repulsed General Dominique Vandamme's attempt to take the town. Eventually, Marshal Grouchy arrived with the rest of his men and flanked Wavre by crossing upstream at Limal, Limalette and Bierges. Thielmann heard of the news of the victory at Waterloo at 8a.m. on 19 June yet Grouchy's forces renewed the fighting that morning. The French finally breached the defences of Wavre at 9a.m. and Thielmann ordered a retreat soon after realising Grouchy would have to retreat himself once he learned of the defeat of Napoléon.[63] Clausewitz played an important part in helping defeat Napoléon. Though they technically lost the battle of Wavre, III Corps was able to protect the Prussian rear for long enough from French Marshal Grouchy for the flank march of Marshal Blücher to succeed and defeat Napoléon's forces at Waterloo.

Clausewitz was promoted major general in 1818 when he accepted the post of directorship of the Prussian Staff College. Starting in 1819, he began his most famous work, *On War*.[64] He wrote this book while writing several others on Napoléonic history, including one on Napoléon's Italian campaign and a work on Waterloo.[65]

Clausewitz may have felt it was his duty to write about Waterloo and the Prussian involvement in the campaign. General Fredrich Bülow died in 1816; Marshal Gebhard Blücher died in 1819; and Johann von Thielmann died in 1824. All three – who may have had the most to say about the campaign – died before writing their memoirs. August von Gneisenau and Clausewitz both died from cholera in 1831. Otto von Pirch died in 1838 and Hans Zieten died in 1848; both without having written anything on the campaign. The Prussian commanders filled out their combat reports and they deposited them in the archive. Others would write the history of Waterloo.[66]

The only other Prussian who wrote anything on the campaign of 1815 was Carl Müffling. He was Wellington's Prussian liaison officer during the campaign but was not with Prussian forces on 17–18 June.[67] Müffling's account did reveal two things; first, Wellington ordered a general advance after the repulse of the French Guards to make sure it would seem the Prussians only helped after the battle had been won and, second, Wellington had already intended to call the action the battle of Waterloo by the time Wellington met Blücher at La Belle Alliance.[68] If anything, Clausewitz was helping fill a gaping hole in the history of Waterloo from the Prussian point of view.

Clausewitz's work on Waterloo was originally released in eight volumes from 1832 to 1837, after Clausewitz's death. He examined the role of Wellington and the relationship between the British and Prussian armies during the campaign of 1815. He was openly critical of Wellington's conduct during the campaign.

Clausewitz started with the initial dispositions of the allies. He was critical of both Blücher and Wellington for having the armies so spread out. The allied forces took longer to concentrate than either commander thought. Wellington was more at fault in this regard and his slow concentration of forces led to him not being able to support Blücher on 16 June. Blücher made mistakes in his initial deployment and it nearly cost him his army at Ligny. Bülow's IV Corps had the longest distance to march to the concentration point at the Sombreffe crossroads and insufficient time was allotted to the corps to make the march to concentration point.[69]

Clausewitz argued Blücher's decision to fight on 16 June was with the understanding that some British troops would be made available to support his right flank via the Quatre Bras–Namur Road.[70] Furthermore, Clausewitz defended Ney's actions of 16 June. Ney's men forced the British to concentrate on Quatre Bras and not march to aid Blücher. In many ways, Ney's mission was a success and Napoléon was able to fight the Prussians free of British intervention. Clausewitz discounted the idea that D'Erlon's forces could have made a huge difference in the battle. The Prussian army could have easily changed its facing and intercepted the new troops coming in on their flank.[71] He argued the Quatre Bras position was not as important as others who applied algebra in their analysis of the battle. The crossroads were not as important an objective which would have changed the campaign. The position was not the point; it was important Ney occupy Wellington's forces long enough for Napoléon to defeat the Prussians at Ligny.[72]

During 17 June, Clausewitz organised the retreat of Thielmann's corps to Wavre. His corps covered the rest of the Prussian army's retreat. He wrote that Napoléon's assertions on Saint Helena about this day and the whereabouts of Marshal Grouchy were hardly credible and not to be believed.[73]

As for the battle of Waterloo, Clausewitz's main criticism of Napoléon was he never imagined the Prussians would arrive on the battlefield. According to Clausewitz, how the battle of Waterloo was fought demonstrated this assumption by Napoléon.[74] Napoléon believed in two things; first, Wellington's army was completely concentrated at Mont-Saint-Jean and, second, Blücher would not intervene.[75]

Clausewitz divided the battle into four parts. The first phase was the attack on Hougoumont. The second phase was D'Erlon's attack on the British at 2p.m. The third was the arrival of the Prussians under Bülow. Finally, the attack and repulse of the French Guard was the last phase.[76]

After 3p.m., the British only faced 45,000 men to their front since the Prussians had drawn off significant reserves to retake the village of Plancenoit. Wellington did not have the best troops according to Clausewitz, but they had 68,000 men to face the French attacks. He argued this was a significant factor in the British being able to repulse the French Guard and win the day.[77]

Waterloo was an excellent case study for *On War*. No other battle was so directly linked to state policy and its political outcome. Clausewitz defined war as, 'an act of force to compel our enemy to do our will'.[78] Waterloo clearly demonstrated this principle. Waterloo may have been the genesis of the Clausewitzian trinity which examined the relationship between the people, government and the army, and their enemies. At Waterloo, the allied triangle won over the French triangle. Clausewitz argued the real victory of Waterloo was political. Napoléon was the army and the government of France. With his defeat, the people would not support him for another campaign. Napoléon's failure led to the allied state policy being carried out. Conservatism of the old regime won at Waterloo. Napoléon's political and military mistakes finally caught up with him.[79]

Clausewitz did recognise the genius of Napoléon and that, he argued, could not be reckoned with science. Men can affect changes and 'rise above all rules'.[80] Clausewitz also argued moral forces cannot be ignored in war.[81] The moral force of Blücher led him to make the decision to support the British at all costs because he had experienced the occupation of Prussia under Napoléon. Blücher hated Napoléon and wanted his empire destroyed.

Clausewitz argued few defeats turn into debacles. Battles like Waterloo had political ramifications that magnified the military defeat. What turned them into debacles were:

1. The enemy's greater loss of material strength.
2. His loss of Morale.
3. His open admission of the above by giving up his intentions.[82]

Waterloo demonstrated these points perfectly. Napoléon's army was out-numbered and lost more men than the allied armies. The French army was routed from the battlefield. Finally, Napoléon had to give up his intended goal of securing Brussels.

Clausewitz argued by 1815 the Prussians had learned the French way of war and mastered it. The lessons of the Prussian defeats in 1806 at Jena and Aüerstadt were not lost on Blücher and the Prussian leadership. Clausewitz argued it was the effective pursuit of the Prussian army that destroyed it in 1806. At Waterloo, the Prussians pursued the French, so the defeat of Waterloo was magnified into a rout.[83] Also, Waterloo demonstrated fighting to the end prevented any effective means of organised retreat. After the French Imperial Guard was committed to the attack, Napoléon had no reserve to break off the action and fight another day.[84]

Clausewitz's experiences and memory of the Waterloo campaign changed his perspective on war. *On War* was an unfinished work and only published after his death in 1832 by his widow. Still, his works on Waterloo demonstrated how to use history to understand how future wars were to be fought. His writings were not initially as popular as Jomini's and his analysis on Waterloo was rejected by Wellington.

Perhaps one of the most important lessons of Waterloo was how war was analysed and framed as an intellectual pursuit. The battle was studied by the military theorists of the 19th century to learn the lessons of war on the strategic and tactical level. Antoine Jomini tried to understand

Napoléon's way of war through science and reason. Carl von Clausewitz, meanwhile, understood war as an act directly connected with politics. Waterloo offered lessons for both men and still offers us insight today regarding the relationship between politics and war. Clausewitz and Jomini challenged Napoléon and Wellington's versions of Waterloo.

They renegotiated a space for discourse in which one could be critical of Napoléon and Wellington while recognising their martial talents.

CHAPTER FIVE

Victor Hugo's Waterloo

The outcome of the battle of Waterloo cast a long shadow over the 19th century. As the men who fought in the wars started to die, the next generation began to look for the meaning in the post-Waterloo world. They could read Jomini or Clausewitz, but it gave them little solace that they could have won the battle. Conservatism had won, and Frenchmen could read about the ideals of the revolution and glorious victories of Napoléon but could not experience them for most of the 19th century. Victor Hugo and his family were a part of the epic events of the 19th century and exemplified the transition from greatness to defeat and back again. To understand Waterloo and to move beyond it, Victor Hugo wrote a semi-autobiographical historical fiction novel that the world has come to know and love as *Les Misérables*.

The main characters of the novel were drawn from Hugo's own remarkable life and his experiences during the 19th century. He wanted to make France great once again. He chose as his protagonist for the novel a man called Jean Valjean, a convict. As Valjean's antagonist, he chose a man who represented Napoléonic justice, Inspector Javert. Valjean was like France after Napoléon's defeat at Waterloo. France was miserable and had to bear the burdens of her past transgressions on Europe. Valjean, who becomes a man of virtue, tried to cope with his own past and atone for his sins. For France, Waterloo was a part of the healing process to bring France back into the family of nations. Hugo argued Waterloo was the necessary price to eventually bring what Hugo hoped for, a republic.

Woodburytype of Victor Hugo by Étienne Carjat (Bibliothèque nationale de France, public domain)

The battle of Waterloo was a beginning, not an end, for France. France could be great once again, but it had to forget the excesses of the revolution, Bourbons and empire. Although France's innocent people paid the price for the country's sins and they enabled it to harness a new power; the virtue of self-sacrifice. *Les Misérables* demonstrated how love and hope can overcome misery and history. A person could be more than his or her past in Victor Hugo's *Les Misérables*. Hugo felt the weight of Waterloo in his own life as did millions of others who lived and died during the 19th century. It was *the* battle, it cast a pall over France's glory and its future. Hugo hoped by giving voice to what injustice and avarice arose in the world from men of power,[1] he could help ease the pain of those who suffered from such men, not just in the past, but in the future as well. Napoléon, Louis XVIII, Charles X, Louis-Philippe and Napoléon III all oppressed the common man; their only defence was in the establishment of a republic that protected the 'miserable'.

Napoléon III after Franz Xaver Winterhalter (unknown, public domain)

The pen of Victor Hugo was ultimately mightier than Napoléon's sword. Napoléon did not win the battle of Waterloo. Victor Hugo's *Les Misérables* transformed and transcended the defeat and made it a victory not for Napoléon, but for France. Hugo used the theme of justice throughout the novel. He learned during his life the often unequal and haphazard way justice manifested itself. He incorporated this lesson; serve an idea, not a man.

Hugo's *Les Misérables* is arguably one of the greatest novels of 19th-century French literature. Although a work of fiction, much of it was autobiographical in nature. In *Les Misérables*, Hugo expressed his own inner struggle about his family, his relationship with his mother (Sophie Trébuchet Hugo), who was an anti-Bonapartist, his godfather (the ardent republican General Victor Lahorie) and his father (General Joseph Hugo).

Additionally, two events, the 'Malet Conspiracy' and the battle of Waterloo, were essential for the formation of Hugo's masterpiece *Les Misérables*.

Hugo's work was his legacy and commentary on 19th-century France. It is also an attack on Louis-Napoléon or Napoléon III and his Bonaparist ideas. The novel's serial approach made it accessible to the general public and was a huge hit. His work on Waterloo expressed the solidarity with the dead of Waterloo and with the living to fight misery and overcome injustice. Nineteenth-century France was wracked with political turmoil. The victims of this turmoil were often labeled 'the miserable'. Hugo wanted to prove through his prose that the defeat at Waterloo was God's judgment on the Napoléonic Empire. In the book, Hugo seems to come to terms with these facts and the complex relationships of his family. Hugo had to come to terms with his father, step-father and his younger self.

Victor Hugo's father, Joseph Léopold Sigisbert Hugo, attended the Royal College in Nancy and enlisted in the regiment of Beauvais in 1787 at the age of 14 but was rejected for being too young. Contemporaries said he was a born soldier and preferred military exercises over his studies. He tried again, two years later, and entered the regiment of the king on 1 February 1789.[2] When the revolution broke out, he enlisted and changed his name to Brutus.

Brutus Hugo, along with his unit, was transferred back to Paris after the Vendée rebellion. He rose from the ranks to command a battalion of the 20th Demi-Brigade.[3] However, his promotion was short lived; politics intervened, and his old battalion was given to another man.

He was happy to end his service in the 20th Demi-Brigade by May 1797. Once detached, he remained in Paris. He discovered Sophie Trébuchet, a girl he met while in the Vendée, had arrived in Paris with her brother. They renewed their relationship and on 15 November 1797, they married. It was not a happy match. Soon, Joseph was having affairs with other women. Perhaps Victor Hugo's first Waterloo was his own parents' disastrous marriage.

While in Paris, Joseph made an important connection that he thought would help his career; one day while taking a walk, he spotted Victor Lahorie. Hugo and Lahorie had first met when they fought together in the Vendée in 1793. Also, during Joseph's time in Paris, he met Adjutant General François-Nicolas Fririon. He made friends with Fririon, who served under General André Masséna. Later in life, Joseph regretted his friendship with Lahorie and cherished that of Fririon.[4] The men's careers would go in two different directions under Napoléon Bonaparte.

In 1799, Lahorie was assigned to the Army of Italy under the orders of General Jean Moreau. He became Moreau's chief of staff and followed Moreau when he became commander-in-chief of the *Armée du Rhin* in 1800. Lahorie soon asked for his friend, Captain Joseph Léopold Sigisbert Hugo, to be attached to the *Armée du Rhin* and to bring his young wife along with him.[5] Hugo was promoted to the rank of major for his new assignment. Victor was now a colonel and attached to General Jean Moreau's staff. The old acquaintances were friends once more and Lahorie asked for Joseph to join him on General Moreau's staff.[6] Joseph thought he was on his way to a promotion and advancement. Now First Consul, Napoléon Bonaparte promoted Lahorie to brigadier general on 28 April 1800 for his service in Italy and to the Republic.[7] After the battle of Hohenlinden in 1800, General Moreau requested promotions for several officers. At the top of the list was General Lahorie. However, Lahorie insulted General Charles Leclerc, Napoléon's brother-in-law, during the campaign.[8] Pauline Bonaparte made sure that word of the insult to her husband reached the First Consul's ears. The First Consul never signed Lahorie's promotion to divisional general[9] and Moreau never forgave Napoléon for this injustice to Lahorie and the perceived insult to himself.

The newly promoted Major Hugo aided Joseph Bonaparte in working out the Peace of Lunéville with the Austrians, while Moreau and Lahorie were sent back to Paris. Major Hugo made a close friend of Joseph Bonaparte. The friendship saved Major Hugo from Lahorie's fate.[10]

The Hugos had three children. Abel Hugo was born in 1798 and Eugène Hugo was born in 1800. In January 1802, Sophie Trébuchet Hugo wrote to General Victor Lahorie to ask him to be the godfather of her third child. She added in the letter that it would be named Victor or Victorinne.[11] Victorinne was expected, but Victor arrived on 26 February 1802. Technically he was the son of Joseph Hugo, but General Lahorie may have been more than a godfather to the infant – Lahorie was Madame Hugo's lover while Major Hugo had liaisons with other women.

Major Hugo did not completely escape the wrath of Napoléon for the *Armée du Rhin*. He was transferred to a depot regiment at Besançon. Soon

Joseph Léopold Sigisbert Hugo attributed to Julie Hugo (parismuseescollections.paris.fr, public domain)

Major Hugo got into a disagreement with his superior and, in a twist of fate, he was sent to the island of Elba in military exile.[12]

In 1803, Joseph Hugo was recalled to the mainland to serve in General Masséna's VIII Corps[13] and he participated in the 1805 campaign in Italy. In 1806, Joseph Bonaparte, now king of Naples, requested Major Hugo be his aide-de-camp. While in Italy, Hugo got lucky and captured the Italian bandit and guerrilla leader Fra Diavolo. As a result, he was promoted to the rank of colonel.[14] Joseph Bonaparte was made king of Spain in 1808 and requested Colonel Hugo come with him. In Spain, Joseph Hugo received his promotion to general after the battle of Talavera in 1809.

Lahorie's days as a battlefield general were behind him after 1800. He had many friends, but they were watched by the minister of police, Joseph Fouché. Generals Fririon and Bellavense were still Lahorie's friends and

Sophie Trébuchet (1772–1821) was the mother of Victor Hugo (parismuseescollections. paris.fr, public domain)

worried what would happen if he was found by Fouché. Since they were public figures, Lahorie could not stay with them. Upon hearing of Lahorie's return to Paris, Sophie Hugo insisted he stay with her.[15]

General Lahorie was the model for *Les Misérables'* main character, Jean Valjean. Like Valjean, Lahorie was a wanted man in hiding. From 1809 to 1810, the address of 12 Passage des Feuillantines in Paris (the chapel at the Feuillantines Convent) became a refuge for Lahorie. The chapel was both a refuge and a prison.[16] He was able to hide from the authorities, but he was not free to move about Paris. However, it was near Sophie Hugo's apartment. He was able to sneak off to visit Victor and Madame Hugo since they lived so near eachother. Lahorie loved Sophie Hugo and especially loved playing with young Victor. He instructed Victor on the importance of freedom and liberty. In the protection of the gardens, Lahorie taught Victor Latin and the classics of antiquity.[17]

On 30 December 1810, Lahorie was tracked down and arrested by the police.[18] He was held at La Force Prison, even though he was not charged with anything, and there he sat for nearly two years. This was Napoléonic justice.

On Friday 23 October 1812, General Claude Malet set out to launch a *coup d'état* against Napoléon Bonaparte. General Malet had strongly opposed Napoléon's elevation to First Consul in 1799. His vocal opposition alienated him from the new government. Malet was arrested and sent to La Force Prison because of his involvement with an émigré group in Philadelphia in the United States. He was moved to an insane asylum in 1809 but escaped to launch the coup.[19] Malet put on his general's uniform and called himself General Lamotte.[20] He proclaimed Napoléon had been killed in Russia and a provisional government now ruled France. The new government was to be headed by General Moreau with Malet as Minister of War and Lahorie as Minister of Police.[21] Malet was able to secure the aide of two other former generals he met while in La Force, Lahorie and Emmanuel Maximilien-Joseph Guidal, by bluffing his way in and out of La Force Prison. Guidal was in La Force for being suspected of spying for the English.[22] Generals Guidal and Lahorie captured the minister of police, General Anne Savary Duc de Rovigo while in his bedclothes. Meanwhile, Malet was himself taken prisoner by Colonel Jean Doucet, the chief of staff of the Paris Garrison, who realised Napoléon was not dead since he had received dispatches from Napoléon dated after his supposed death. The plot collapsed; soon Lahorie and the other conspirators were arrested.[23] However, it had shown how one man could come close to toppling the government in Paris.

Minister of War Henri Clarke convened a military tribunal and Jean-François Dejean presided over the trial of the conspirators. Aiding the persecution was Pierre Fouchér; the Hugos' neighbour and Victor's future father in-law. Sophie Hugo never forgave the Fouchérs for their role in the trial. Generals Malet, Lahorie, and Guidal were found guilty of crimes against the security of the state. They were sentenced to death and were shot at the plain of Grenelle at 4p.m. on 31 October in front of many spectators. Victor Hugo and his brother Eugene were at the trial but did not witness the execution; however, they read how Lahorie bravely faced the firing squad.[24] Lahorie taught Victor Hugo how men could die with pride for a cause in which they believed. When Napoléon heard of the plot, he was most upset that nobody proclaimed his son Napoléon II to be the new emperor.[25]

Napoléon gave Joseph Hugo the duty of defending the city of Thionville in 1814.[26] The city was an important crossroads in north-eastern France and defended the bridges over the Moselle. Joseph Hugo was told to hold the city at all costs to buy time for Napoléon to gather reinforcements to defeat the allied invasion of France in 1814. The fortress was eventually bypassed by Marshal Blücher.[27] General Hugo, like Napoléon at Waterloo, had the distinction of facing both Wellington and Blücher, fortunately not at the same time.

In February of 1815, Victor's mother filed for divorce from his father. Sophie had had enough of Joseph's philandering.[28] Victor and his siblings became pawns in a vicious fight during the couple's divorce. Victor would not speak to his father again until after his mother's death.[29]

In March 1815, all hopes of a quick divorce evaporated when Napoléon arrived in France. General Hugo was asked by Marshal Davout to defend the city of Thionville.[30] Despite overwhelming odds, General Hugo held the city against the invading Prussians and, eventually, the Russians as well. He had only 3,600 men but held out against the invading forces until 13 November 1815.[31] The Jewish citizens of Thionville thanked General Hugo for his defence of the city and for saving it from destruction at the hands of the Prussians and Russians.[32] His troops wrote to him in an act of loyalty and fidelity.[33] General Hugo's popularity soared. The citizens and troops hoped the king would not punish Hugo for fighting so hard against the allies.

Meanwhile, in Paris, the teenage Victor Hugo soaked up all the news from the battlefield. When he heard of the defeat of Napoléon, he rejoiced. He thought his father a tyrant just like Napoléon.[34] In 1815, Waterloo seemed like a blessing to Victor.

The divorce of his parents shaped Victor Hugo's attitude towards his father in his early years. He became a committed monarchist in his early years thanks to his mother. Sophie's influence ensured Napoléon and Joseph's name were synonymous. Victor's mother was confident her position was secure as a (by now) committed anti-Bonapartist after the fall of Napoléon. From 1815 to 1818, Victor attended the monarchist school, Lycée Louis-le-Grand, in Paris. While there, the 13-year-old wrote a song in November 1815 on Napoléon's defeat and exile to Saint Helena. The song was not flattering towards Napoléon. His mother's hatred of Napoléon and his father had a powerful effect on Victor. Napoléon's name could have easily been substituted for that of his father.[35] In his poem, 'Vive La Roi, Vive La France', Victor expressed no sympathy for the Jacobins or the soldiers who followed Napoléon:

> Corsica has bit the dust
> Europe has proclaimed Louis
> The bloody and perfidious Eagle
> Falls before the flowers of the lily
> At last, this perfidious field marshal, This Ney is going to march to his death.
> Tremble, cohort regicide;
> Jacobins, here is your fate.[36]

The battle of Waterloo affected all of France. It had to accept defeat and for three years it was occupied by the allied forces. To wipe away this insult, Louis XVIII paid off the reparations to the allied powers as quickly as possible and he had the allies depart France in 1818. For the young Victor, Napoléon was responsible for the humiliation of France.

In 1821, Victor Hugo's life changed when both Napoléon and his mother died. Now Napoléon was dead, Victor started to re-evaluate the emperor's place in French history. His mother's death freed him from her domination, and he re-established relations with his father. In 1822, Victor married the woman his mother had forbidden him to marry: Adèle Fouchér. She was the daughter of Pierre Fouchér who had reportedly alerted the Minister of Police, General Savary, in 1810 that General Lahorie was in Paris. Sophie had never forgiven Pierre or the family for the treachery.[37] Neither General Hugo nor his new wife, Catherine Thomas Hugo, attended the wedding. The wedding reception was held in the rooms of the Conseil de Guerre where, nearly ten years before, General Lahorie had stood trial for his life.[38]

In 1823, General Hugo wrote his memoirs to try to recoup the financial losses he incurred from Napoléon's downfall. These memoirs became a vehicle in which he reconnected with his son, Victor. His father ignited

Victor's love of the legend of Napoléon. He reunited with his paternal uncles, Colonel Louis Hugo and Major Fançois Juste Hugo, who were also officers under Napoléon. They filled Victor with stories of the myth and legend of Napoléon. From 1823 to General Hugo's death, Victor slowly changed his mind about Napoléon. General Hugo died in 1828 and was buried in Père-Lachaise Cemetery.

General Hugo's death had a more profound impact on Victor than his mother's death. As young Hugo matured into manhood in the late 1820s, he became disillusioned with the French monarchy of Charles X. As a result, Victor transformed into a wholehearted admirer of Napoléon but was not a Bonapartist like his brother Abel. He saw the oppression and injustice of the monarchy. Victor distrusted the concentration of too much power in one person's hand.

Victor Hugo examined the theme of justice in his 1829 work *The Last Day of a Condemned Man*. This short work became the foundation for his great work, *Les Misérables*. He continued distancing himself from his monarchist and Catholic connections in *The Hunchback of Notre Dame* in 1831. *The Hunchback of Notre Dame* demonstrated Hugo's populist leanings. He began work on *Les Misérables* in the late 1830s and it took him nearly 25 years to complete. It was released as a book series and a new installment was released over the years only to be completed in 1862.

Meanwhile in 1830, Charles X tried to curry favour with the army by launching an invasion of Algeria; he wanted to avenge the defeat of Waterloo and instructed the leader of the expedition, General Louis Bourmont, to invade Algeria on 14 June.[39] No sooner had the expedition landed in Algeria when a revolution erupted in Paris. Charles X was deposed, and Louis-Philippe proclaimed the new king.

Victor Hugo detested the new government under King Louis-Philippe. After the censorship of one of his plays, *Le Roi s'amuse*, in 1832, he publicly stated he preferred Napoléon's empire to Louis-Philippe's bourgeois kingdom. Hugo was a bystander in the revolt of 1832 that was the literary climax of *Les Misérables*. Hugo loved lost causes. They reminded him of his father and his uncles. Hugo wanted a republic, but he wanted to wait for the right opportunity.[40] He reveled in the myth of Napoléon during the 1830s and thought of Napoléon I as the champion of the poor.[41]

Hugo was fascinated with Napoléon and was repelled by Louis-Philippe's bourgeois monarchy. To placate the popular writer, Louis-Philippe made Hugo an officer of the Legion of Honour in the summer of 1837.[42]

Louis-Philippe and François Guizot arranged for the body of Napoléon I to be returned from Saint Helena and to be interred in Les Invalides in 1840. Hugo witnessed the grand parade and dedication of the Arc de Triomphe. However, he was disappointed his father's name was left off the monument. Victor admired Napoléon but his political leanings during the 1840s demonstrated a leftward drift towards the establishment of a new republic. The sun of Austerlitz shone but gave no warmth.[43]

Napoléon's funeral in 1840 was like going to a country fair. Amidst the cries of '*Vive mon grand Napoléon!*' could be heard '*Tabac et Cigars!*'[44] The procession was grand but lacked substance. Hugo called the procession Satan coming home.[45] From beyond the grave, Napoléon still had his grip on the imagination of France. Hugo thought it a false one like the empire itself. The memory of the empire was better than its reality. The funeral stands listed among Napoléon's greatest victories.[46] What Hugo remembered was that the entire spectacle was cheap and tawdry. British author William Makepeace Thackeray thought the day cold but grand and critised Hugo for his lack of poetry on the day.[47] Hugo reserved his poetry for Napoléon on this day he thought it was God's judgement of the Napoléonic era, 'the angel of judgment blowing his trumpet upon sleeping St. Jerome, – that is what I saw in a flash, that is what one minute burned into my memory for all my lifetime.'[48]

France, like Hugo, was tortured by the memory of greatness. The parade was trying to blot out Napoléon's failures in favour of his victories. They were hollow in the face of Waterloo; a façade much like the funeral itself. Victor realised nostalgia could be dangerous if mixed with politics and power. Bonapartists used the myth and legend of Napoléon to gain control of France once more.

Napoléon's tomb became a monument, as did the Arc de Triomphe. Napoléon had started the Arc de Triomphe and it was finished by Louis-Philippe. The monument listed the victories of the Revolutionary and Napoléonic Wars. Waterloo was not mentioned on the monument. Hugo begged for the inclusion of his father's name on the Arc de Triomphe but to no avail.[49]

Perhaps, Hugo's greatest honour under Louis-Philippe was his election to the Academy in 1841. It was high praise for Hugo. The poet Honoré de Balzac refused to challenge him for the election of the open seat of the deceased Louis Lemercier. As customary, Hugo gave the eulogy for Lemercier. In the eulogy, Hugo praised both Lemercier and Napoléon. The eulogy made Hugo even more popular, yet this popularity made him politically dangerous. Perhaps to pacify Hugo, Louis-Philippe made him a peer of France in 1845. As a member of both the Academy and Chamber of Peers, Victor began to exert his political power.

In 1839, Louis-Napoléon Bonaparte wrote *Napoléonic Ideas,* which attacked Louis-Philippe's regime. Louis-Napoléon claimed the political legacy of Napoléon for himself after his cousin Napoléon II died in 1832. Although Victor initially liked the young Bonaparte, he detested his book. In time, Hugo would attack both the man and the book in *Les Misérables.*

Napoléonic Ideas outlined Louis-Napoléon's thoughts on an ideal government. Louis-Napoléon thought the best two governments on the planet were those of Czarist Russia and the United States. He believed they merited praise for two different reasons. Russia maintained a centralised all-powerful government and the United States possessed grass-roots democracy and liberty. Both nations were respectable because they fulfilled their mission of civilising their parts of the world and advanced civilisation. Napoléon I bridged the chasm between the two governments. Governments since 1815 were an utter failure and doomed France to ruin.[50]

Louis-Napoléon argued Napoléon I reunited France by protecting liberty and restoring Christianity. Napoléon I completed his mission by bringing the warring factions of the revolution together and made peace with the Catholic Church. He noted the Republicans and Jacobins wanted liberty only for certain groups within France, while Napoléon wanted it for all Frenchmen. The problem with the revolution was there was too much change too fast; this inspired fear instead of hope. Napoléon I took the best of the revolution and jettisoned the rest. He made the ideas of the revolution acceptable to France because the ideas he retained were practical ideas all Frenchmen could agree on.[51] Napoléon was a champion of the common man.

According to Louis-Napoléon, Napoléon should be regarded as a messiah of new ideas. Napoléon's real purpose was to protect liberty. Louis-Napoléon and Napoléon drew on the example of Rome. Napoléon I preserved liberty by adhering to the form of a republic while maintaining a monarchy. France had liberty and glory under an Emperor. It was only Waterloo and Saint Helena that prevented Napoléon from fulfilling his mission for France.[52] Louis-Napoléon looked to Napoléon's victories, not his defeats, for inspiration. To discern Napoléon's true genius, one had to examine the problems faced by him in 1800. He reshaped France on a new model based on liberty. In his book, Louis-Napoléon wrote that Napoléon reorganised the country on the principles of 'equality, order, and justice'.[53] These were the ideals of Napoléon and for a time Victor Hugo agreed with them. Indeed, these three themes were examined in *Les Misérables*.

In 1848, he was about to release *Les Misérables* as a two-volume work when events in Paris paused the printing.[54] Revolt swept across France. The uprising called for reform and the end of the Ministry of Guizot.[55] The Revolution called for universal suffrage for all men. Guizot who famously said, 'Not to be a republican at 20 is proof of want of heart; to be one at 30 is proof of want of a head,'[56] found himself out of office on 24 February 1848 and replaced by a Republic on the next day. Guizot, who had so much heart for constitutional monarchy, was lucky not to lose his head. He went to Belgium in exile.

Victor Hugo was instrumental in creating the Second French Republic. He was elected to both the Constitutional Assembly and the Legislative Assembly. He also created a monster. Hugo, in seeking to harness the memory of Napoléon, lifted up his nephew Louis-Napoléon to the Assembly. Victor aided Louis-Napoléon by supporting his candidacy to be President of the new Second Republic. Victor welcomed Jérôme Bonaparte, the only living brother of Napoléon, back to France. Louis-Napoléon and Victor Hugo made sure the veteran of Waterloo became governor of Les Invalides and his brother's tomb.[57]

On 10 December 1848, Louis-Napoléon was elected president by nearly five million votes. By identifying with Napoléon I, Louis-Napoléon hoped the people of France would follow him as a man who could establish social order. While in the National Assembly, Hugo met often with Adolphe

Thiers, Henri Lamartine and General Louis-Eugène Cavaignac.[58] Hugo was in the inner circle of Louis-Napoléon's friends. He was friends with the second Prince of Moscow (Ney's Son)[59] and Charles Napoléon, son of Jérôme. Commenting on a mistress of Charles Napoléon and Louis-Napoléon, Hugo joked 'To change from a Napoléon to a Louis is an everyday occurrence.'[60]

Jérôme Bonaparte had misgivings about his nephew and thus relations between the two men were less than completely cordial. Jérôme detested Louis-Napoléon's strangulation of universal suffrage in France. While at the theatre, Jérôme said to Hugo, 'No one knows what is at the bottom of that man!'[61] Hugo turned against Louis-Napoléon when his two sons were arrested for printing seditious articles. Even as president, Louis-Napoléon acted as an emperor. On 2 December 1851, Louis-Napoléon launched a *coup d'état*. It was the anniversary of Napoléon's coronation as emperor of the French. Louis-Napoléon took every effort to link himself with Napoléon I. Paris was occupied by troops loyal to Louis-Napoléon. Victor opposed Louis-Napoléon's seizure of power in 1851 and was exiled from France. The Assembly was dissolved, Thiers and Cavaignac arrested and a price of 25,000 francs put on the head of Victor Hugo, dead or alive.[62] Louis-Napoléon established the Second Empire and proclaimed himself Napoléon III.[63]

Victor escaped Paris in disguise and headed for Belgium. However, his sons were less fortunate and were arrested. Hugo declared Louis-Napoléon a traitor to France and became Napoléon III's most ardent enemy abroad. In 1851 Hugo experienced his personal Waterloo. For the next 20 years, he was an exile from his beloved France.

Failing to protect France from the Bonapartists, Hugo set out to write his revenge on Napoléon III. His first work was *L'Histoire d'un Crime*, in which he detailed the events of December 1851.[64] In 1852, Hugo wrote *Napoléon le Petit*, which contrasted Napoléon I's greatness in comparison to Napoléon III's mediocrity. He attacked everyone associated with the new empire and anyone who helped Napoléon III come to power. He took aim at the rightwing military establishment.[65] The book caused such a stir within Belgium that the Belgian government asked Hugo to leave to pacify the new empire.[66] He travelled to England and on to the island of Jersey.[67]

Hugo wrote his next attack on Napoléon III, *Les Châtiments,* whilst on Jersey. Published in 1853, the work purposely exalted Napoléon I. In this work, Hugo acted as both historian and satirist. Hugo evoked images of Napoléon I as a great man who, through his own efforts, transformed France, while Napoléon III was merely a pale shadow of Napoléon I's greatness. Victor Hugo called Waterloo 'Atonement' for the empire. Waterloo was the price Napoléon I had to pay for the empire and his own greatness. Hugo credited God, not the British nor the Prussians, for the defeat and that his true punishment would be exile on Saint Helena.[68] In his book *The Sewers,* Victor Hugo attacked Napoléon III by depicting the Lion's Mound at Waterloo as laughing at Napoléon III.[69] *Les Châtiments* second chapter's first line, 'Waterloo! Waterloo! Waterloo! Somber plain!' often shows up on the guest books at the Battlefield of Waterloo by visitors.[70] Although his satire exposed many truths about the regime, Victor Hugo's bitterness towards Napoléon III came at a price. In 1855, Hugo was asked to leave the island of Jersey for the island of Guernsey[71] after an article protesting about Queen Victoria's government allying itself with France during the Crimean War (1853–56). He had to, once again, start over on a new island. Hugo began to understand Napoléon I's bitterness of exile.

Like Napoléon did after Waterloo, Hugo wrote about his own life. *Les Contemplations* were meditations on his life written in 1856. His next major work, *La Légende des Siècles,* published in 1859, was a collection of poems that confirmed Hugo's fascination for being a poet historian.[72]

In 1859, Hugo, among others, was offered amnesty by Napoléon III. He decided not to take it. Hugo believed his exile was one of principle and he should continue to oppose the regime from the outside. Hugo set about completing his great tome, *Les Misérables.* The work was partially released in installments but remained incomplete for a while.

Hugo decided to give a literary and philosophical Waterloo to Napoléon III. He had to fight both the legend and myth of Napoléon. The best way to do that was with another myth and legend. For that purpose, he chose to rewrite *Les Misérables.* Hugo wanted to invent a new collective history of the 19th century. Accordingly, the new novel was,

> Collective, familial, and personal memories; invented remembrances; analyses of earlier institutions and events, both real and imagined – all are synthesized into

a new national *histoire* whose legendary quality renders it much greater than the sum of its parts. Hugo offers a collective fictional (but not fictitious) version of the past with which to begin forging France's future identity.[73]

Hugo set out to both understand and transform what had happened to France during the first half of the 19th century. The character Jean Valjean represented the first republic, Fantine the second and Cosette the hoped-for third republic. The character of Javert represented reaction, the establishment and Napoléon's civil code. Bishop Myriel represented God and forgiveness of past sins.[74] Finally, the Thénardier family represented both the best and worst of the Bonaparte family.[75]

Jean Valjean's and the republic's imprisonment started with the rise of Napoléon. From 1796 to 1815, Valjean served his sentence for stealing a loaf of bread.[76] As Napoléon falls at Waterloo, Valjean was freed. At Waterloo, Wellington was described as a cold and calculating man who beat Napoléon with scientific precision. Wellington, like Javert, has come to put Napoléon in prison at Waterloo by relentless pursuit of his enemy.[77] Hugo chose October 1815 as the opening of the novel in which Bishop Myriel transforms Valjean from a convict into an honest man. This date was chosen because it was the month in which Napoléon arrived to serve out his imprisonment at Saint Helena. After this, events change for Valjean in 1821 when the Bishop dies and so does Napoléon. In the novel in 1821, Valjean has a Waterloo of sorts in which he must flee his beloved village Montreuil-sur-Mer.

Victor decided the best place to finish the novel was to go to the source of so much misery for France – Waterloo. Hugo travelled to Waterloo, Belgium, in 1861, via London. He arrived on 7 May 1861 and stayed at the Columns Hotel at Mont-Saint-Jean, run by the innkeeper Joseph Dehaze. The hotel's best room had a balcony in which Hugo could view the Lion's Mound to his right, the road to Charleroi to his left and a view of the broad plain of the battlefield in front of him.[78] This room's view provided the best vantage point for Hugo's imagination to run wild with visions of the battle.

The use of guide books for tourists was one way in which people could describe journeys to Napoléonic sites. The historian Victor Hugo chose to use as his guide to the battlefield was Lieutenant Colonel Jean Baptiste

Charras and his account of Waterloo. Charras's account drew many conclusions from the writings of Napoléon and his fellow exiles on the island of Saint Helena. Charras sent Hugo a copy of his work, Histoire de la campagne de 1815: Waterloo. Charras was the minister of war during the second republic and a fellow exile like Hugo.[79] Hugo decided to use his history for the basis of his chapter on Waterloo in Les Misérables. Hugo used Napoléon's myth and legend of Waterloo against the Bonapartists by subverting it.

The main character of Les Misérables, Jean Valjean, was a character partially of imagination and of fact. His model for the character was General Lahorie and the ideals of the French Republic; in essence, a myth. Like Valjean, Lahorie knew what it was to be imprisoned, love the woman of another man, raise a child of questionable parentage and die for a principle. Valjean and Lahorie had a conscience. 'An awakening of conscience is the greatness of soul.'[80] Lahorie and Valjean were caught in a moral conundrum as were the men of the Revolution. Their conscience was their only rudder. Though both men were doomed to die, they did so for the cause of liberty. Valjean's grave was simple and had no name on it like many men of Waterloo. Valjean's tombstone only had an inscription that read:

> He sleeps. Although his was a strange fate.
> He lived. When he died he had no angel.
> The thing itself just arrived
> Like night coming for the day.[81]

The epitaph could have been just as well applied to Lahorie or the men who died at Waterloo or for the Revolution. Hugo expressed his sense of loss for men who had died for their principles and it was the duty of the living to continue their work.

Hugo, through the character of Jean Valjean, expressed his own regret and remorse over his inability to thwart the demise of the character of Fantine. For Hugo, Fantine represented the fall of the Second Republic. Valjean, like Hugo himself, was too preoccupied with self-preservation and self-absorption to prevent her death.

Not only did Victor Hugo include the history of France in the book, but he also incorporated his own family's history. The character of Marius

Pontmercy was a reflection of himself as a younger man. Through this character, he tried to reconcile with his father, Joseph Hugo. Victor chose the name Marius for the character. It was a fitting name for the son of Brutus. To illustrate how Victor Hugo wanted reconciliation with his father, he called two characters in the book Pontmercy. Joseph was the model for the character of Colonel George Pontmercy.[82] Marius Pontmercy, like Hugo, had thought his father was a scoundrel. It was only after the character George Pontmercy died that Marius found out his father was made a baron, promoted colonel, and made a member of the Legion of Honour on the battlefield of Waterloo.

> At Waterloo he led a squadron of cuirassiers in Dubois' Brigade. It was he that took the colors of the Luneburg battalion. He carried the colors to the Emperor's feet. He was covered in blood. He had received, in seizing the colors a sabre stroke across the face. The Emperor, well pleased, cried to him: 'You are a Colonel, you are a Baron, you are an Officer of the Legion of Honor!' Pontmercy answered: 'Sire, I thank you for my widow.' An hour afterwards, he fell in the ravine of Ohain. Now who was this George Pontmercy? He was that very brigand of the Loire.[83]

In Hugo's imagination, George Pontmercy personified his own father. Hugo noted the pain of many because promotions and awards given by Napoléon were annulled by Louis XVIII upon his return to power and caused much bitterness among the military.[84] After Waterloo, many of the Napoléonic veterans wished they had died at Waterloo rather than live under the Bourbons.

Hugo expressed his remorse for having a bad relationship with his father. In *Les Misérables*, Marius was surprised to find out how much his father loved him, even though they were separated from each other. George Pontmercy could not see his son, much like Joseph could not see Victor. Victor thanked his father and his sacrifices for him through the novel, 'He sacrificed himself that his son might someday be rich and happy. They were separated by political opinions … . Bless me! because a man was at Waterloo does not make him a monster.'[85]

Like Hugo, Marius read *Le Mémorial de Sainte-Hélène* and the *Moniteur* for accounts of the battle and read all the bulletins of the army.[86] Hugo was consumed with reading everything about Waterloo in preparation for writing the section on Waterloo.

However, in *Les Misérables*, it was not with George Pontmercy who young Marius would have his most important relationship. Marius' most important relationships were with young Cosette and Jean Valjean.[87] Marius' life was saved by both characters in the novel. The character of Javert, the personification of the law, relentlessly pursues Jean Valjean. The law as Hugo describes it is detached from human emotion. It was Napoléon's law, the civil code, which chased Jean Valjean in the form of Javert. It was this same pursuit of blind justice that condemned General Lahorie in 1812. Hugo presented readers of his day a problem through the character of Inspector Javert. Could they condone an illegal act and still be moral? Through Javert, Hugo responded, no. As the only reconciliation between morality and the law, Javert commits suicide. The implication of this suicide was that the people of France should move to right the wrong of Napoléon III's coup and act morally to restore the republic. The myth that Napoléon was a great lawgiver and friend of the poor was not true.

For Victor Hugo, the battle of Waterloo assumed a political quasi-spiritual event. He made the pilgrimage to Waterloo while writing *Les Misérables*. Waterloo was the perfect place to refute Louis-Napoléon's *Napoléonic Ideas*.[88] He went to Waterloo to finish *Les Misérables* in May of 1861.[89] In the first book of the section titled, 'Cosette', he offered his version of Waterloo to readers.

In *Les Misérables*, Hugo employed a plot device to insert himself within the novel and to offer readers a certain history of the battlefield – his. Some of it was true and some of it was not. According to Hugo, 'Waterloo was not a battle, but a transformation of the universe.'[90] Hugo could not resist the temptation of starting his tour of the battlefield with the chateau of Hougoumont.[91] At Hougoumont, Hugo saw the handiwork of both the combatants of 18 June but also fellow tourists like himself. He found the nature of Hougoumont was transformed from a large farmhouse with an orchard to a veritable ruin. The battle had left its mark on the building but so had the tourists. They had left so many messages by 1849 that the walls in the chapel had to be whitewashed. It was a battle of wits among the visitors with each taking a side.[92] Perhaps one of the greatest fictions of Hougoumont was the well in the grounds contained the bodies of 300 dead soldiers. Some of the 300 were, according to Hugo, not yet dead when deposited in the well. This is one of the stories Hugo put in *Les Misérables* from the locals and was intended to earn them a few extra coins for telling ghost stories. It was a healthy business and one Hugo was aware of. He condemned it yet believed them nonetheless.[93]

Hugo wrote in the chapters of book one of 'Cosette' in *Les Misérables* a history of what happened at the battle. He drew upon works by Napoléon and those of his friend Charras. He argued he was not writing history but merely passing by and making observation and history should be left to the art of historians.[94]

Many of today's tourists still use *Les Misérables* while touring the battlefield. Hugo's analysis of the battle and his many walks of the battlefield gave the reader a clear basis on which to imagine the battle. He used the letter 'A' to describe the battle.

> The Left Stroke of the A is the road from Nivelles, the right stroke is the road to Gennape, the cross of the A is the sunken road from Ohain to Braine l'Alleud. The top of the A is Mont Saint Jean, Wellington is there; the left hand lower point is Hougomont, Rielle is there with Jerome Bonaparte; the right hand point is La Belle Alliance, Napoléon is there. A little below the point where the cross of the A meets and cuts the right stroke, is La Haie Sainte. At the middle of this cross is the precise point where the final battle-word was spoken. There the lion is placed, the involuntary symbol of the supreme heroism of the Imperial Guard. The triangle contained at the top of the A, between the two strokes and the cross, is the of Mont Saint Jean. The struggle for this plateau was the whole of the battle. The wings of the two armies extended to the right and left of the two roads from Genappe and from Nivelles; D'Erlon being opposite Picton, Reille opposite Hill. Behind the point of the A, behind the plateau of Mont Saint Jean is the forrest of Soignes.[95]

The use of the 'A' helped both the reader and tourist understand the battle. This description was so helpful gift shops continue to sell this account by Hugo at Waterloo.[96]

Many visitors to Belgium, including Hugo, observed there are often three seasons in a day. In summer, there is torrential rain that makes the plains of Belgium vast quagmires of mud. For the foreigner, walking the fields around Waterloo allows one to easily imagine the problems the armies had moving about in the mud.[97] Many soldiers and tourists have found their shoes so deeply sucked into the mud they were unable to retrieve them. The battle was a wet affair full of mud and muck. Hugo blamed the weather and the wet ground for starting the battle late.[98]

The allied victory was not a forgone conclusion. In Hugo's opinion, the French had a chance to win the battle. The chance occurred when Wellington feigned his retreat and Ney charged with the heavy guard cavalry. Twenty-six squadrons charged the allied line. According to Hugo, it was the hope and chance that Napoléon could win Waterloo. Hugo blamed a sunken road that was unknown to the riders and a great multitude fell in the sunken road crushing both horse and rider.[99] This sunken road near Ohain would eventually be the meeting place of Sergeant Thénardier and Colonel Pontmercy. Pontmercy was buried alive under the piles of bodies of horses and men. Hugo used Honoré de Balzac's story of *Le Colonel Chabert* as a blueprint for Pontmercy's fate at Waterloo.[100] In Hugo's account of Waterloo, the sunken road helped explain how the French lost, but no such sunken road existed near Ohain in 1815. To be fair, Hugo was writing a story, not a factual history of the battle.[101] This sunken road filled with dead men may have been Hugo's own way of dealing with the multitude of good men like his father who followed Napoléon blindly over the abyss to dictatorship.

Offering an analysis of the battle, Hugo noted the misfortune of the French. He blamed Ney for his tactical formations during the battle.[102] He blamed Grouchy for not showing up on the battlefield.[103] 'On both sides somebody was expected and it was the exact-calculator (the best gambler) who succeeded. Napoléon waited for Grouchy, who did not come; Wellington waited for Blücher, and he came.'[104]

In his analysis, Hugo argued only God could have defeated such a genius and it was providence that intervened to save the allied forces time and time again.

> Was it possible for Napoléon to win the battle? We answer, no. Why? On account of Wellington on account of Blücher? No; on account of God. Bonaparte, victor of Waterloo, did not harmonize with the law of the nineteenth century... It was time for this vast man to fall; his excessive weight in human destiny disturbed the balance.[105]

Napoléon had 'vexed God'.[106] In Hugo's opinion, the turning points of the battle were the failure of the great cavalry charge, the arrival of the Prussians, and Grouchy's failure to arrive at the battlefield.[107]

The true victor of Waterloo was General Cambronne. While the army routed off the battlefield, General Cambronne and the old guard stood like a dyke trying to stem the tide of fleeing men. One journalistic account of the destruction of the last square had General Cambronne uttering 'The Guard dies and does not surrender.' when British General Coleville asked for the square's surrender. Victor Hugo did put it more bluntly – 'shit'.[108] In France, after its publication, soldiers accused Hugo of profaning the memory of Waterloo with that word. A French soldier even earned a Legion of Honour for refuting Hugo's words.[109] Whatever the exact words, the last square of the Old Guard was fired upon by several cannons at point blank range and most of them were killed. Cambronne was severely wounded but did not die.[110] Hugo took 'Cambronne's word of Waterloo' to symbolise France's scorn for reactionary Europe.[111]

Hugo's interpretation of Waterloo maintains it was a battle between opposites, with God intervening. God's role made the English win in the short term, but the victory was Liberty's. Waterloo was the price Europe and France had to pay for the cause of liberty.

> Let us render unto Fortune the things that are Fortune's, and unto God the things that are God's. What is Waterloo? A victory? No. A prize.
>
> A prize won by Europe, paid by France.
>
> It was not much to put a lion there.[112]

In Hugo's Waterloo, the vanquished could be the victors.

Hugo asked the question, 'Must we approve of Waterloo?' Waterloo was the egg of liberty laid by an imperial eagle. He argued that the counter-revolution won against Napoléon, the Robespierre on horseback involuntarily had to become liberal to win. Yet in defeat, Napoléon became greater than he was in victory. According to Louis-Napoléon, he was a martyr to liberty. That was what made him so dangerous. A dead Napoléon with the aura of liberty could be wielded by less men, particularly Louis-Napoléon.

> The future, the jest of the emperor, made its appearance. It had on its brow this star, liberty. The ardent eyes of rising generations turned toward it. Strange to tell,

men became enamored at the same time of this future, Liberty, and of this past, Napoléon. Defeat had magnified the vanquished.[113]

Waterloo as a symbol was more important for Louis-Napoléon. Hugo's point was to illustrate how Louis-Napoléon would say he was for liberty while denying it at the same time. Hugo also noted that in defeating Napoléon, the European powers united for the first time like no other, bringing an, albeit counter-revolutionary, United States of Europe.[114] Hugo hoped from the quagmire of the Second Empire a United States of Europe could be established.[115] During Hugo's stay in Waterloo, he often walked on the battlefield. He stayed at the Hotel des Colonnes where he wrote part of *Les Misérables*. The hotel provided Hugo with the necessities of life. The hotels of this period even appealed to certain clientele. There were 'English' and 'French' hotels that provided different amenities to travellers based on national origin.

Hugo opened his chapter on Waterloo with a stroll. He wanted readers to experience the battlefield as he did a tourist looking for ghosts. His first encounter with the battlefield was to walk up from the Nivelles road towards Hougoumont. He described the ghostly terrain of the battlefield in 1861.[116] He went looking for ghosts; he found them on the battlefield in the stories of the locals.

The local inhabitants of Mont-Saint-Jean realised soon after the battle there was money to be made in items left on the battlefield. Everything was stripped from the dead to make money from the tourists flocking to the battlefield. Even the elm Wellington stood under during the battle was chopped down to make souvenirs.[117]

Several families also realised there was profit in accommodating visitors at the place where Napoléon was defeated. The hotels on the battlefield were owned by several families including the Brassine, Nicasse, Pirson and Crauwels. These hotels offered gifts, mementos and tours of the battlefield. Hugo used the death of one of the Nicasses, Matthew Nicasse, to illustrate how deep the ravine coming into Braine l'Alleud was by relating the story of his death.[118]

These families' hotels had an advantage over their competition because they were located next to the 'Butte du Lion'. They offered tours to visitors and Hugo was no exception. Locals often made spare change by offering to tell stories to tourists. Hugo took walks with his mistress and muse, Juliette Drouet.[119] Indeed, fierce competition among the innkeepers may have been another source of inspiration for the infamous Sergeant Thénardier. In *Les Misérables*, after the battle, Sergeant Thénardier became an innkeeper with a dubious reputation.

Although the real families of Waterloo were dedicated and honest innkeepers, they all knew they could make money from the myth of Napoléon. While on a walk with Juliette, Hugo encountered Florentin Cloquet of Braine-d'Alleud, an eyewitness to the battle, who saw many people robbing the dead after the battle for trinkets. These people were models, but it was Napoléon III who Hugo had in mind for the villain of his masterwork. The villainous character of Sergant Thénardier was the embodiement of Napoléon III. It was Thénardier who robbed the good men of Waterloo of their glory and lied to them to profit from their death. The Bonapartists were the great thieves of Waterloo.

Thénardier was central to Hugo's story. For Hugo, Napoléon III and Sergeant Thénardier represented the villainy of all men. Hugo made the character a sergeant in jest to Napoléon III. Napoléon I often wore the dress uniform of a corporal and underscored Hugo's contempt for Napoléon III as a charlatan. The character of Thénardier was a buffoon throughout the book like Napoléon III, only instead of being a little corporal, Napoléon III was a sergeant.

On 30 June 1861, Victor Hugo wrote to a friend, 'This morning at 8.30, with a beautiful sunlight in my windows, I have finished *Les Misérables*.'[120] Later he would add, 'I finished *Les Misérables* on the battlefield of Waterloo and in the month of Waterloo. I spent two months at Waterloo so that I could do an autopsy of a catastrophe. I have spent two months on the cadaver.'[121] In a letter to his friend Auguste Vacquerie. he wrote, 'It's on the plain of Waterloo and in the month of Waterloo that I have fought my battle. I hope I have not lost it.'[122] His work was now complete.

Hugo made France able to come to terms with Waterloo and move on with liberty. It served as a catharsis for France and for Hugo. *Les Misérables* changed how visitors experienced the battlefield from that time forward. Victor Hugo gave to France a Waterloo that it could live with and put away the memory of the past. Hugo had exorcised the ghost of Napoléon.

Waterloo was God's punishment for Napoléon's empire. Hugo hated the new one that it inspired and somehow felt it would meet its fate the same way. Waterloo swept away the old empire and the old monarchy at the same time. Never could they be repeated.

> Swords, as we have said, insulted each other; the sword of Fontenoy was ridiculous and nothing but rust; the sword of Marengo, was hateful, and nothing but a sabre. Formerly disowned Yesterday. The sense of the grand was lost, as well as the sense of the ridiculous. There was somebody who called Bonaparte Scapin.[123] That world is no more. Nothing, we repeat, now remains of it. … It has disappeared under two revolutions. What floods are ideas! How quickly they cover all that they are commissioned to destroy and bury, and how rapidly they create frightful abyss.[124]

In abridged versions of *Les Misérables,* sometimes the chapter on the battle of Waterloo is taken out but this omission misses the point of why Hugo put it in the book in the first place. The mood of the book takes on a macabre turn in the chapter, with bodies piled up in the fictitious bloody lane near Ohain. Hugo eased back readers into the overall narrative of the novel by introducing Sergeant Thénardier, who saves Colonel Pontmercy from the pile of bodies. Sergeant Thénardier is the antithesis of General Cambronne – a coward and a thief. In this way, Hugo shows the real nature of the French army: it had its heroes but also its villains.

Les Misérables was an immediate hit and paid all of Hugo's outstanding debts.[125] He received 300,000 francs for eight years and all rights to the translations. The original edition was illustrated by Emile Bayard. However, celebrated artist Alphonse de Nueville illustrated later editions with 20 imprints.[126] The book went through several editions in 1862 alone. A pocket edition, printed in 1862, allowed tourists to take the book along while touring the battlefield.[127] However, in some editions, the digression on Waterloo was left out to avoid the censors.[128] Even publishing success had its limits.

To celebrate the success of the book, the publishers held a grand banquet. Louis Blanc was the featured guest to speak in Hugo's honour. It was Blanc's work on the revolt of 1832 that inspired the climatic event of *Les Misérables.*[129] The death of General Maximilian Lamarque (a Bonapartist) in 1832 sparked the uprising in June to overthrow Louis-Philippe.[130]

Ironically, General Georges Mouton Comte de Lobau, commander of VI Corps at Waterloo, suppressed the revolt.

The book was such a commercial success it was translated into several languages. Many soldiers in the United States read it during the American Civil War. The book was popular on both sides and even transcended the conflict at times.[131] The wife of General George Pickett remarked, 'How we fought over and over the wonderful battle of Waterloo and compared it with other contests of which we knew.'[132] Robert E. Lee's men even called themselves 'Lee's Miserables' during the siege of Petersburg.[133]

There have been movies, plays and musicals based on *Les Misérables*. There have been many theatrical adaptations. The first movie of *Les Misérables* was made in 1905[134] and there have been at least 30 movies up to 2019 including a recent BBC adaptation. The most popular musical version simply called '*Les Mis*', was first staged in 1980 in Paris and continues to be popular worldwide. In most adaptations, the Waterloo digression has been removed for clarity and time considerations.[135] Hugo finally returned to France in 1870 after Napoléon III's defeat and capture at Sedan – his Waterloo. He lived in Paris during the siege and was elected to the Senate. Victor Hugo thought of running for the office of president of the Third Republic, but his advanced age persuaded him to bow out to let younger men take over. He wrote other works, but none came close to the popularity of *Les Misérables*. Victor Hugo died on 22 May 1885 in his beloved Paris.[136] The two giants of France lay on opposite sides of Paris, Napoléon in Les Invalides and Hugo in the Panthéon. Bonapartist and Republican separated forever.

Victor Hugo's contributions to the history and formation of the popular imagination of the battle transformed Waterloo for Frenchmen. Belgians, in recognition of Hugo's work and for his time at Waterloo, erected a unique monument to him – a pillar in honour of a man who did not fight in the battle. The monument's dedication took place on the 50th anniversary of the publication of *Les Misérables*.[137] The building of the monument was organised by The Society of Friends of Waterloo. However, it was the initiative of local Belgian historian Hector Fleischman and artist Maurice Dubois who made the monument possible.[138] The Hugo monument was to compliment the 'wounded eagle' monument dedicated to the last square

The portrait at the base of the Victor Hugo monument in Waterloo, Belgium (Olnnu, Creative Commons license)

of the old guard. The monument to Hugo was to be completed by 1915 for the centenary of the battle. On top of a great pillar was to be a large rooster symbolising France. The idea was to have the rooster face east and greet the sun and look forward for a new beginning for France. It was a rooster, not an imperial eagle.

Hector Fleischman laid the first stone at the monument's dedication ceremony. Like Hugo, Fleischman maintained France was not defeated at Waterloo but reborn.[139] Fleischman reflected force conquers nothing. Poets and artists in the end will win over force. The battle was not, according to Lord Byron, a 'field of bones' or 'the tomb of France'; it was much more. Fleischman wanted people visiting the battlefield to remember the ghosts of the men who fought on that day and, somehow, they were still with them on the battlefield.[140] In Hugo's work, those ghosts came alive.

However, the project nearly failed. The sculptor for the rooster was not paid in full and so he destroyed the piece. The pillar was built, but without

The Victor Hugo Column at the battlefield of Waterloo (EmDee, Creative Commons license

the rooster. Like *Les Misérables,* Fleischman's work was interrupted. Only two short years from the dedication ceremony, new more terrible battles erupted in Belgium. The monument was put on hold during World War I. It was nearly forgotten. In the meantime, a half-built monument stood until 1956.[141] A new effort to complete the work also symbolised the rebuilding of a Belgium torn apart by two world wars.

A simple plaque remains on the column there today dedicated to Victor Hugo; the true victor of Waterloo. There is neither a grand monument to Napoléon nor Wellington on the battlefield but there is one to Hugo.[142] Hugo's chapter on Waterloo in *Les Misérables* made a defeat into a victory and hope for a better day. The monument is dedicated to Hugo as much as it is to *Les Misérables* and the miserable who inspired him.

Les Misérables transformed Waterloo both physically and historically. The book provided tourists with a way to tour the battlefield that made sense. Hugo's 'A' can be used even today to tour the site. The lives of his father, mother and of his godfather all contributed to Victor's understanding of what it meant to be miserable. They, along with Victor himself, were witnesses to the Napoléonic era. For nearly 100 years, the battle was *The battle*.

Historians, authors and poets tried to encapsulate the Napoléonic era. None did it better than Hugo. As the centenary of the battle approached, it was *Les Misérables* that formed visitors' opinions about the battle. Victor Hugo was able to do in *Les Misérables* what Napoléon could not. He won the battle of Waterloo for France, not for Napoléon.

CHAPTER SIX

Imagining Waterloo

After the battle of Waterloo, the British wanted to see the battlefield. Travelling, however, was an expensive luxury most people could not afford. For those who could not make the trip, Sir Walter Scott wrote in such a way that people could imagine themselves at the battle. Meanwhile, Henry Barker and William Siborne provided visual representations of the battle to the British.

For those who made it to the battlefield, William I of the United Netherlands built a monument visitors could climb and enjoy a panoramic view of the entire battlefield. Louis Dumoulin painted a panoramic painting of the battle located at the base of the monument. All the artists interpreted the battle with different art forms, but all tried to convey what they considered to be the most important part of the battle. The attempt at memorialisation differed from art form to art form and the interpretations caused friction.

Each artist tried to portray Waterloo in their own unique way. Together, they presented a multinational, yet nationalistic, perspective of the battle. These depictions helped people experience the battle without having fought in it.

By the time of the battle of Waterloo, Walter Scott was already a literary star. He had always wanted a military career, but his right leg was injured as a baby, so he walked with a limp for the rest of his life. He became a lawyer and writer. Scott earnestly tried to do his part in the Napoléonic Wars and was a member of the Volunteer Royal Edinburgh Light Dragoons.[1]

Sir Walter Scott by Henry Raeburn from 1822 (The Bridgeman Art Library, Object 68272, public domain)

His interest in the battle was much like that of other Britons, but for him, it became even more important to assess what role the Scots played in defeating Napoléon's forces. Scott started his journey from England on 28 July 1815. He boarded a ship that had been specially commissioned for the hordes of visitors travelling to Waterloo to see where the great battle took place.[2] Arriving in August 1815, Scott travelled to Waterloo and then Paris. He kept a journal of his visit and the journal would form the basis of his novel, *Paul's Letters to his Kinsfolk*.[3]

While on his trip, he toured the Waterloo battlefield and met the Duke of Wellington in Paris. The Duke of Wellington was the one man Scott met during his life who truly overawed him. The Duke invited him to a ball in Paris where he met the Prussian royal family, the Duke of Orange and several other eyewitnesses to the battle. For Scott, these were the true 'Knights' of the Roundtable who protected the world from Napoléon.[4]

Truth was better than fiction. Wellington was what the best of England was and could be.

In this aura of euphoria, Scott penned his poem, *The Field of Waterloo* and rushed home to publish the work. He wanted to have the poem printed as soon as he returned from his trip.[5] Scott hoped to raise some money for the widows and orphans of the men lost at the battle, while raising interest in his *Paul's Letters to his Kinsfolk* project. They priced the epic poem at five shillings and made 6,000 prints.[6] The first edition sold out immediately and they ran several more editions to meet the demand.

However, there was a problem with the printing. To meet demand, James Ballantine, Scott's business partner's brother, agreed to let John Murray Publishing print extra copies. An argument soon broke out between the two publishers over copyright. Murray had insisted they had publishing copyright forever on the work. In opposition to that idea, Scott wrote to John Ballantine, 'I will see their noses cheese first.'[7]

Scott's poem on Waterloo supported the Duke of Wellington's account and barely mentioned the Prussians. He gave the Prussians credit for pursuing the French but in no way mentioned Bülow's contribution to the battle.[8]

In addition, Scott mixed fiction and fact in his descriptions of Waterloo, partly due to his close connection with the Duke of Wellington. Scott's work *Paul's Letters to his Kinsfolk* described the journey he took shortly after the battle of Waterloo. Published in January of 1816, Scott wanted to describe in detail how the great battle was won. The narrative closely followed Wellington's own accounts and downplayed the role of the Prussians during the battle.

The Duke of Wellington did not like to add or detract from his account – the 'Waterloo Dispatch'. Sir Walter Scott wrote his own account of the battle of Waterloo. In *Paul's Letters to his Kinsfolk*, Scott wrote a series of letters to various relatives and took on the pen name of Paul. The work described his travels over the battlefield and his journey from the battlefield to Paris. Scott met with and interviewed several eyewitnesses for the narrative of the battle including the Duke of Wellington. Though organised as letters, the information provided more of a journalistic type of prose and was primarily a narrative. Scott's hope in writing such a work of fiction was to 'make the past live'.[9] Wellington did not have to boast about winning the battle of Waterloo; Scott did that for him. Scott liked twists and turns in his writings and he knew there was not only plenty of drama in the story of Waterloo, but also in the days preceding it in France.

Scott chose to interview French Minister of Police Joseph Fouché for his information on the intrigues of France during the campaign. Fouché served both Louis XVIII and Napoléon. He was described as the best man to 'ride on the whirlwind and direct the storm'.[10] Most of the information in letters three and four were regarding the political situation just before and during Napoléon's return from Elba. For that, Fouché was an excellent source. Most of the information in letters one to five was either from Scott's own travels or from information provided by Fouché.

In *Paul's Letters to his Kinsfolk*, Walter Scott described the Waterloo campaign in letters six, seven and eight. Letters six and seven outlined the battles of Ligny and Quatre Bras. Scott paid attention to the contributions of the Scottish regiments during 16 June. In Scott's account of the battle of Ligny, he claimed the French outnumbered the Prussians.

The Prussians, according to Scott, felt they were cheated of their right of vengeance on the French in 1814 and were glad to fight them again.[11] Scott did give Marshal Blücher credit for his personal bravery and leadership during the battle.[12]

As for the battle of Quatre Bras, Scott was critical of Marshal Ney for not taking the crossroads. He attributed Ney's inability to take the crossroads from failure to receive proper support from Napoléon. He added, 'If, in the conjoined assault of the 16th, Ney failed in success over an enemy far inferior in numbers, it can only be accounted for by the superior talents of the English general, and the greater bravery of the soldiers whom he commanded.'[13] In letter seven, Scott analysed the campaign as being won on the night of 16 June and on 17 June. The battle of Waterloo still needed to be fought, but the outcome of the campaign itself was reversed by the events on those days. He insisted Wellington had planned to attack on the day of 17 June but wisely did not. It was this threat that forced Napoléon's hand to not pursue the Prussians with his army. Scott credits Wellington in forcing Napoléon to advance towards him and allowing the Prussians time to regroup on 17 June.[14]

Scott incorrectly guessed the size of the force under Marshal Grouchy at 25,000 men and assumed it was headed towards Wavre beginning on 17 June. Further, Scott concluded that by leaving such a small force, the French could not have effectively pursued the Prussians since they retired from Ligny in good order. Scott argued it was Ney's fault for failing to take Quatre Bras.[15]

According to Scott, Wellington sensed the danger by staying at Quatre Bras and retreated to the Mount-Saint-John position. Napoléon's forces were slow to follow their retreat.[16] The weather also played an important role in the battle of Waterloo and compared the night before the battle to a tempest that was little abated. Scott compared how low British spirits were and how high the French ones before the battle and were reversed the next day like at Agincourt.[17]

The battle of Waterloo was the subject of letter eight. Scott reported Wellington was in communication with Bülow's corps before the battle started.[18] Scott alleged a traitor told Wellington of an impending attack on the right of the British position at Mount-Saint-John early in the morning of 18 June would consist of cavalry and infantry.

Scott argued the battle was fought primarily by British troops with little support from their allies. The attack on the chateau of Hougoumont was easily repulsed since it was occupied by members of the British Guards. Scott reflected the mood of the some of the generals was not good, fearing there were too few British troops to hold Napoléon's army at bay. They did not trust their Dutch-Belgian allies and were suspicious of some of their German contingents.[19] Scott held the Dutch-Belgians in low regard and mockingly referred to them as 'Les braves Belges' when they fled the battlefield.[20]

The valour of the British soldier was on parade at Waterloo in the eighth letter. Scott cited the example of Corporal Shaw who was a member of the Life Guards and a former boxing champion and duelist. Shaw killed and wounded ten Frenchmen before being killed from a pistol shot. According to Scott, even the officers of wealth and privilege fought with extraordinary vigour. Scott noted in one remark of one officer to another:

> 'You are uncommonly savage to-day,' said an officer to his friend, a young man of rank, who was arming himself with a third sabre, after two had been broken in

his grasp: 'What would you have me do,' answered the other, by nature of one the most gentle and humane men breathing, 'we are here to kill the French, and he is the best man to-day who can kill the most of them;' – and he again threw himself into the midst of the combat.[21]

Had it not been for the British, the whole affair would have gone Napoléon's way. The Dutch, Hanoverian and Brunswick troops only held on because of the determination of the British regiments were interspersed between them.[22] Scott continued to argue it was only the first line of troops, which was made up of primarily British troops, that did most of the fighting.[23] Perhaps Scott's boldest claim was, 'With 80,000 British troops, it is probable the battle would have not lasted two hours.'[24]

Scott's love for the Duke of Wellington showed in *Paul's Letters to his Kinsfolk*. He cited the personal bravery of Sir Alexander Gordon to save Wellington's life and the wounding of Sir William Delancey as simply heroic. They both died. Scott continued that his love of Wellington was shared by the men of the army. 'Lieutenant-Colonel Canning, and many of our lost heros, died with the Duke's name on their expiring lips.'[25]

Regarding the issue of the Prussians at the battle, Scott accepted Wellington's version of events and even rejected the thought that the British needed the Prussians' help on 18 June.

According to Scott, Wellington was asked if he looked for the Prussians to arrive from the Bois de Ohain during the battle. Wellington claimed to have looked more to his watch than to the woods. He knew if he could hold his position the whole of the Prussian army would arrive the next day. United, the two armies would sweep Napoléon from the field.[26]

Scott blamed losing the battle squarely on Napoléon. He argued that Napoléon sent Grouchy away from his army to pursue the defeated Prussians but never imagined Blücher's Prussian army would march in the direction of the British army. When the Prussians of Bülow did arrive, Napoléon thought Grouchy was right behind them even though they had no communication from Grouchy. Scott argued Napoléon sowed the seeds of defeat with his own men when he spread the rumour, via General La Bédoyère, that the troops arriving on the battlefield were Grouchy's men. Scott condemned this action, because the men had already been verified as the Prussians. Scott added, 'The real error was sufficient for his destruction (believing Grouchy was coming to the battlefield while ordering him to Wavre at the same time), without exaggerating it into one which would indicate insanity.'[27] Worse for Scott was Napoléon became self-deluded that Grouchy was near, and/or at least on his way, and could intervene before the battle's end. It was in this calculation Napoléon made his greatest error. Thinking Grouchy was almost on the battlefield, he committed his old guard in one last gamble to sweep the British from the field and catch Blücher between his army and Grouchy's men arriving on the battlefield. Scott further criticised Napoléon for not having taken personal command of his Imperial Guard himself and lead the attack. Scott thought it would have been better for Napoléon to at least have tried to die as a hero, instead of being jailed on Saint Helena.[28] Scott fully credits the repulse of Napoléon's guards to Wellington and the British army. Wellington's leadership allowed him to concentrate more men at a critical point than Napoléon, and he was in such a strong position he was able to both repel the attack and follow it up with a counter-attack of his own to put the French to flight.[29] To capture the moment, Scott wrote: 'Headed by the Duke of Wellington himself, with his hat in his hand, the line advanced with the utmost spirit and rapidity.'[30] What Scott did acknowledge was the arrival of the Prussians only 'gathered in the harvest, which was already dearly won and fairly reaped.'[31] Even upon seeing the British troops, the Prussian bands began to play *God Save the King*.[32] The last scene of the battle was the heroic French General Cambronne's refusal to surrender the guard with, 'The Imperial Guard can die but never surrender.'[33]

The account Sir Walter Scott portrayed of the battle of Waterloo made it seem as if it was a British affair that only they could have won. Indeed, the British spirit on the battlefield was what won the day. It was the moral leadership and inspired actions of the troops who won the battle.

The book was well received and a commercial success. Again, the topic of Waterloo sold well. It was a critical hit and over three editions sold out during 1816.

Scott's writings even influenced Jane Austen. She was so excited to hear of Scott's work *The Field of Waterloo* she wrote to her publisher John Murray for an advanced copy *of Paul's Letters to his Kinsfolk*. Delighted by both works, Waterloo became the backdrop for her own novel *Persuasion*.[34]

Walter Scott wrote several histories. After years of success, Scott was ruined by his continued business dealings with James Ballantine. Scott met with financial ruin and he needed money to pay off his debts. He knew anything associated with Napoléon or Waterloo sold. He started writing a number of short articles in 1825, which blossomed into his nine-volume work *Napoléon*. It was not a work of fiction and was hoped to be a commercial success. He drew on sources that were already available to the public and simply rehashed old familiar stories.[35] Even Scott admitted the work was unbalanced and not impartial. His work traced the outbreak of the revolution to the rise and fall of Napoléon.[36] It was a commercial, but not a critical, success.

The part of the work that dealt with Napoléon's defeat at Waterloo centred on Napoléon's plans for the battle. He had hoped to defeat the English and then turn and defeat the Prussians while strung out on the march with Grouchy in their rear.[37] Since the Paul project, several other accounts argued many of the British squares had been broken by the French, to which Scott took great umbrage.[38] In this work, he praises Wellington as usual but singles out the leadership and lauds the gamble Blücher made when realising his rearguard was under attack. He left the men of the Prussian III Corps isolated and on their own to take on Grouchy at Wavre and hurried the rest of the army towards Waterloo.[39]

In Scott's new analysis of the battle, he criticised Napoléon for using the French Imperial Guard the way he did. He argued it was the gambler in Napoléon that made him do what he did. Napoléon had no reserve and the Prussians were arriving on the battlefield in force and on the right rear of his lines and to his front. Desperate to get out of the vice he now found himself in, Napoléon decided to try to break the English by any means possible; this meant committing the Imperial Guard, despite the odds of success.[40] Scott clearly gave credit to Wellington for ordering his men to advance and seize the opportunity to completely overwhelm the French without the Prussians.

Scott responded to new accounts about the battle that he wanted to dispel. The circumstances of the end of the Old Guard at the end of the battle had created some controversy. He wanted to make two points clear. First, the battle was not lost because some unknown parties had cried 'Save

Yourself' that caused the panic which routed the French army; it was the advance of the British army that caused the rout. Second, Scott challenged some of Napoléon's friend's versions of how the last square of the Old Guard met its fate. 'The Guard can die but cannot yield' was now (in 1828) taken for truth as the reply from General Cambronne when requested to surrender. Scott denied the event ever took place. He challenged it took place, but he did not doubt the valour of which the last square fought. He wrote even though it did not happen, it was a fitting epitaph for the men who died fighting to the end. What Scott objected to was the story that the men of the last square turned their guns on one another: 'the battalions made a half wheel inwards, and discharged their muskets into each other's bosoms to save themselves from dying at the hands of the English.'[41] The thought of the men committing suicide was abhorrent to Scott and he wanted to make sure everyone knew Cambronne did not die but surrendered his sword and lived after the battle.[42]

It was Napoléon's character who lost Waterloo. Scott judged that men such as Napoléon deserve their fate. Napoléon showed his true face when he tried to blame the defeat on Ney and Grouchy. In doing so, he illuminated his character and his own downfall. This was not leadership.

Scott defended both Grouchy and Ney; he wrote this scathing attack on Napoléon:

> The account of the battle of Waterloo, dictated by Napoléon to Gourgaud, so severely exposed by General Grouchy, as mere military romance, full of gratuitous suppositions, misrepresentations and absolute falsehoods, accuses the subordinate generals who fought under Bonaparte of having greatly degenerated from their original character. Ney and Grouchy are particularly aimed at; the former by name, the later by obvious implication. It is said that they had lost their energy and enterprising genius by which they had been formerly distinguished, and to which France owed her triumphs. They had become timorous and circumspect in all their operations; and although their personal bravery remained their greatest object was to compromise themselves as little as possible. This general remark, intended, of course, to pave the way for transferring from the Emperor to his lieutenants the blame of the miscarriage of the campaign, is both unjust and ungrateful. Had they lost energy, who struggled to the very last in the field of Waterloo, long after the Emperor had left the field? Was Grouchy undecided in his operations, who brought his own division safe to Paris, in spite of all the obstacles opposed to him by a victorious army, three times the amount of his

own in number? Both of these officers had given up, for the sake of Napoléon, the rank and appointments which they might have peacefully borne under the Bourbons. Did it indicate the reluctance to commit themselves, which they are charged, that they ventured on the decided step of joining his desperate career, not only abandoning al regard to their interest and safety, but compromising their character as men of loyalty in the face of all Europe, and exposing themselves to certain death, if the Bourbons be successful? Those who fight with a cord around their neck, which was decidedly Grouchy and Ney, must have headed the forlorn hope; and is it consistent with human nature, in such circumstances, to believe that they, whose fortune and safety depended on victory, personally brave as they are admitted to be, should have loitered in the rear, when their fate was in the balance? He who was unjust to his own followers can scarce be expected to be candid towards and enemy.[43]

While defending Grouchy and Ney, Scott also defended the role both Wellington and Blücher played in the campaign. According to Scott, 'the British won the battle; the Prussians rendered and achieved the victory.'[44] Scott argued Napoléon underestimated Wellington and Blücher's march to aid the British. The defeat was Napoléon's, but it was also in line with his character to blame others for it.[45]

Scott had a huge success with his work on Napoléon's life. He made a profit of £18,000 and was able to pay back his creditors. However, while writing the nine-volume work, his health began to fail, and he died four years later.[46] Scott's work on Waterloo would influence other artists. His poem and book *Paul's Letters to his Kinsfolk* influenced one of the most popular of London's attractions of the late Georgian era – *The Panorama of Waterloo.*

Panoramas were a form of entertainment most people in Britain had not seen before and were a modern marvel when first displayed. Going to see a panorama became a fashionable and entertaining thing to do in the late-18th and early-19th century.[47]

Henry Aston Barker was perhaps one of the most entrepreneurial men of the Napoléonic Wars. A panorama painter like his father Robert Barker, he pioneered the panorama art form and held a patent on it until 1802. His panoramas made money and lots of it. The Barkers made money from the Napoléonic Wars by painting scenes people wanted to see. They offered a 360-degree view for visitors of the subject.[48] Robert Barker built the Panorama Rotunda in 1793 near Leicester Square.[49] There was a large rotunda of 90 feet in diametre on the lower floor and an upper floor of 50 feet in diameter in a smaller rotunda. The building was designed by architect Robert Mitchell.[50]

Henry Barker's panorama opened in May 1793, nearly three months after Britain declared war on the French Republic. King George III and Queen Charlotte attended the opening of the first panorama. The subject of the larger painting on opening day was the British Fleet assembled for review at Spithead in 1791.[51] The Queen was so moved by the display she felt seasick.[52]

The essential aspect of the panorama was to engulf the viewer in the scene. Panoramas made the viewer a part of the landscape or seascape. They also lent themselves to particular views. Skylines of cities, naval battles and battlefields were all subjects of the Barkers' panoramas. From 1793 to 1815, the Barkers brought several scenes for the viewing public to appreciate. Henry Aston Baker's panoramas were part of a new visual culture offering scenes the populace could enjoy.[53] The most important thing was that the scene had to be realistic. Among the military themed panoramas were Nelson's attack on Copenhagen, the battle of Trafalgar,[54] the siege of Badajoz, the battle of Vitoria and the battle of Paris. Upon hearing of Napoléon's return in 1815, Henry Barker prepared to produce another painting that demonstrated the might of the British Empire. He knew there would be a battle and he would paint it.

As soon as the news broke of the victory of the battle of Waterloo, Barker made his way to the battlefield. He intended to make money by painting a panorama of Waterloo and cash in on the excitement of the victory. Almost immediately there was a frenzy for prints, paintings and caricatures of the battle.[55] Barker chose the moment of victory as his subject of the painting. He wanted to show his audience the moment the British forces triumphed under the leadership of the Duke of Wellington.

Barker sketched the painting and John Burnet actually painted the panorama. It took nearly a year to complete and the *Panorama of Waterloo* opened to the public on 25 March 1816. The panorama of Waterloo was on the lower rotunda and accompanying it was a smaller panorama in the smaller rotunda – the battle of Paris. Admittance was one shilling for each painting and the exhibit was open from 10am until dusk.[56]

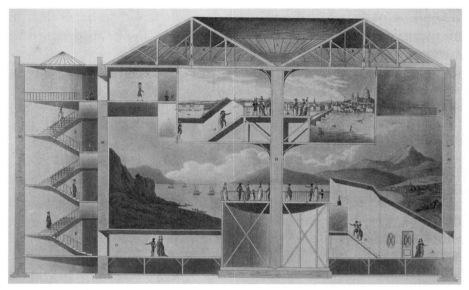

Cross section of Barker's Panorama in London by Robert Mitchell from *Plans, and views in perspective, with descriptions of buildings erected in England and Scotland; and ... an essay to elucidate the Grecian, Roman and Gothic Architecture. (Plans, descriptions et vues en perspective, etc.)* (British Library, public domain)

A visitor to the panorama entered through a dimly lit corridor and upon entering the exhibition rotunda was greeted with a burst of light from the open dome. Whereupon, the first thing one saw of the panorama was the Duke of Wellington with his staff.[57]

For six pence, a guide was available for the painting. The guide had over 60 explanations of the images in the panorama, an order of battle for the British forces engaged and the contributions of each unit involved. In its description of the battle, only one of the guide's nearly 70 items depicted the Prussians being in the battle. The guide made it seem like British units were the only ones involved against the French. The Prussians and Dutch-Belgians were given little canvas space and were barely mentioned.

The guide borrowed from Sir Walter Scott's *The Battle of Waterloo* to describe the battle. Scott's poem praised Wellington, the British troops and their fighting spirit.[58] In the poem, Scott describes the British troops as being outnumbered, wet and cold; however, it was their fighting spirit that pulled them through. The French numerical superiority and the charges

Coloured cartoon from the *Glasgow Looking Glass*, 25 June 1825, advertising the Panorama of Waterloo at a rotunda theatre in Buchanan Street, Glasgow (Barker's Panorama on Tour, Edinburgh, 1825)

the French cavalry made were negated according to Scott because 'But on the British heart were lost, the terrors of the charging host; for not an eye that the storm view'd chang'd its proud glance of fortitude.'[59]

Wellington's fortitude and leadership were praised by Scott. He described the repulse of the French Imperial Guard and the moment of crisis: 'Then, Wellington, thy piercing eye, this crisis caught of destiny. The British host had stood that morn' gainst charge of sword and lance, as their own ocean rocks hold stance; but when thy voice said "Advance" they were an ocean flood.'[60]

Barker's Panorama also depicted the charge of the Highlanders and the Scots Greys at the battle. Though the actual events took place several hours before the crisis point, Barker chose to include them in the overall panorama.[61] The panorama tried to depict as best it could the sequence of events, while at the same time reinforce the idea that Waterloo was an epic British victory. The actions at Hougoumont and La Haye Saint were depicted as heroic struggles. In the final act of the battle, it was the British Guards who defeated the French Imperial Guard. According to Barker, the British Guards fired several volleys into the French Guards and then charged the French Guards, throwing them into confusion and eventual flight.[62] Wellington ordered a cavalry charge and ordered the entire army to advance on the retreating French Guards.

According to Barker, this was what broke the spirit of the French Army.[63]

Barker did include the Prussian involvement in the battle as a light skirmish between the French right flank and Bülow's men. However, it was only an asterisk to the entire battle. The Prussians are depicted as being on the horizon when the moment of crisis happened.[64] The panorama was an expression of the pride the British felt in having finally defeated Napoléon and Revolutionary France after nearly 20 years.

Barker's guide also let visitors know they could subscribe to a national painting of Waterloo commissioned by the Prince Regent. Barker was extremely smart in his design of the building, because as people exited, they could buy a set of eight prints to take home for only one guinea painted by John Burnet.[65] By doing so, visitors could contribute to a national commemoration. He knew he could raise additional revenue by advertising the panoramas with the sales of the prints and get more people to come and see the panoramas.

The Waterloo Panorama was extremely popular; however, the crowds were less than pleased with the room in which it was displayed. The room was so crowded that shorter people could not see the picture at all. After the complaints, Barker installed a central raised stage for visitors to be able to see over the heads of their fellow visitors.[66] The painting was a commercial success and made £10,000 within the first few months of display.[67] This feat was even more remarkable since Britain was in a period of economic depression. After the defeat of Napoléon, the government cut expenditures drastically. Men who had fought in the wars now found themselves on half-pay and out of a job.[68] Still, many people paid the price of admission and merrily enjoyed their visit.

One visitor, by the name of Lady Mary, accompanied her uncle to see the Waterloo Panorama in Leicester square. She felt so moved by the panorama and her uncle's explanation of it she felt like bursting out saying, 'Scotland Forever!'[69] She felt as if the scene was so real she would have to bivouac with her uncle upon the field. Writing to her friend, Felix M'Donogh, she added:

I advise you go and see it: and I trust the scene will have interest for a Briton for a century hence, when we, and when ours are no more. Our heroes have gathered their laurels in vain, unless the dews of immortality, failing from on high, preserve them: the brave but sleep and the coward perishes and is forgotten[70]

Felix M'Donogh, an art critic and local journalist, took Lady Mary's advice and went to see the panorama for himself. M'Donogh discovered the panorama was crowded, just as Lady Mary had described. The British were cutting down the French and the Prussians were on the horizon. M'Donogh was lucky enough to have one of the officers of the Scots Greys provide him with an explanation of the painting. M'Donogh remarked the officer was an excellent guide to the painting and the officer's presence lent an air of credibility to the painting.[71]

M'Donogh's most striking commentary on the panorama was perhaps on the people who went to see it:

In all assemblages of people, a spectator may learn much. Here there were groups of all classes, and feelings of as many descriptions: – the man and woman of quality, proud to distinguish on the canvass some hero who added lustre to their name, – the female of sensibility, who heaved the deep sigh for some relative or bosom friend left on the bed of glory, – the military spectator, who had been an actor in the scene, and who, pride beaming in his countenance, yet wrapt in silence, looked on the representation of that awful and eventful reality, – or the garrulous but worthy veteran, who saw his own deeds of arms live again in the pictured story, and who, bereft of an arm, or leg, and leaning on a friend, indulged in the gratifying account of what his country owed him, whilst,
> Thrice he routed all his foes,
> And thrice he slew the slain.

There also was the exquisite militaire, youthful and blooming, affected and vain, lounging with an air of *sans souci*, a toothpick or a violet in his mouth, a quizzing glass either suspended round his neck or fixed in the socket of his eye, seeming to disdain taking an interest in the thing, yet lisping out,

'Upon my thoul, it's d—d like, d—d like indeed, – yeth – that's just the place where we lotht tho many men, – it's quite ridiculouth, how like it ith.' What a contrast! So much valour, yet so much feminine conceit, starch and perfume, whalebone and pasteboard! It is, however, not less true, that these fops, who take so much care of their pretty persons out of the field, took no care of them in it. Here were idlers looking at the action merely as a picture; and there were vacant countenances staring at nothing but the company. In one place a fat citizen came in merely to rest himself; and in another, a pretty brunette of the second class, whose only business was to meet my Lord. In a third corner, I could see a happy couple enjoying the short space previous to a permanent union, and who came here for fashion's sake, or to be alone in the world, and thus to escape the attention of a smaller circle; for there exists a certain retirement or solitude in crowds, known only to the few. This couple took as much interest in the battle of Waterloo as in the fire of London.[72]

At the entrance were some jealous painters looking out for defects in the piece and, in the doorway, was a covey of beauties surrounded by fashionables, who seemed scarcely to know why they came there, and enjoying nothing but their own conversation… and on my exit, I perceived some wry faces and some discontented looks at the door. These were French people come over here, all with a view of gain, in some shape or other, but who sickened at anything which lowered France, *avec ses armies victarieuses*, which so long gave laws to the greater part of Europe, but could never dictate them to us. As much was said by the French, about their Ligion d'Honneur and Napoléon's Invincibles, as ever ancient history has trumpeted concerning the sacred battalion commanded by Pelopidas: but I did not stay long to listen to them – I left the Panorama more of a Briton than ever: I had, on many occasions, considered myself as a cosmopolite but upon this one, I confessed myself to be wholly an Englishman; and I was proud of the title. Divers ideas of my country's glory rushed on my brain at the same instant: and as I was sauntering along the pave of London, so eulogized by Voltaire as an emblem of our constitution, and formed equally for the little and for the great, I caught myself in a reverie, and was actually muttering 'Soldiers, stand firm,' exclaim'd the chief, 'England shall tell the fight.'[73]

Barker did his job well. *The Panorama of Waterloo* was a place to see and be seen. It was highly fashionable and cut across all sections of society. The message of the painting was clear: the British won the battle of Waterloo. The Prussians were on the horizon and did not contribute materially to the moment of crisis when the battle was won. Every Briton, for a price, could experience Waterloo without having to go to the battlefield. For a price they could visit the field and experience the greatness of being British. By seeing the panorama, everyone could take pride in knowing their country beat Napoléon and the French. Even with his commercial success, some people did not like Barker's work. The poet William Wordsworth took exception to the panorama. Wordsworth was put off by its attempt to overawe the senses. He thought the panorama suppressed the imagination and was an evil to be avoided.[74] Wordsworth feared such a panorama would cheapen the meaning of the event and lessen the poetic medium.[75]

Barker was in the business of capturing trends and moving on to what the public wanted. In August of 1816, a British fleet bombarded the city of Algiers to free some Christian slaves. In response, Barker set out to paint the scene. The Waterloo Panorama had two profitable years, but Barker closed the exhibit in London on 9 May 1818 to display a work on the attack of Algiers.[76] Nevertheless, Barker was not done with the Waterloo Panorama and he wanted to continue to profit from the work.

Even though the panorama closed in London, it travelled to other cities for display in 1818 and again in 1820. It toured England and Scotland. In Edinburgh, Barker allowed the 42nd Highlander Regiment free admission to enhance the realism of the painting. Eventually, the panorama was shipped across the ocean to Boston for an engagement before being returned to London in 1820 to be displayed again until May 1821.[77]

To celebrate the fifth anniversary of the battle, Barker's company painted another panorama. This time it was movable and shown outside. They had John Buford paint a series of paintings on rollers. It was a display that moved in order of the events of the battle. Much like a modern movie, but to add to the excitement, Barker enlisted a band and fireworks to celebrate the anniversary. The people attending the event cheered Wellington's painting when the band played 'See, the Conqu'ring Hero Comes'.[78] Barker's spectacles evoked an emotional response that physically demonstrated Briton's emotional connection with the battle and the pride they took in defeating Napoléon.

The original panorama eventually fell to pieces by 1825 because of exposure to humidity.[79] A new panorama was made and displayed again from 1842–43 and 1852–53, following the Duke of Wellington's death.[80] The new panorama added scenes that were, according to the artist, 'amendments suggested by time, experience and additional information.'[81] Barker's new panorama depicted Wellington as pointing the men forward and making the entire scene more dynamic than the first by adding the words 'Up, Guards, and at them.'[82] The only objections to the new panorama arose from Napoléon's prominence in the work. Despite the objections, *The Times* review wrote that everyone should go and see it.[83]

Other panoramas on Waterloo were made by various artists and displayed in London until the 1890s. One artist to innovate the panorama art form was Philip Fleischer, who added models to the foreground of his paintings to create an illusion of depth. He created another work for his employer entitled *Panorama of Waterloo,* borrowed from William Siborne's model, which depicted the British and Prussians advancing together on the defeated French.[84]

Legions of paintings entitled 'The Battle of Waterloo' continued to be made until World War I owing to the popularity of the topic. These artists depicted the battle with great élan. George Jones painted the battle so many times in the 19th century he earned the nickname 'Waterloo Jones'.[85] Like Jones, Barker depicted things the British people wanted, and the period from 1820 to 1850 was artistically dominated by scenes from the Napoléonic Wars. The battles of Trafalgar and Waterloo were the events that were most often depicted.[86]

The last panorama displayed at the Barker building was in 1863. It still stands today as 5 Leicester Place, London. Today, perhaps fittingly, it is a French Catholic church called Notre Dame de France. Though the rotunda's open ceiling has been covered with glass, light still shines in the building to give it a sense of its grandeur.[87]

Henry Barker had a successful business model to keep people coming to see his panoramas. His success was built on images the British public wanted to see, and he made sure those topics were shown in titanic scale. The people did not want to see the Prussians on their battlefield, and they wanted to believe Waterloo was not just Britain's victory over Napoléon but also theirs.

Siborne tried to use the science of topography and eyewitness accounts to challenge the accepted version of the history of the battle. Siborne attempted an accurate visual memory of the battle by making his model. This visual memory was rejected by the Duke of Wellington over the involvement of the Prussians at the critical moment of the battle. What the Duke may have missed was that the critical moment of the battle was from his own memory of the action. Siborne's method used the collective memory of the combatants to depict the battle. In many ways, this was typical of the conservative era trying to hold back the forces of democracy.

What Siborne exposed was that one man's memory was more prone to error than aggregate memory of those involved.

The fight over the memory of Waterloo had been in full swing for nearly 50 years when, in 1830, a fastidious lieutenant named William Siborne was given the task by the Commander in Chief of the army, Sir Rowland Hill, of collecting information to make a scale model of the battlefield of Waterloo. The model hoped to preserve the memory of the battle and exist as a centerpiece of the new United Services Museum.[88] In 1826, a monument had been constructed called the Lion's Mound. It changed the landscape of the battlefield. Upon seeing the Lion's Mound monument in 1828, the Duke of Wellington remarked, 'they have ruined my battlefield'. In 1830, Wellington was the prime minster and news of a new housing development on the battlefield spurred Hill into action.[89]

William Siborne's specialty was cartography and it was for this reason he was commissioned to make the model. He loved making maps and honed his skills at the Royal Military Academy at Sandhurst where he graduated with honours in 1815. Siborne served in the occupation forces of Paris in 1815 with his father, Benjamin Siborne.[90] However, neither father nor son fought at Waterloo.[91] Siborne set out to make a model that was both topographically correct and historically accurate. Siborne used his scientific training in cartography and applied it to the study of Waterloo.

It was a fine example of a rationalist project. He wanted to categorise each fact into a comprehensible version of events. The units were divided by nationality, type and function. The project's first phase was topographical while the second was historical. The project's first phase went as planned and without incident. The second phase did not go as planned. Siborne hoped to produce something that would be praised as the 'truth'. He wanted to find out the who, what, when and where of the battle in detail. He was not aiming to entertain, but to educate the masses about the battle.

Siborne wanted to describe the moment of victory. He spent eight months on the battlefield staying at the farmhouse of La Haye Sainte. He walked over the battlefield many times during his stay while making a detailed map for the model; however, Siborne also needed to become a historian, cartographer and an artist to complete his work. According to the Duke of Wellington, the critical moment of the battle was the repulse of Napoléon's Imperial Guard. Siborne wanted to get as much information as he could about the moment. He sent out a letter to the officers who were veterans of Waterloo.

> Sir,
>
> Having for sometime been occupied in constructing a Model of the Field and Battle of Waterloo, upon a scale sufficiently large to admit of the most faithful representation of the memorable Action, I have accordingly the honour to request you will have the goodness to reply to the following queries, as far as your recollection and circumstances of your position at the time will admit. What was the particular formation at the moment when the French Imperial Guards, advancing to attack the right of the British Forces, reached the crest of our position? What was the formation of the Enemy's Forces?
>
> Would you have the goodness to trace these formations, according to the best of your recollection, upon the accompanying Plan?
>
> If Officers will, however, but I trust that, by fairly weighing and comparing the data thus afforded me, I shall be enabled to deduce a most faithful and authentic record of the battle, the surest means of imparting to the Model that extreme accuracy which in a work of this nature, not dependent like a pictorial representation on effect for excellence, must always constitute its real value.
>
> I have the honour to be, Sir
>
> Your most Obedient, humble Servant,
>
> W. Siborne[92]

The response to his letter was overwhelming. He collected nearly six volumes of correspondence from the veterans. Some Prussian and French veterans wrote him too.[93] He tried in vain to get a response from Marshal Soult who he thought could shed the most light on the battle. Despite trying five times to gain an audience or any information with Soult, he gave the attempt up.[94] Soult wanted nothing to do with anything dealing with Waterloo. Soult would not be the only veteran of Waterloo who would have problems with Siborne's request for information.

Siborne wanted to depict a triumph but he ended up starting a feud between brother officers. General Sir Hussey Vivian, who was also Siborne's direct boss, commanded the British cavalry who attacked the Imperial Guard after it was repulsed by the British Guards and swept it from the field at the moment of crisis. Lieutenant George Gawler challenged Vivian's account. He asserted it was his regiment, the 52nd, and General Adams' brigade who repulsed the attacks, not General Peregrine Maitland's guards. The two men sparred in the *United Services Journal* (which in time became the *United Services Gazette*) for the next year.[95] Siborne was in a predicament since Vivian was his boss, but he wanted to be exact. Eventually, he sided with Vivian and, by extension, Wellington too, as Wellington had credited Maitland's guards, not Adams' brigade, for repulsing the attack.

Siborne soon found out sorting out the truth would be hard some 15 years after the battle. Wellington's version stated the British had won the battle and the Prussians had arrived only to help pursue the defeated enemy. However, Siborne soon questioned this narrative. He posed the question, 'Who won the battle of Waterloo?' Was it the British, the Prussians or a combination of the two armies? What Siborne wanted to recreate with his model was the central crisis point of the battle.[96] He wanted the viewers of the model to see the moment of victory. Researching the Prussian role in the battle caused problems. First, the questions about the Prussians made many veterans uneasy. Second, the significance of their involvement was counter to official British history. The most significant problem was how to depict the Prussians.[97] Wellington's 'Waterloo Dispatch' did not to hold up to scrutiny.

At the same time, uncomfortable questions were surfacing about the level of the Prussians' contribution to the victory. There were financial problems for Siborne as well. After three years of research and mapmaking, the project ran into financial trouble. When the project started, the Tories under Wellington had been in control of the government and approved of the project, but when Wellington opposed parliamentary reform, Wellington lost a no confidence vote and was replaced. Charles Grey, a Whig, became Prime Minister. For the next decade, the Whigs were in power and cut funding for the model since they thought it would enhance Wellington's prestige. In 1833, the new Minister of War, Edward Ellice, decided not to fund the project at all.[98]

To make the model a reality, William Siborne invested his own money into the project.[99] Even Siborne's own resources could not finance the entire £1000. He was so deep in debt by the end of 1834 that he appealed to the public for financing the project. In doing so, he opened the project up to ordinary people.[100]

The Duke of Wellington did not like the idea of anyone challenging his version of events. He had never endorsed any books written on the battle and believed all the history needed to be written about the battle was already contained in his 'Waterloo Dispatch'. By going public with the model, Siborne inadvertently created an enemy of the Duke of Wellington. The Duke was a politician and he wanted to write his own place in history as well. He did not like anyone questioning his victory.[101]

Perhaps Siborne's biggest problem was how to reconcile Wellington's 'Waterloo Dispatch' and the information he received in response to his circular. Wellington claimed no knowledge of the Prussian intervention at the moment of crisis; however, Vivian told him he was aware of the Prussian's arrival on Wellington's left flank. Vivian was ordered to move to the centre of the British lines by Henry Paget, Lord Uxbridge, who commanded the cavalry and was Wellington's second in command. The Prussian corps of Hans Zieten had arrived and linked up with the British left.[102] They not only freed the British cavalry to move to the centre of the British line but also additional infantry units. If the Prussians were not there, Wellington would not have intentionally created a gap in his lines. Napoléon surely would have launched an attack to exploit the gap. The only conclusion could be the arrival of the Prussians before the moment of crisis on the battlefield allowed Wellington to strengthen his centre to receive the charge of the Imperial Guard; therefore, the Prussians had made a significant contribution to the moment of crisis. It occurred to Siborne that the 'Waterloo Dispatch' could be wrong.[103] Siborne had a rival in both Wellington and Colonel John Gurwood, Wellington's personal secretary. Gurwood was completing his multi-volume work, *The Dispatches of Field Marshal the Duke of Wellington*,[104] and did not want interference from Siborne. Wellington tightly controlled Gurwood's work but had little control over Siborne's work. Nevertheless, he could use his influence within the army to block his promotion and thwart his work. Gurwood's 12th volume on Waterloo came out in 1838; the same year the model was ready for public viewing.[105]

In the meantime, several members of the British military elite tried in vain to persuade Siborne to depict the beginning of the battle rather than the end. There certainly were no Prussians on the battlefield at the start of

Colonel John Gurwood by William Salter (1834–40) (National Portrait Gallery, London, Image 3719)

the battle and it would avoid disagreeing with the Duke's account.[106] The British military establishment tried again to have Siborne concentrate on the fighting around the chateau of Hougoumont where the defence of the chateau could be glorified as a British victory. Siborne refused again and defended the idea the model should represent the entire action not just one part of the battlefield.[107] He responded to his critics by writing defiantly,

> ...there are insurmountable obstacles to an abandonment of my original design. More than a hundred of my circulars have already been issued and I continue issuing them daily. I have made application to the French and to the Prussian military authorities for information with respect to the 'Crisis'.
>
> I have made and have in hand, houses represented as on fire, others as shattered with shot and shell. I have several thousands of figures, representing men in the act of firing and such, and as my alteration now would be attended with incredible inconvenience, sacrifice of labour, great loss of precious time and very heavy expense, I trust that in expressing my earnest wish to complete my work

upon the plan with which I at first set out I may not be deemed deficient in proper deference and submission to the military authorities or undeserving of their favourable countenance and support.[108]

Furthering his critics' outrage was the fact that Siborne's circular letter had made its way to the Prussians and they responded with numerous eyewitness accounts. He was gathering enough evidence to accurately depict the Prussian involvement in the moment of crisis.[109] Colonel Wagner of the Prussian General Staff had made a complete study of the battle and knew where each of the Prussian units were and when they were there.[110]

Wellington's allies had enough. In 1836, they wanted to settle the matter of the Prussians once and for all. F. H. Lindsay, a friend of Lord Fitzroy Somerset, the Duke's nephew, wrote to Siborne to inform him that the Duke of Wellington would like to speak to him about his model and the Prussian matter. Siborne did not refuse to meet Wellington; he simply could not afford the travel expense to go to London.[111] The state of his finances was so dire that the cost was too much for him to attend a secret meeting to discuss the placement of the Prussians. Besides, it was too late for discussion: the model was almost complete.

The Great Model started in 1833, measured 21 feet 4½ inches wide by 19 feet 8¼ inches long and was made of plaster of paris divided into 30 compartments attached to each other with brass plates and screws.[112] The horizontal scale of the model was 1:600 and its vertical scale was 1:180, with each model soldier representing two real soldiers in the battle.[113] The Great Model had thousands of hand-painted miniature soldiers. No detail was spared from the houses to the trees and even the colours of the crops in season at the time.[114] It took a year longer than expected to complete, but the work was finished in 1838.[115]

Siborne's military career was virtually over by the time the exhibit opened. He was still a lieutenant after 23 years of service. The model had absorbed his time and money, thus limiting his chances of promotion. His situation was also made public.

> If anything can add to the credit due to Lieutenant Siborne for the attention which he has bestowed on this elaborate work, it is the fact that it has been accomplished without at all interfering with his official duties, and we are more the particular in mentioning the circumstance having heard a contrary opinion prevailed at headquarters.[116]

He planned to open the exhibit in time for the anniversary of the battle in 1838 but missed the deadline.

The Times gave the model a favorable review when it opened in October 1838 at the Egyptian Hall in Piccadilly. The review noted the size of the model as being 420 square feet and everything seemed as it was on 18 June 1815. The fields, woods, and general landscape were reproduced with attention to detail.[117] The brochure that was provided to visitors guided the guest to what was called the 'time chosen'. What was most interesting about *The Times* review that was it barely mentioned the Prussians at all. *The Times* review praised Siborne for depicting the attack on the British right flank and it seems they thought this attack was the moment of crisis. *The Times* credited Siborne for doing service to the public and the battle.[118]

Papers and magazines praised Siborne's work. *The Morning Post* strongly recommended people go to see the model. The *United Services Gazette*, the official newsletter of the British armed services, praised it for its 'perfect representation' of the scene.[119] There was even a suggestion in the magazine *Fine Arts* that the model be housed beneath a memorial dedicated to the Duke of Wellington.[120] Apparently, the editors of *Fine Arts* were not aware of the irony of the suggestion.

The model was not the only attraction from Waterloo in the Egyptian Hall. Napoléon's coach had been on display since 1816. It had been a rousing success with nearly 200,000 people paying one shilling each to see the coach and Napoléon's horse, Marengo.[121] People wanted to see something of Napoléon's life, rather than a model of his downfall. Still, with its exhibition in the Egyptian Hall a hundred thousand people came to see the model.[122]

The 12th volume of *Wellington's Dispatches*, published in 1839, treated Waterloo. In the volume, there was no deviation from the original 'Waterloo Dispatch'. It stated again that the battle had already been won and British forces were going forward when the Prussians' main force, under Marshal Blücher, arrived on the battlefield. What Wellington did reaffirm in *Wellington's Dispatches* was it was the Prussians who continued the pursuit of the French after the battle.[123] *Wellington's Dispatches* did not shed any new light on the moment of crisis. For Wellington, he and the British army won the day, but appreciated the Prussians' arrival as they had promised.

Wellington refused to see the model because of the way it depicted the Prussians. It depicted a victory of two armies over one and he did not want to be seen at the Egyptian Hall looking at the model. He thought by visiting the model he would be imparting approval to it.

> I was unwilling to give any sanction to the truth of such a representation in the model, which must have resulted from my visiting it, with protesting erroneous representation. This I could not bring myself to do on (any) account; and I thought it best to avail myself of my absence from London, and of indisposition, never to visit it at all.[124]

The failure to receive Wellington's endorsement may not have been a surprise, but his endorsement would have made the model more profitable. Economic reality hit Siborne as the model failed to make enough money to recoup his costs.[125] Siborne learned a lesson that accurate history does not always entertain. His model was too complicated for the average man. He was forced to close the exhibit in London and put it on tour, thinking he could make money somewhere else. Soon, events would give Siborne hope of finally being reimbursed for his expense of making the model.

Conservative Robert Peel was elected Prime Minister in 1841. With the Whigs out of office, Siborne thought Peel's ministry would be more willing to help him out by buying the project than Peel's predecessors. Siborne got a lesson in politics as well. He soon found out his requests for compensation would have to go through Fitzroy Somerset, Wellington's nephew. Somerset promptly refused to buy the model or compensate Siborne for his expenses.[126] Nevertheless, Siborne did seem to be able to buy a captaincy after he closed the exhibit.

Siborne had already collected thousands of documents and began to compile them into a narrative history of Waterloo. In another effort to raise cash, he decided to write a book with the information he had collected for the model. In 1842, the history received a huge endorsement when Queen Victoria allowed Siborne to dedicate the book on Waterloo to her.[127]

He published his *History of the Battle of Waterloo* in 1844. *The Times* reviewed his book and praised Siborne for his analysis of the battle. According to the review, Siborne was one of the first historians who was able to pull together all of the elements to present a convincing account of the entire campaign. With the endorsement and review, the book sold out immediately and went through three editions within three years of its original publishing.[128]

For Siborne, the French lost the campaign after Ligny. He argued Napoléon wasted an opportunity while the Anglo-Allied and Prussian armies were separated on 17 June. Had Napoléon united his entire force and fought Wellington at Genappe then the campaign may have turned out differently. It was Napoléon's inactivity on 17 June that lost him the campaign.[129] Siborne exonerated Marshal Grouchy from losing the battle and weighed in on the controversy.

> Another point of dispute has been the conduct of Grouchy in remaining at Wavre, notwithstanding Napoléon's injunctions that he was so to maneuver as to join the right of the main French army; but those who censure Grouchy seem to overlook the fact that the delay in the pursuit of the Prussians had enabled Bülow's corps to leave Wavre before he had arrived – that he not only held in check, but fought and defeated Thielmann with 35,000 men, and that if he had joined Napoléon with his whole force, he would have been followed to the field by a Prussian body of still greater number.[130]

Siborne also explained to British audiences in detail the meeting at Sart-a-Walhain between Grouchy, Vandamme and Gérard.[131] While explaining how the French lost was one thing, explaining how the British won it was another matter.

Siborne's version of Waterloo now was in line with what the British public thought of Waterloo. The book was not only a commercial but also a critical success. It was praised for being a real history of the battle rather than a collection of antidotes. Siborne praised Wellington, 'It would, however, be unjust to the abilities and to the fame of the Duke, to ascribe such victory solely to the defeat of the attacking columns of the imperial guard upon his own position... .'[132] Siborne credited Wellington for being in the moment of crisis and quickly thinking to capitalise on the defeat of the French Guard.[133] The Prussians had nothing to do with the defeat of the French Guard and subsequent Anglo-Allied advance. It had already happened when the Prussians arrived. Siborne called the follow up of the defeat of the French Guards 'which in truth was a march of triumph, not an attack, since all fled before its approach.'[134]

There was one weakness in the book mentioned by the critics; namely, missing from all the eyewitness accounts was the commander-in-chief's own viewpoint. However, the critics by now had learned of the public disagreement between the two men and few could blame Siborne for not including Wellington. The duke already had his version of Waterloo in the 'Waterloo Dispatch' and in Gurwood's *Wellington's Dispatches* and that version was already well known by the public.

In *The Battle of Waterloo*, Siborne changed his mind about the Prussians. Why? New information had been provided to him about the arrival of the Prussians. It happened at the same time as the repulse of the middle guard. He acquiesced to Wellington's version that the Prussians arrived after the Imperial Guard had been defeated and the British army was advancing on the enemy.[135] Siborne even removed the 40,000 soldiers from the model to placate Wellington. The duke never acknowledged the gesture.[136] Siborne also made it clear in his writing that while the arrival of Bülow at Plancenoit early in the battle was an important diversion, it was not the deciding factor in winning the battle. The victory, according to Siborne, was exclusively an affair of the Anglo-Allied army (minus the Dutch-Belgians).[137] Yielding to the enormous pressure exerted by Wellington and his friends, he changed his position to stop the fighting. Unfortunately, for Siborne, the fight was not done over his version of events.

Even with the major concession about the Prussians by Siborne, things had become personal and the concession was too little too late. A friend of the duke and Fitzroy Somerset, the Reverend George Gleig, wrote a book entitled *The Story of Waterloo* in 1847. In the preface, he acknowledged Siborne and Gurwood for their work about Waterloo and was merely complimenting their endeavours. All the while, Gleig's intent was to discredit Siborne's work.[138] The book was a part of a series called, 'Mr. Murray's Monthly Library' in the Home and Colonial collection and sold for six shillings.[139] It was an affordable book compared to Siborne's work, which cost £2.2s.[140] According to Siborne, Reverend Gleig copied the *History of the Battle of Waterloo* with only minor changes. Those changes enhanced the role of the duke's leadership in winning the battle and downplayed the role of the Prussians. In the preface of Siborne's third edition of his book, he attacked Gleig for the act. He stated Gleig had done Siborne and his publisher, T. and W. Boone, great financial harm.[141] Gleig's work robbed Siborne of the financial success he thought the book would bring for him. Gleig's book was published in large quantities and was cheap. Few people bought Siborne's much more expensive book. T. and W. Boone were smaller printers than Murray, and Siborne could never hope to compete with Gleig's book on the mass market.[142]

Siborne skillfully insulted Gleig by complimenting him on providing the masses with cheap literature. The way Siborne repudiated Gleig in his third edition demonstrated his frustration and hostility to Wellington's supporters. Siborne was particularly upset by Gleig's apparent underhandedness. Before the printing of Gleig's book, the two men met; Siborne was totally ignorant of Gleig's book at the time. Siborne mentioned to Gleig a factual error of another author and Siborne's observation that Wellington could not have seen the battle of Ligny from Quatre Bras because the heights of Marbais where between the two locations.

Siborne retold the account in the preface to illustrate the duplicity of Gleig.

> When the book was published, I became curious to see what he had written upon this particular point, and I was not a little amused to find in his desire to follow the wake of the writer in the 'Quarterly' and, at the same time, to overcome the difficulty which I had pointed out, he had represented (In *Story of Waterloo*, 106) 'the fields of action were near enough the one to the other to permit his (the Duke's) seeing, from each height as he ascended it, the smoke of the battle of Ligny rise in thick volumes over the intervening woods.' This is the first time we have heard of the Duke having ascended *each* height on his own field, to see what Blücher was about at Ligny. However, in the third sentence beyond the one quoted, Mr. Gleig forgets the woods which, as if with some magic wand, he has caused to spring up between the two fields of action, and borrowing that extraordinary telescope which the writer in the 'Quarterly' puts in the Duke's hands, and which at once levels both woods and heights, and clears away smoke, mist, and even darkness,[143] he actually enables the Duke to *see* 'the failure of that cavalry-charge which led to Blücher's misfortune, and immediately preceded the general retreat of his army' – which charge, be it recollected, took place at a distance of seven miles and after darkness had set in!144

Siborne challenged Gleig to disclose how certain 'facts' came into his book. Siborne asked him if he could provide any other sources before the publication of his work in which he could find the same 'facts'.[145] Siborne provided several side-by-side examples of Gleig's 'piracy' in the third edition's preface. By the end of the preface, Siborne made several convincing proofs that Gleig had borrowed from his work and presented as his own. In concluding his preface, he wished Gleig (and indirectly Wellington) had shown him professional courtesy of not stealing his work.[146]

His book's success led him to be able to make another model, but this time it would be a specific scene and be much smaller in scope. This allowed for the models themselves to be larger and more visible. He used a 25mm scale or one to one-inch scale to depict the action. He purposely chose a popular subject for his model; the charge of the British heavy cavalry led by General Ponsonby who died during the charge but heroically broke up an attack by the French on the British. The new model was 18 feet 7 inches by 7 feet 9 inches and was modular like Siborne's first model.[147]

Once again Siborne's work was displayed in the Egyptian Hall for one shilling. It opened in late December 1844. This time Siborne's model faced competition with Madam Tussaud's. For the same price, one could see at Tussaud's a variety of things that belonged to Napoléon.[148] Wellington helped Tussaud take away some of Siborne's business by visiting the Tussaud's Napoléon exhibit and not going to Siborne's.[149] Siborne had been snubbed once again.

The new model suffered the same fate as the first model. Attendance was not what Siborne expected and it was a financial failure. He tried to boost sales in 1845 by displaying both models together in the Egyptian Hall at Christmas and, again, he tried to sell the models with similar results; no one wanted them. Siborne even removed the offending Prussians from his first model to try to get it sold.[150]

Despite the lack of commercial success for Siborne, people did see the models and they did have an effect. The models were famous. People could imagine themselves on the battlefield and remember Waterloo. A visitor from Poughkeepsie, New York, to the battlefield of Waterloo would remark some years later:

> Some forty years ago I met in America a Captain Soabey of the Royal Artillery who was at Waterloo. Speaking with him respecting the Model of the Battle ex-hibited some years ago at the Egyptian Hall, London, he assured me that a dis-

mounted gun represented in it, he Captain Soabey having (served) recollected on
the field of Waterloo and had received a charge in line by the cavalry.[151]

William Siborne died on 13 January 1849. The Duke of Wellington died
three years later on 18 November 1852.[152] For Wellington and Siborne,
their duel over Waterloo was over.

Siborne's Waterloo model was eventually bought and displayed for the
public by the United Services Institute. The new model was shipped back
to Ireland and was put in storage for nearly a century. The models were
great to look at if you could not get to the battlefield, but at the battlefield,
quite another visual awaited.

King William I of the United Netherlands decreed on 11 December 1815
a monument would be built on the battlefield of Waterloo to commemorate
the victory.[153] 18 June was an official holiday in the Kingdom of the
United Netherlands. For 15 years, the Kingdom of the United Netherlands
consisted of Holland and Belgium. The King wanted a pyramid but due
to costs and concerns the stone would crack during the Belgian winter,
the idea was scrapped. In 1819, architect Charles van Straeten proposed
to build an earthen mound out of part of the battlefield 'to make the soil
itself contribute to the composition'.[154] He continued in his proposal that:

> (It) would be surmounted by the monument proper, composed of a colossal
> lion set upon a marble pedestal. The lion is the symbol of victory; by resting
> (its paw) on the globe, it proclaims the tranquility which Europe has won on
> the plains of Waterloo. The monument, standing 43 meters above ground lev-
> el, would stand out majestically on the horizon, producing the greatest effect.
> No maintenance or surveillance would be needed for its conservation.[155]

King William I decided in 1820 to build Straeten's vision for the monument. However, he had to first buy the land from its current owner. The
Count von Velthem, the owner of La Haie Sainte farm, agreed to sell
enough land to build the monument in 1821. The king commissioned
the sculptor Jan van Geel to design and make the lion. The placement of
the mound was exactly where the French cavalry had attacked Wellington's
line and where William I's son, the Prince of Orange, had been wounded
in the shoulder.[156] The lion was made to sit at top of the mound facing
France.

The statue of the lion – the symbol of both Britain and the Netherlands – weighed nearly 30 tons.[157] William had hoped the British would like the colossal monument to commemorate their united victory. Instead, the monument would alienate the British for disturbing the battlefield, become an object of division within his own country and was derided by the French.

The monument was started in 1824 and finished nearly three years later. The monument was made of a brick interior and an earthen exterior. The project altered the battlefield significantly. The dirt taken from the surrounding ridge lowered it by several metres and filled in the sunken road where the monument was built. During the construction a tourist wrote:

> The monument, as it is called, has a very imposing effect, even in its unfinished state. It is an earthen mound or hill, of a conical form, resembling the one on the Bath road, near Kennett, but of larger size, being upwards of 700 feet diameter at the base, or 2160 feet circumference. It is 206 feet high, and 109 feet in diameter at the top; the is a double carriage road winding round it, in a spiral form, and supplying them an easy means of ascent for carriages to the very to; and by this road the materials have been and are, conveyed to complete the work. In the centre is a shaft of brickwork, which have been carried up from the bottom, and is still going on. It is 60 feet higher that the top of the mound, making the while height 260 feet long, and 12 feet high, which is ready to be put up when the work is finished. This mound has been 18 months in hand, and is to be complete in six more, and from what had already been done little doubt remains that it will be so. For the first twelve months 2,000 men, 60,000 horses, and so many carts as could be kept at work, were employed on I, and the number has only been reduced as the termination of this great undertaking approaches. At present, the works are going on, at the top it has a pleasing appearance, from the great number of horse carts, and people ascending and descending by the winding road.[158]

The mound did not please everyone. Reverend William Falconer visited the battlefield in 1825 and was upset the construction had disturbed the dead and there were people collecting bones as souvenirs.[159]

Louis XVIII crossed into the Kingdom of the United Netherlands to escape France in 1815. After Waterloo, many of the men who joined Napoléon fled to the United Netherlands and settled in Brussels. Thus, the Netherlands went through three invasions from France in one year.

One prominent Napoléonic officer who escaped to live in Brussels was General Étienne Gérard, the former leader of IV Infantry Corps during the Waterloo campaign. He lived in Brussels and knew the surrounding countryside well. He was allowed to return to France in 1817 and was elected to France's Chambers of Deputies in 1822. However, Gérard was not done with his travels in the United Netherlands.[160]

In 1830, the revolution that overthrew Charles X in France sparked an independence movement in Brussels. The Belgians were Catholic and the Dutch Protestant. The Belgians were united in religion but not in language, the Flemish north spoke Dutch and the Walloons in the south spoke French. In Wallonia, there was support for independence and the 'French Party' was formed to seek independence from Holland. Between 1830 and 1832, Belgium was in political turmoil. The United Netherlands was breaking apart.

The Lion's Mound of Waterloo was a symbol of the merger and the French Party was not fond of it. A revolution broke out in Brussels during an opera called *La Muette de Portici*. The tension between the Belgians and the Dutch was such that in September of 1830 a crowd marched on Brussels from Braine l'Alleud and Waterloo to support the revolution and independence but detoured first to plant the Tricolor on the top of the monument.[161] By the end of 1830, both sides were stalemated. William I withdrew Dutch forces to the fortresses of Antwerp. Meanwhile, Belgium had declared independence on 4 October 1830. In December 1830, a conference was called in London to try to settle the dispute. The London Conference of 1830 decided to split the Kingdom of the United Netherlands into the kingdoms of Belgium and Holland.[162] William I did not agree to the partitioning of his kingdom. Tensions were high, and, on the anniversary of the battle in 1831, a mob marched on Waterloo to destroy the Lion's Mound. However, the local inhabitants assembled an armed force to protect the monument and the lucrative tourist attraction. Only the timely intervention of the police and army prevented bloodshed.[163]

In June 1831, Leopold of Saxe Coburg was chosen by the provisional government of Belgium to become the King of the Belgians. Leopold I had to call on his French allies after William I sent troops into Belgium after rejecting the partition of the Netherlands. The French King, Louis-Philippe, decided to make Étienne Gérard a marshal of France and give him command of the *Armée du Nord*. Marshal Gérard's forces stopped the Dutch invasion of Belgium in 1831. While marching on Brussels, Gérard's men began to fire on the Lion's Mound as a symbol of the French defeat at Waterloo. Gérard

The erection of the Lion's Mound (1825) engraving by M. Jobard, after a drawing by Bertrand (public domain)

stepped in and ordered his men to stop firing on the monument. In ten days, the Dutch forces had been pushed back to their starting positions by Gérard's men. Gérard had saved the Lion and Belgium, but the citadel of Antwerp would not surrender to Belgian authority. General David Chassé was a veteran of Waterloo and defended the citadel of Antwerp. Gérard's forces laid siege to the fortress. Outnumbered, Chassé surrendered 'with the honors of war' after nearly a month of bombardment in December 1832. The French evacuated Belgium a few days later.[164] After the surrender of Antwerp, a bill was introduced in the Belgian Chamber of Deputies to melt down the Lion and use the material for making ammunition for liberty. A new memorial would be placed on top of the mound flying the flags of France and Belgium. The bill did not pass, but it embarrassed the Belgian government by annoying both the French and British governments.[165] When Napoléon III founded the Second French Empire in 1852, the Waterloo monument again became an international issue. The minister to Belgium, Prince De Bassano, demanded the monuments at Waterloo be destroyed. Napoléon

III thought the monuments were an insult to the honour of France. By the 1850s, the Lion's Mound was firmly established as a tourist destination, and the request was refused. However, to minimise tension within Europe, the Belgian government decided to limit the celebrations of Waterloo during Napoléon III's reign.[166] The 50th anniversary was marked by the celebration of brotherhood in an effort not to antagonise Napoléon III.[167]

In the 1860s, Victor Hugo visited the Lion's Mound and included the grand French cavalry charge in his novel. After the publishing of *Les Misérables*, the Lion's Mound became a must-see sight for many tourists. In 1875, an American tourist commented on her experience to the Lion's Mound as:

> The summit of the mound, which we reached by a toilsome climb, affords a comprehensive view of the great scene of the conflict, but a high tower would have served as well as this impertinent young mountain … By the way, an old guide born near Waterloo, and who at the time of the battle was a lad of seventeen and helped bury the dead, told us that he first conducted Victor Hugo over the field. He said that the novelist stayed at a farm house in the neighborhood for two months and walked again and again over the ground to make his marvelously vivid scenes. That is how an artist works.[168]

Other Americans wanted to see the Lion's Mound and Waterloo. Buffalo Bill decided to take his Wild West show on a tour of Europe in 1891. He wanted to visit Waterloo as well as the 604 members of the travelling show. Accompanying Buffalo Bill were soldiers from the United States, Britain and Germany, along with 100 Sioux Indians, 37 musicians of the famous Buffalo Bill Cowboy Band and, of course, Annie Oakley.[169] Spies were on board Buffalo Bill's train while in Europe. The Germans learned from Bill's methods and applied them nearly 20 years later during the invasion of Belgium.[170]

The show did have some relative newcomers. On 29 December 1890, the Indian Wars had officially ended with the massacre of Native American Indians at Wounded Knee. Some of the survivors would travel with Buffalo Bill on his European Tour. The leaders of the 'Ghost Dancers' and two of the so called 'Three Wise Men', Kicking Bear and Short Bull, joined the show, along with 100 Sioux Indians.[171] Other famous Indians like Johnny Burke, called No Neck, and Lone Bull also travelled with the show.

Buffalo Bill at Waterloo with Native Americans and his all-cowboy band (Buffalo Bill Museum)

On 2 June 1891, the Wild West Show arrived at the battlefield of Waterloo. They stayed at the Hotel du Musée and were honoured guests. They posed for a picture on the Lion's Mound on 4 June and the Buffalo Bill's Cowboy Band, led by William Sweeney, played the *Star-Spangled Banner* for the first time on the battlefield.[172] To mark the occasion, they raised an American flag there as well.[173] The survivors of Wounded Knee could identify with Waterloo. They too had a lost cause. Buffalo Bill's show celebrated the defeat of Indian culture and yet it was that culutre was what drew in the crowds. Even American identity found expression at Waterloo with the *Star-Spangled Banner* and the American flag.

The battle was depicted several times and in new ways to keep the public's attention. Scott's poetry and prose captured the public imagination. The new art form of the panorama allowed people to experience faraway places in a virtual setting and be a part of the landscape of what was being observed from the horizontal view. Whereas, viewing the

Detail of Lion's Mound picture (Buffalo Bill Museum)

battlefield from the Lion's Mound monument or William Siborne's model gave the viewer a vertical top down observation of the battle. Buffalo Bill sensationalised the battlefield and made it a spectacle for tourists. All these interpretations were made to capture the popular imagination of their audience and to keep the memory of Waterloo alive.

CHAPTER SEVEN

Waterloo During Two World Wars and Beyond

Wallonia anticipated an economic boon for the centenary of the battle. Even before the centenary, tourism of the site was important to Wallonia. To accommodate the visitors, in 1874 a railway stop was added at Waterloo. To that end, the Belgian government financed a new railroad station in Waterloo in 1895. The plan included an electric street-car connection from Waterloo station to the battlefield with stops at the Gordon Monument and the Butte du Lion. Visitors could take a train from Brussels and be at the battlefield in a matter of minutes. The railway station is still in service today. However, the street car connections were replaced by buses in the 1960s.[1] The planners of the centenary had more improvements instore.

In 1910, efforts started to get underway for the celebration of the 100th anniversary of the battle. To complement the Lion's Mound for the centenary, artist Louis Dumoulin secured a lease for 18 years to build a panorama in 1910 at the base of the monument.[2] Louis Dumoulin's Panorama of Waterloo opened on 2 May 1912.[3] It was to be a tourist attraction for the visitors for the centenary of the battle in 1915. For the project, a special building had to be built to house the exhibition of the panorama.[4] The main building measured 35 metres in diameter and 15 metres high and housed the panorama which was 12 metres high, 110 metres long and made of 14 sections of canvas.[5]

The painting of the panorama was done by building a scaffold on wheels that could move around the interior of the building. It was painted by a team of artists. Helping Dumoulin paint the panorama were the artists: Desvreux, Robiquet, Malespina, Meir and Vinck. Dumoulin painted in secrecy behind locked doors.[6] Even though Dumoulin's work strove for historical accuracy, it did make an error in the landscape. He painted trees lining the Brussels road – trees that were there in 1912, but not in 1815.[7]

Dumoulin chose for his topic the French cavalry charges, which took place between 4p.m. and 6p.m.[8] The choice of subject matter was influenced by Victor Hugo's *Les Misérables*, and the location of the panorama was supposedly where many French cavalry units fell into a sunken road. However, Hugo grossly exaggerated both the size and effect of the sunken lane on the cavalry charge. The sunken lane was about ten to 15 feet deep, but it was only in one part and was for the most part a minor obstacle for the cavalry. No such piling up of horses and men occurred as in *Les Misérables* at the site.[9]

When the panorama was ready for display, an umbrella was placed over the main viewing area to block from the visitor's view the interior lighting and the edge of the painting. Dulmoulin's panorama gave them what they all wanted – a chance to be a part of the action. On entering the panorama, visitors had to climb a staircase that led to the main viewing gallery. Once in the main viewing gallery, visitors would notice a foreground made up of models and figures that blended into the middle ground of the painting. The effect combined two dimensional and three-dimensional images to trick the viewer's eyes into believing they were witnessing the battle.[10] Finally, a rail separated the viewer and the panorama to limit the vertical view angle, while providing a 360-degree horizontal image.[11] Brand Whitlock was the American minister to Belgium and was in Belgium when World War I broke out in August 1914. He toured the panorama before the war and wrote:

> Once, before the war, down at Waterloo, the old English lance-sergeant who lectured on the panorama of the battle described to me that engagement, not then dwindled into the skirmish it has since become. He was in uniform, with waxed moustaches, and an odour on his breath and in all the air about, that was of the essence of all the alcohol distilled in the British Isles since the Crimean War; he had, of course, a little swagger stick and as he said, poising it horizontally, delicately, before my eyes; 'Now sir, look sharp sir. This is Napoléon's left and Wellington's right; this, Napoléon's right, Wellington's left. Do you follow me sir?' I nodded with the inane acquiescence of one dazed under instruction … Half an hour later he said, again poising the swagger stick horizontally: 'And now, sir, I shall describe to you the Battle of Gettysburg.' But for once I was firm.

The exterior of the Panorama with the Lion Mound behind (EmDee, Creative Commons license)

> 'Pardon me', I said, 'You will do no such thing! I spent my youth hearing of that battle from original sources.' And I gave him his half crown and went out, past the catchpenny booths and cheap museums with their squalid trinkets and trash souvenirs, into which all earthly glory soon or late dwindles.[12]

During World War I, Waterloo was in German hands from 22 August 1914[13] to 20 November 1918.[14] When the war started, people in Belgium thought there would be another great battle like Waterloo to decide it. Some hoped the British and French would arrive to defeat the Germans on the field of Waterloo.[15] Indeed, German General Otto von Emmich called for the Belgians to support the Germans in the war because they had helped secure Belgian independence at Waterloo. But this did not happen, and the Germans occupied the battlefield site for most of the rest of the war. The victorious Germans celebrated the centenary of the battle of Waterloo in Brussels in the Royal Palace. The German Governor General of Belgium, General Moritz von Bissing, said of Prussia's role in the battle and on the state of the current war:

The Panorama rotunda as seen from the Lion's Mound (EmDee, Creative Commons license)

> We are celebrating in the capital of Belgium the centenary of the victory of June 18. That seems to me, is a wonderful dispensation of Providence without comparison in the history of the world … That seems to me we entrust our just cause, so that victory and the spirit of victory, which since the Battle of Waterloo has become ever more and more he common property of our people, may procure a peace which will give us for a long time to come the possibility of healing the wounds of war and of carrying out our tasks of civilization.[16]

The celebration of the centenary of the battle was not as Dumoulin had envisioned. Luckily, both the Lion's Mound and the panorama survived the war intact.

The centenary of the battle of Waterloo was not celebrated on the battlefield because of the war. In June 1915, World War I was in its first year of dreadful conflict. Waterloo was quickly becoming insignificant compared to the casualty reports coming in from the trenches. By June 1915, there were a dozen or so such Waterloos in terms of casualties.[17] There would

The Panorama entrance (EmDee, Creative Commons license)

Painting detail of Marshal Ney of France leading a charge from the Waterloo Panorama
(Dennis Jarvis, Creative Commons license)

be many more casualties. The trenches were nearly 100 kilometres away from Waterloo, but the war would visit the battlefield on its anniversary. The Germans had banned any form of celebration of the 'British' victory. The Germans believed it to be a source of British pride and the curfew they enforced would make sure that there were no celebrations. However, the relatively new monument of the Wounded Eagle (the place of the last square) became a secret meeting place on the night of 18 June 1915 for Walloon resistance to the German occupation.[18]

These projects had a lasting effect. They helped form a memory of the battle and led people to realise the battlefield of Waterloo was worth preserving and protecting. That the battle field and Belgium were worth saving. Shortly before World War I, Albert, the King of Belgium, declared the battlefield was not to be built upon or any trees planted on it.[19] The panorama was one of the last buildings to be built before the law took effect. The panorama was an important artistic medium for the depiction of the Napoléonic Wars and it still merits visiting today. Besides the Waterloo Panorama in Belgium, the panorama of Borodino in Russia and the panorama of the battle of Mount Isel in Austria depict other Napoléonic-era battles.

The panorama had its zenith as an art form in the 19th century and was a popular art form to depict battle scenes. In the United States, the battles of Gettysburg and Atlanta were also commemorated by painting panoramas. The art form of the panorama too had its own nemesis. Movies soon made panoramas obsolete. Moving pictures could bring action to the battlefield in ways paintings and models could not. The battle of Waterloo was the subject of several 20th-century films and the panoramas were all but forgotten.

What would replace Waterloo in the popular imagination was already evident to Brand Whitlock in 1919. Waterloo, in comparison to World War I, had become a skirmish. The battle of Waterloo's 'Waterloo' was World War I. For the British, Waterloo was forgotten, and the new battlefield horrors of World War I were to be commemorated and mourned. The memory of the Napoléonic Wars in Europe faded in the face of the new history of the 'Great War'.

Viewing these visions of Waterloo became a fashionable thing to do in the 19th century. Whether it was to go to panoramas, seeing the models of Waterloo, visiting the battlefield or reading about the battle, they all reflected the importance the battle had on national identities prior to World War I. Often, visitors of these displays became part of shaping the memory of Waterloo. Perhaps the lasting impression of these works was its contribution to keeping Waterloo in the public imagination for nearly a century. However, World War I changed all of that. The bloodletting of the Great War eclipsed the memory of the Waterloo.

Post-World War I, Waterloo returned to a sleepy little village. The farms of La Haye Sainte, Hougoumont and La Belle Alliance were all in private hands as was most of the land of the battlefield. The battlefield itself covers a patchwork of municipalities and jurisdictions. Tourism dropped off and the village struggled to survive economically after the war, even though it was spared much of the destruction of the war. The great depression of the 1930s did not help Waterloo either. No new projects were envisioned during this period of economic crisis. The automobile increased access to the battlefield but people curtailed their travel. However, there was hope that things would get better during the 1930s with passage of many new laws increasing paid vacation for workers.[20] This was hoped to increase and democratise tourism. Waterloo was not the main destination of battlefield tourists in the 1930s, instead Verdun, Ypres, the Somme and other World War I battlefields took precedence. However, one lasting effect of the new laws was that people had time to spend on leisure activities and it was a right not a privilege of the few. This eventually impacted Waterloo by allowing tourists not only to visit but be part of the commemoration activities through reenactments of the battle. People in France, for example, could take up to 15 days' paid leave to pursue leisure actives and the eight-hour work day allowed people to spend time outside of work.[21]

On 10 May 1940, Belgium was invaded for a second time by German forces. The fighting was brief, lasting only 18 days, and King Leopold III surrendered Belgium on 28 May. Waterloo was, once again, occupied by the Germans. Marie Threes Brassine was a young girl when the Germans arrived. She lived on the battlefield for many years on the second story of the Wax Museum at the base of the Lion's Mound. She saw the Germans occupy the buildings of the battlefield and saw them plant potatoes in the base of the Lion's Mound to make vodka and schnapps.[22] The occupation was not without resistance though. The Wounded Eagle monument became again a clandestine meeting place for the Belgian resistance movement. The Belgians were inspired by Charles de Gaulle's message of resistance on 18 June 1940.[23] The war was hard on Belgium. The battlefield was a billet for German officers and there was a listening post atop the Lion's Mound. The British and Americans liberated most of Belgium in September 1944. The liberators took time out to visit the battle, most notably Field Marshal Montgomery.[24] Allied soldiers visited many of the battlefield's attractions in 1945 after Germany was defeated and it became a popular attraction for many of them.[25]

After World War II, life in Waterloo returned to a sleepy town once again. Many of the actions fought in Belgium during the war were fought to its south and, once again, battlefield tourists in the1950s and 1960s went to view the places of action in World War II. After the war, improvements in transportation and the new European Common Community made it easier than ever to visit the battlefield. Soon visitors, especially from Great Britain, once again, descended on Waterloo. However, the visitors were often school-age children off on holiday with their teachers and parents. 'Vive La Beatles' was their battle cry.[26] They cared little for Wellington or Napoléon.

Norbert Brassine was a leading citizen of Waterloo in the 1960s and wanted to bring something new to the 150th celebration in 1965. He began to dress up as a Napoléonic soldier to interact with visitors and get students more interested in history. He soon began to recruit others and soon the group was able to have the first of many reenactments on the battlefield.[27]

In 1974, a Swedish pop group named ABBA had their first major hit, 'Waterloo'. The song's lyrics had an element of truth about the battle that resonated with young people and local Belgians alike. The group soon made a triumphal tour; they went to Waterloo. ABBA was given the royal treatment in the town and the battlefield.[28]

ABBA were not the only famous 20th-century tourists to visit Waterloo. After World War II, presidents, premiers, heads of state and dignitaries visited the site. Japan's Emperor Hirohito visited in 1960. Britain's Queen Mother visited in 1986 and Queen Elizabeth visited in 1993.[29]

A huge change came to Europe in 1994 when the Channel Tunnel was completed. Now tourists from Britain could cross the channel with ease and visit the continent. However, not all Frenchmen were happy about the journey. Florent Longueppee, a conservative French politician, objected to the British terminal's name where French visitors to Britain arrived. The name of the station was Waterloo.[30] 'Forget Waterloo' became an ad campaign to eventually move the Eurostar train to St Pancras station in 2007. No longer would the French people have to arrive in London and be reminded of the battle.[31]

The fight to preserve Waterloo's history is an ongoing affair. As the bicentennial approached, local and regional authorities believed that tourism of Waterloo could be improved. The site needed a new visitors' centre and plans to renovate the buildings for the expected rush of visitors for the 200th anniversary began in earnest. The Brussels firm BEAI were in charge of the renovation to clear the land and start over. The old Cotton Inn, across the street from the visitors' centre, was now a wax museum and that too was slated for renovation.[32] However, there was considerable resistance to the plan since the planned renovations could pose a risk to archeological remains.[33] During the refurbishment of the visitors' centre in the 1980s, the site took on a pro-French attitude to reflect local Walloon politics. In 2003, the local government bought the farmhouse of Hougoumont and began to restore it for the public.[34] In 2004, a pan-European company took over the project. The plan was championed by the mayor of Waterloo, Serge Kubla.[35] His influence and vision for a new visitors' centre was popular with many Walloons but not all. Some residents of Mont-Saint-Jean objected, mostly because how things were being handled by local government officials.

In addition to the plans for welcoming vistors to commemorate the battlefield, the planners of the 200th anniversary had to deal with a new and powerful force in battlefield tourism, the reenactors. Reencactors come in many shapes and sizes. There are three main varieties of how reenactors chose to portray the soldiers of the era they are representing. The first are mainstream reenactors, who care about authenticity but not to the extreme where the modern world is completely shut out. Then there are what are called campaigners who have been doing reenacting for several years and who have perfected their impression so that they are extremely believeable as a soldier of the era. The last group are called 'stitch counters'; this is often a derogatory term because the meticulous nature of the reenactors' attire.

Literally, it means that these reenactors will only wear clothes or items made using period materials and fashioned using period-correct methods. Perhaps the most often word dreaded amonst reenactors is the word 'farb'. A farb is something incorrect for the period that is being portrayed. For instance, a modern item like sunglasses being worn at an event would be frowned up by other reenactors. A farb is also something out of place for a particular era.

Reenactors spend much time and money perfecting their impressions. Some Napoléonic unforms can cost the equivalent of several months' salary. There are also numerous hours of research on battles, uniforms, food and guns of the period, all in the pursuit of being as authentic as possible for an event. For many reenactors, the hobby is an escape from the nine-to-five world, that allows them to camp in the outdoors and share comradery with people who enjoy history and telling the stories of their unit to spectators or each other. New recruits are often gained at reenactments and one of the greatest draws to the hobby is what can only be described as suspension of disbelief for a split second that the reeactor is in the period that they are portraying. This time-warp effect is what drives many reeactors to try to authentically portray the soldiers as best as possible. They do it for the enjoyment of learning, having fun and for the spectators.

Modern reenacting is a phenomenon that has its roots in commemoration and access to more leisure time since World War II. In the United States, the American Civil War is the most often reeacted period. Starting in the 1950s and growing during the 1960s, civil war reenacting became progressively larger. Most reenactment units are based on a unit that existed in the time period. Soon an industry was born. It started with indivduals selling handmade items but soon blossomed into arms manufacturing and manufactured uniforms. The people selling these wares are called sutlers. Some are authentic, while others cater to those who want affordablity over authenticy. In 1998, the largest reenactment on record occurred at Gettysburg for the 135th anniversary with over 15,000 reeactors and over 50,000 spectators. In the United States, the most popular reenactments are those of the American Civil War but World War II reenactments are gaining in popularity. Other popular time periods include the Roman Empire, the English Civil War, and Napoléonic reenacting.

The immense Lion's Mound on the battlefield of Waterloo (Jean-Pol Grandment, Creative Commons license)

For the 2015 reenactment of Waterloo, there were roughly 5,000 reenactors to refight the battle. About half of the reeactors represented the French at the battle. Interestingly, many French reenactors are not French but are from many other countries most notably from Russia. The British and Prussian reenactors tend to be from Britain or their former colonies and the Prussian reenactors are generally from Germanic speaking countries. Another group well represented at the event were the Dutch-Belgians. This group is primarily made up of local Flemings while local Walloons tend to fall in with the French. The reenactors of the Napoléonic Wars are mainly European but have significant participation outside of Europe as well. For the 2015 commemoration, Alan Larsen portrayed the Duke of Wellington and Blücher was portrayed by Klaus Beckert. However, there was an intense competition to see who would portray Napoléon. Mark Schneider, an American and living historian from Williamsburg, vied to be Napoléon for the 2015 commemoration.

The lion on top of the mound at the site of the battle (Foroa, Creative Commons license)

He had been Napoléon for the 2005 reenactment and was popular with many reenactors with an uncanny resemblance to Napoléon. Mark took his inspiration for his role from many of the people who portrayed Napoléon before him. He especially enjoyed the portrayal by Albert Dieudonné in the 1927 film *Napoléon* and that of Herbert Lom in the 1956 version of *War and Peace*.[36] The other contender for the role of Napoléon for the reenactment was a Frenchman, Frank Samson. Samson spent most of his time researching Napoléon and paid close attention to his every detail.[37] Eventually, the contest of who would play Napoléon for the 2015 commeration went to Frank Samson. The contest within the reenactment community became so heated it even spawned a documentary film called *Being Napoléon*. The 2015 reenactment was well attended with over 50,000 spectators there. Waterloo still mattered in the 21st century.

Mark Schneider portraying Napoléon by Joeri de Rocker

Commemoration of Waterloo still goes on every year with a reenactment. However, the bigger gatherings are every five years. Wallonia still draws on the name of Napoléon and Waterloo for tourists' money. It seems the economic impact of battle of Waterloo has overshadowed both Napoléon and Wellington in the 21st century.

Conclusion

The history of Waterloo will never escape the myth and legends of Wellington and Napoléon. These two men tried to control the memory and history of the battle of Waterloo. Each of them and their followers waged a vicious war on those who opposed their version of events. Others fought to protect certain legends of Waterloo because they had built perceived notions of their national identity upon them.

In Chapter 1, Wellington wanted to establish a history for his country that could be celebrated as a British victory. The British version of events commemorated and honoured Wellington and the British men who fought there. The Prussians wanted to document, but not commemorate, the heroism of the men who fought against Napoléon and for the Fatherland. Louis XVIII's objective in ordering trials for those who collaborated with Napoléon was to restore order in his army. He also wanted to punish those responsible for Napoléon's return and discredit Bonapartism.

Chapter 2 demonstrated how Napoléon and his supporters protected Napoléon's legacy at all costs, even if it meant destroying one of their former comrades. Napoléon's mission on Saint Helena was to protect his legacy for his son, Napoléon II. Napoléon used Emmanuel Las Cases and Gaspard Gourgaud to help him develop his political and military myth. Napoléon intentionally lied to protect his legacy and his son, Napoléon II. Anything and anyone who challenged the myth of Napoléonic infallibility was an enemy of both Napoléon and his supporters. Marshal Grouchy was vilified by Bonapartists, Republicans and Royalists. The Bonapartists shunned him for not being at Waterloo and abandoning their political cause; the Republicans shunned him for his association with Napoléon and for being an aristocrat and the Royalists despised him for siding with the revolutionaries and Napoléon.

Chapter 3 examined the effect of challenging the political myth and legend of Napoléon. Marshal Grouchy's abandonment of the Napoléonic cause and Napoléon II by 1819 made him an outcast, particularly to the Bonapartists. Napoléon argued he made a mistake in appointing Grouchy to a position of leadership in the *Armée du Nord* and making him a marshal. Grouchy was blamed by Napoléon and France for losing Waterloo. Grouchy's public fight with Generals Gérard and Gourgaud only made things worse for himself. He transformed into a bitter man who had to defend himself from all sides. He was perhaps the biggest loser of Waterloo; he died unloved and despised by his country for which he fought for so nobly.

Chapter 4 examined scholarly attempts to discern the objective truth of Waterloo. The battle was studied by the military theorists of the 19th century to learn the lessons of war on the strategic and tactical level. Antoine Jomini tried to understand Napoléon's way of war through science and reason. Carl von Clausewitz, meanwhile, understood war as an irrational act and connected directly with politics. Waterloo offered lessons for both men and still offers us an insight today regarding the relationship between politics and war.

The fifth chapter examined the political relationship to Waterloo of those who grew up with its memory. Victor Hugo's entire life was spent in the shadow of both Napoléon's legend and Waterloo. He fought his own fight against Bonapartism through the publication of poetry and novels. Hugo's attack on Bonapartism and Louis-Napoléon in his masterpiece *Les Misérables* transcended the 19th century and helped lay the foundation for the French Third Republic. Waterloo was central to Hugo's understanding of the 19th century. It is fitting he has a monument dedicated to him at the battlefield of Waterloo.

The sixth chapter explored how Waterloo was visualised. Monuments do not have to be physically on the battlefield to commemorate it. Walter

Scott, Henry Barker and William Siborne made monuments to Waterloo in their own way for Britain. They let people visit Waterloo without having to go to the battlefield. Artists transformed the battle of Waterloo's mythic interpretation into something that could be understood by the common man of the 19th century. By reading novels, poetry, going to art exhibits and travelling to Waterloo, one could vicariously experience the battle. The Lion's Mound tried and failed to ignite popular support for the Kingdom of the United Netherlands, yet it has become the most enduring monument and symbol of Waterloo at the battlefield.

In Chapter 7, the 20th and 21st centuries saw Waterloo's importance diminish as it was eclipsed by the sheer carnage of the two world wars. Waterloo's romantic image of the 19th century was replaced by the gritty reality of war. The Waterloo Panorama, at the base of the Lion's Mound, was made to help celebrate the centenary of the battle and was hoped to help the French come to terms with their defeat. Waterloo's centenary was not celebrated as it was planned. Tourism at Waterloo picked up after World War II and Waterloo benefited from the long European peace and improvements in transportation to the continent. With leisure time increasing, a new passion arose, reenacting.

If one contributed to the prevailing myths and legends, great rewards awaited. In Britain's case, men like Sir Walter Scott sold books and Henry Barker sold tickets to the panoramas. Both made fortunes. In France's case, men like Gérard were given their marshal's batons. Political adherence to what the people wanted to hear in both countries made financial and political sense. During the 19th century and until World War I, articles, books, paintings and panoramas made money. People wanted to hear the story of Waterloo and believe what they wanted about it. The different interpretations of what happened at Waterloo were popular during the 19th century. The subject of Waterloo was the leading topic of publications and works of art concerning the Napoléonic era. The interpretation of the battle has always been political and continues to be political in nature.

To dispute Wellington's and Napoléon's myth of Waterloo often brought sharp criticism from the people of Britain and France. William Siborne was financially ruined for his feud with Wellington. Marshal Grouchy was ridiculed for the rest of his life by his comrades and countrymen for being incompetent.

Perhaps the country that paid the greatest price for interfering with the battle's place in history was the Kingdom of the United Netherlands. The Lion's Mound destroyed the topography of the battlefield. In the end, it failed as a monument of unity and the Kingdom of the United Netherlands dissolved.

Belgium inherited Waterloo and the Lion's Mound. The Lion's Mound was rescued as a symbol of the battle by the local inhabitants of Waterloo and Mont-Saint-Jean. The locals realised British tourists came to celebrate the battle and, though they did not like to celebrate France's defeat, they did take the money those tourists brought in. The Lion's Mound was a tourist attraction, and it eventually became the most identifiable symbol of the battlefield. Besides the memory of Napoléon, Belgians have profited the most from the battle. Tourism of the battlefield was its ultimate gift to Belgium and Wallonia.

The smartest of those who resisted the myths and legends of Wellington and Napoléon was Victor Hugo. He realised to take on the myths and legends of Wellington and Napoléon was folly. Instead, he accepted such stories and turned them on their head.

Napoléon was not a friend of the poor or the army. He was an opportunist like his nephew, Napoléon III, and Sergeant Thénadier. Hugo transformed the Bonapartists' political agenda and exposed it as a fraud. Hugo wanted Republican France to sail like Odysseus between the Scylla and Charybdis of the Monarchists and Bonapartists. He meant for France not to be guided by hereditary or charismatic leaders but by ideas that protected people from injustice and provided liberty of conscience. The political effects of Waterloo are still with us. The debate over Waterloo opened a space for political discourse during the 19th century over what was good government. The debate has not ended. Politically, Waterloo was a beginning not an end.

For France, the debate over Waterloo in its role in national identity crystalised long ago around the person of Marshal Grouchy. Paris persists in refusing to name a street after him.[1] It is doubtful it ever will. The Grouchy family still tries from time to time to clear their ancestor's name despite the evidence of Napoléon's deceit about the loss of the battle. To this day, the family continues the tradition of military service to France.[2] The memory of Waterloo in French history is still painful for its national identity. The historiography and the popular interpretations of the marshal's role in the campaign have, in the 21st century, begun to be re-assessed.

The movie *Waterloo* (1970) went a step further in attacking Grouchy. The marshal was portrayed as dogmatically adhering to his orders, while ignoring the sage advice of General Gérard. Worse yet, Grouchy was depicted as not being engaged with the Prussians at Wavre. It depicted him wandering in the countryside with his men eating strawberries. The depiction in the movie was as inaccurate as it was insulting. The movie favorably depicts Wellington, Blücher and Napoléon. According to the movie, it was Grouchy's fault for not winning the battle.

In 1965, the battle of Waterloo was reenacted for the first time, and since 1979, it has become an annual event. The event draws several thousands of people each year. Napoléon is the focus of the event. The cult of Napoléon still survives today. Looking at the visitor centre guest book one realises how few people remark on Wellington, except visitors from Britain. Grouchy is almost never represented at these events.

Even fewer mention Blücher. All the other remarks left by visitors reflect a love of Napoléon. British visitors complain the visitors' centre is like entering the temple of Napoléon. In the 21st century, it seems Napoléon won the battle. At the reenactments, people cheer for Napoléon, and in 2009, nobody even showed up to play Wellington or Blücher. 'Napoléon is still a mythic figure – there are lots of people in France who are hooked on him.'[3]

The battle was reenacted in 2015. Nationalism influenced the event. There was concern in France, Napoléon would not be played by a Frenchman at the 200th anniversary reenactment.[4] For many French reenactors the thought of Napoléon not being French was unacceptable. Frenchman Frank Samson challenged Schneider for the role in 2015 and won. For

France, Napoléon is a national symbol of the glory of France even today. His many victories overshadow his defeat at Waterloo for them. The role of who portrayed Napoléon became an issue of national pride not just for Frank Samson but for France as well.

Some historians have argued Napoléon's defeat at Waterloo irrelevant. According to historian Alexander Grab, Europe was transformed by the time of Waterloo. Nationalism had already taken root in all of Europe. The Hundred Days was more of a brief interruption of what would be Reactionary Europe.[5] Grab's view of Waterloo is also shared by other many historians.

The argument Waterloo was irrelevant seems to miss the point; Waterloo defined the age and ushered in an era of peace. Waterloo marked the beginning of the Pax Britannica that lasted nearly a century. Waterloo mattered to the people of the 19th century as evidenced by the popularity of the subject in various art forms. The myth Napoléon created about the battle is as strong as ever. Compounded with the myth and legend of Wellington, the story of Waterloo will always be one that ignites the imagination.

Both Wellington and Napoléon sought to control history and their place in it, even at the expense of truth. Two men got in their way, the first was Marshal Grouchy and the second was Captain William Siborne. Each paid a price for their interference. One was defamed and the other bankrupted. However, their challenges to the Napoléonic and Wellingtonian versions of the battle of Waterloo are important for understanding the complex relationship between memory and history.

It was only in the wake of two world wars that nationalism's effects partially abated. In the 21st century, Britain, France and Germany are allies and economic partners. Belgium is the home capital of the European Union, which de-emphasises nationality in favour of a new European identity.

However, nationalism's popular appeal led to Great Britain's referendum of 2016 to leave the European Union. It was a very close vote to leave the European Union and upset many, particularly in Scotland and Northern Ireland. The politics of disunity may undo what Waterloo initially did in the 19th century. For Britain, Waterloo can still be a source of unity. An Irish lord who led Irishmen, Scotsmen, Welshmen and Englishmen into combat against their continental foes. However, the same nationalistic forces may split Britain as the memory of the battle fades.

Endnotes

Introduction

1   Linda Colley, *Britons: Forging a Nation 1707–1837* (New Haven, Connecticut: Yale University Press, 1992), pp 5–7.
2   Kaiser Wilhelm II attended the dedication ceremony.
3   During World War I, Germany tried to win the war in 1918 in one last attack called the Michael offensive.
4   Russian troops were also present in large numbers at Leipzig, but the Russians viewed the Battle of Borodino as the beginning of the end for the French Empire. The Prussians were proud of their actions in the Waterloo campaign and that they ably assisted their British allies in winning the battle.
5   There are over 25 towns or cities named Waterloo in the United States and Canada. There are more in parts of Africa, India and in Australia. The largest of these are Waterloo, Ontario, and Wellington, New Zealand.
6   There is one dedicated by the Italians though.
7   The 'Wounded Eagle' monument is on the spot of the Imperial Guard's last stand.

Chapter 1

1   The centre of the fighting between the armies took place at Mont-Saint-Jean.
2   The 'Waterloo Dispatch', *The Times*, 22 June 1815.
3   In reality, they outnumbered the French – nearly 100,000 Prussians to 70,000 Frenchmen.
4   Whether not that was true has been a source of much recent controversy.
5   'The Waterloo Dispatch', *The Times*, 22 June 1815.
6   Colonel De Lancey did die of his wounds some weeks later.
7   *The dispatches of Field Marshal the Duke of Wellington*. Wellington to King of Netherlands VIII (London: John Murray 1852), p. 146.

8   Emilio Ocampo, *The Emperor's Last Campaign* (Tuscaloosa, AL: University of Alabama Press, 2009), p.23. Ney and La Bédoyère were tried and convicted of treason and subsequently shot by a French firing squad.

9   One myth that flourished during the period and for some time was that Nathan Rothschild made his fortune this way. Rothschild earned his fortune in government contacts before the battle. Indeed, he would have profited more had the campaign been longer.

10   It was much larger than what Wellington thought.

11   *The dispatches of Field Marshal the Duke of Wellington*. Wellington to Earl Bathurst VIII, p. 160.

12   *Battle of Waterloo: Collected from Official Documents* (New York: Jon Evans and Co., 1819), pp. 280–82. Proclamation to the men of the *Armée du Rhin*, 19 June 1815.

13   Ibid.

14   Ibid., p. 283.

15   Ibid.

16   Ibid., p. 288.

17   Ibid., p. 284.

18   Ibid., p. 291.

19   Ibid., p. 267. Official Battle Report of the *Armée du Rhin*.

20   The Prussians used the corps system like the French. The corps were arranged in such a way to be able to defend one another or attack at a certain point within 24 hours.

21   *Battle of Waterloo*, p. 269.

22   The English division he referred to was at Quatre Bras.

23   Ibid., pp. 270–75.

24   Ibid., p. 275.

25   Ibid., p. 276. Moonlight played a huge part in the outcome of the campaign. On the night of 16 June clouds prevented the French Cavalry to effectively pursue the Prussians, but the skies cleared on the night of 18 June for effective pursuit of the French after Waterloo.

26   *Correspondence of Napoléon I*. From *Le Moniteur Universal*, 21 June 1815, Vol. 28, pp.341–45.

27   *Waterloo*, p. 278. I came, I saw, I conquered.

28   Ibid. This information was confused with the Battle of Ligny.

29   It was the official government newspaper.

30   The account fails to mention that the Prussians had also outflanked the French army. Thus, it fought in a position of being outflanked and outnumbered. This did not deter Napoléon and he chose to attack the British line one more time even after the arrival of all of the Prussian forces.

31   This was not the case, but the rumour had been spread throughout the army to bolster its confidence in fighting superior numbers.

32 *Correspondence of Napoléon I.* 22061. From *Le Moniteur Universal*, 21 June 1815, XXVIII, pp. 341–45.

33 Jean Joseph Regnault-Warin, *Mémoires Pour Servir à la Vie d'un Homme Célèbre* (Paris: Plancher, 1819), Chapter 3, p. 59.

34 Louis-Joseph Marchand, *In Napoléon's Shadow*, trans. Proctor Jones (San Francisco, CA: Proctor Jones Publishing Company, 1998), p. 249.

35 *Correspondence de Napoléon I*, No. 22063, Declaration au Peuple Francais, 22 June 1815, XXVIII, p. 346. This was the second abdication announcement.

36 *Correspondence de Napoléon I*, No. 22064, Bertrand to M. Barbier, XXVIII, pp. 346–47.

37 Ibid.

38 Michael Ross, *The Reluctant King* (New York: Mason/Charter Publishers, 1977), p. 244.

39 Rafe Blaufarb, *Bonapartists in the Borderlands* (Tuscaloosa, Alabama: University of Alabama Press, 2005), p. 1.

40 Alexander Dumas' *The Count of Monte Cristo* also described the 'White Terror'. White being the symbolic colour of the Bourbons.

41 *Battle of Waterloo*, p. 489.

42 Moncey, who remained neutral during the Hundred Days, paid for his refusal by being jailed for three months, stripped of the title marshal and removed from the Chamber of Peers.

43 The officers voted five to two to hold themselves 'non-competent' of judging Ney.

44 'From the Boston Advertiser', *Albany Advertiser*, 30 October 1815.

45 The two powers were the French provisional government and the government of Louis XVIII.

46 'Trial of Marshal Ney', *The Times*, 16 November 1815.

47 *The Battle of Waterloo*, p. 498.

48 The proclamation was to be announced the following day.

49 *The Battle of Waterloo*, p. 491, 'Trial of Marshal Ney'.

50 Ibid.

51 Ibid.

52 Ibid., p. 492. Heudelet was put on the inactive list for appearing for Ney and retired some years later.

53 'Execution of Marshal Ney'. *Niles Weekly Register*, 3 February 1816.

54 The execution was scheduled for the plain of Grenelle but the judge feared a large crowd at Grenelle and chose a less crowded public place.

55 'Execution of Marshal Ney', *Niles Weekly Register*, 3 February 1816.

56 There were rumours that he escaped this fate and travelled to America. There is significant doubt that this occurred. His body was also on display in public for some time.

57 John Elting, *Swords Around a Throne*. (New York: The Free Press, 1988), p. 666.

58   Ibid., p. 6.
59   Nicolas Soult, *Memoirs Justicatif de Monsieur Le Marechal Soult Duc de Dalmatie* (Paris: Le Normant, 1815), p. 25.
60   Ibid., p. 31.
61   Ibid., p. 11.
62   Ibid.
63   *The Battle of Waterloo*, pp. 30–31.
64   Nicolas Soult, *Memoirs Justicatif de Monsieur Le Marechal Soult Duc de Dalmatie*, p. 21.
65   Ibid., p. 24.
66   Ibid., p. 33.
67   Napoléon Hector Soult, *Mémoires du maréchal-général Soult*, pub. par son fils (Paris: Librairie d'Amyot, 1854), p. iii.
68   Ibid., p. 181.

Chapter 2

1   What he failed to mention was that this route bypassed some of the most loyalist areas of France where he would have not been welcomed. In short, he chose the path of least resistance.
2   *Battle of Waterloo*, p. 23. The villagers of Laffey, for several years after 1815, resisted the re-establishment of Bourbon rule.
3   David Chandler, *Waterloo: The Hundred Days* (London: Osprey, 1980), p. 18.
4   Soon to be promoted to the rank of general.
5   Nicolas Soult, *Memoirs Justicatif de Monsieur Le Marechal Soult Duc de Dalmatie* (Paris: Le Normant, 1815), p. 21, 24.
6   *Correspondence de Napoléon I*. Oeuvres de Napoléon Ier À Saint-Hélène. Chapter VIII, III Observation, XXXII, p. 249.
7   Ibid., IV observation.
8   *Correspondence de Napoléon I*. 22056. 'Bulletin De L'Armée', XXVIII, p. 333.
9   Ibid., p. 251.
10   Ibid., pp. 249–50.
11   Ibid., p. 254, VI observation.
12   Ibid., p. 257, VI observation.
13   Ibid., p. 258.
14   Ibid., p. 590.
15   Ibid., p. 591.
16   Emmanuel Las Cases, *Memorial de Saint Hélène. Journal of the private life and conversations of the Emperor Napoléon at Saint Helena* (Boston: Wells and Lilly, 1823), p. 187.

17 *Correspondence de Napoléon I.* Note sur Le Comte De Las Cases. XXXII, p. 311.

18 Ben Wieder, *Assassination at Saint Helena Revisited* (New York: John Wiley and Sons, Inc., 1995), p. 221.

19 Emmanuel Las Cases, *Memorial de Saint Hélène. Journal of the private life and conversations of the Emperor Napoléon at Saint Helena* (Boston: Wells and Lilly, 1823), pp. 13–14.

20 Ibid., p. 111.

21 Ibid., pp. 111–113.

22 Ibid., pp. 13–4.

23 Ibid.

24 Ibid, p. 9.

25 Ibid. p. 10.

26 Ibid., p. 143.

27 Ben Wieder, *Assassination at Saint Helena Revisited*, p. 198.

28 Gaspard Gourgaud, *Talks of Napoléon at Saint Helena*, trans. by Elizabeth Latimer (Chicago, A.C. McClurg & Co., 1903), p. 182. Original published in 1899.

29 Ibid., p. 191.

30 Ibid. pp. 184–85.

31 Ibid., p. 186.

32 Ibid., p. 186.

33 Ibid., pp. 186–87. Gourgaud notes that Napoléon had planned to fight a battle similar to his 1814 victory at Montmirail, only the arrival of Bülow's forces prevented this plan of attack.

34 Ibid., p. 189. Andréossi was Marshal Bertier's chief of staff.

35 Ibid.

36 Napoléon makes this point that Grouchy was an independent commander. However, Napoléon was still the overall commander in the theatre of operations. Grouchy's role as an independent commander has been much debated. Grouchy argued that he was not an independent but a dependent commander in his role to pursue the Prussians and that he was acting under the Napoléon's plan for the successful completion of the campaign.

37 Gourgaud, *Talks of Napoléon at Saint Helena*, p. 189.

38 Ibid., p. 190.

39 Ibid., p. 143.

40 He wounded Philipe de Ségur in a duel over his criticism of Gourgaud in Ségur's work on Russia. He also published a volume rebutting Ségur.

41 Gaspard Gourgaud. *Campagne de dix-huit cent quinze, ou, Relation des operations militaires qui ont lieu en France et en Belgique pendant les cent jours* (London: Ridgeway, 1818), p. 90. The guard dies but does not surrender.

42 Ibid., p. 64.

43 Ibid., p. 70.

44   Ibid., p. 71.
45   Ibid., pp. 75–77.
46   Ibid., p. 84.
47   Ibid., p. 87.
48   Ibid., pp. 87–88.
49   This version of heroes against villains figured heavily in the Bonapartist narrative after Waterloo.
50   Ibid. pp. 91–93.

Chapter 3

1   General Baron Gourgard, *Saint Helene: Journal inedit de 1815 a 1818* (Paris Ernest Flammarion, 1899), II, p. 424. Marshal Louis Suchet, 25 December 1817.

2   The Hundred Days refers to the nearly hundred days of Napoléon's return from exile on the island of Elba and his eventual downfall after Waterloo.

3   Historians, Adolphe Thiers, Henry Houssaye, David Chandler and, as recently as 2005, by Andrew Roberts, among others.

4   Several historians of the 19th century noted this preference for Suchet and most notably David Chandler in the 20th century. However, Suchet was an expert at mountain defence and he was assigned to guard the Alpine approaches. Grouchy, a cavalry expert, was needed in Belgium where cavalry was often the decisive factor in winning battles and campaigns.

5   Chateau de Villette was designed by Le Notre and Marsart who were the architects of Versailles.

6   Emmanue de Grouchy, *Memoires du Marechal de Grouchy*, Tome 1 (Paris, Dentu, 1873–74), p. v. The English branches of the family were members of the House of Lords until the beginning of the 19th century. Their family crest can be seen in the Crusade Rooms in Versailles.

7   Rafe Blaufarb, *The French Army 1750–1820* (NY: Manchester University Press, 2002), pp. 18–19.

8   This company was the oldest cavalry company in the Guard du Corps.

9   Grouchy, *Memoires*, Tome 1, p. 3. De Coigny was made Marshal of France in 1816.

10   Trevor N. Dupuy ed., *The Harper Encyclopedia of Military Biography* (Edison, NJ: Castle Books, 1992), p. 299.

11   Grouchy, *Memoires*, Tome 1, p. x. Condorcet was an accomplished member of the Enlightenment. He became a Girondin member of the National Assembly and died in jail in 1794.

12   Grouchy's sister, Charlotte, married Condorcet and had one of the most famous Salons in Paris. This Salon espoused enlightenment and 'new' ideas. It also had considerable political influence in the National Convention. Marquis de Lafayette was a frequent guest of Charlotte's Salon.

13   Grouchy, *Memoirs,* Tome 1, p. 15.

14   James D. Lunt, 'The Odd Man Out: Grouchy' in David Chandler, editor, *Napoléon's Marshals* (New York, NY: Macmillan Publishing, 1987), p. 140.

15   An anti-republican revolt to restore the monarchy.

16   Trevor Dupuy, *The Harper Encyclopedia of Military Biography*, p. 299

17   Lieutenant General Dumont to the Committee of Public Safety. 18 Brumaire year 3 (18 November, 1794). Service historique, Dossier 6Yd 26a He commends Grouchy for his bravery under General Canclaux but that his noble birth made him suspect of treachery towards the republic.

18   Lunt, 'The Odd Man Out: Grouchy', p. 140.

19   Committee of Public Safety, 30 September 1793, Service historique, Dossier 6Yd 26a. This document is signed by Carnot among others.

20   Report of Service of Emmanuel Grouchy. Service historique, Dossier 6Yd 26a.

21   Grouchy, *Memoires*, pp. 155–160. Since the fall of the Terror Grouchy's friends and political influence increased.

22   Dupuy, *The Harper Encyclopedia of Military Biography*, p. 299.

23   Ibid.

24   R. F. Delderfield, *Napoléon's Marshals* (New York, NY: Cooper Square Press, 2002), p. 30. Politically, Hoche had to find a scapegoat for the failure. Grouchy transferred to the army of Italy since relations were so strained between the two men.

25   R. F. Delderfield. *Napoléon's Marshals*, p. 30.

26   The third of that name.

27   James Arnold, *Marengo and Hohenlinden* (South Yorkshire: UK: Pen and Sword, 2005), p. 148.

28   Lunt, 'The Odd Man Out: Grouchy', p. 140.

29   Grouchy to his father, 8 September 1799. *Memoirs*, Tome 2, pp. 131–32. He spent most of his captivity at Gratz.

30   On 9 November 1799, Napoléon Bonaparte launched a *coup d'état*, replacing France's Directory government with a Consulate with Napoléon as the First Consul. General Moreau was also involved in the coup arresting the two Jacobin directors.

31   Lunt, 'The Odd Man Out: Grouchy', p. 140.

32   Grouchy, *Memoirs*, Tome 2, pp. 137–39.

33   The *Armée du Rhin* was France's largest army responsible for controlling central Germany.

34   On 2 December 1800, only one day before the battle.

35   At the Battle of Marengo, General Louis Desaix arrived in the nick of time to save Napoléon from the jaws of defeat and turned the battle into a triumph. Napoléon would argue later that Grouchy should have done what Desaix had done at Marengo then Waterloo would have been a triumph.

36   Fifteen years later, Napoléon would choose this combination of men to lead the *Armée du Nord*.

37   Lunt, 'The Odd Man Out: Grouchy', p. 140.

38 Marmont was Napoléon's best friend at the time and a logical choice to watch Grouchy.

39 Lunt, 'The Odd Man Out: Grouchy', p. 140.

40 Grouchy to La Ferriere, 25 July 1806, *Memoires*, Tome 2, p. 228.

41 Ibid., p. 237.

42 Harold T. Parker, *Three Napoléonic Battles* (Durham, NC: Duke University Press, 1983), p. 8.

43 Lunt, 'The Odd Man Out: Grouchy', p. 142.

44 Albert Sidney Britt III, *The Wars of Napoléon* (Wayne, NJ: Avery Publishing, 1985), pp. 70–72.

45 Grouchy, *Memoires*, Tome 2, p. 301.

46 David Johnson, *The French Cavalry 1792–1815* (London: Belmont, 1989), p. 82.

47 Lunt, 'The Odd Man Out: Grouchy', p. 144.

48 Grouchy, *Memoires*, Tome 3, p. 315. Letter to his father, 14 March 1807.

49 David Chandler, *The Campaigns of Napoléon* (New York, NY: Macmillan Publishing, 1966), p. 555.

50 Napoléon I, *Correspondance de Napoléon* I, No. 12756, Napoléon to Lannes. 13 June 1807, XV, p. 414.

51 Service historique, Correspondance: Grande Armée, Grouchy to the Duc De Berg, 15 June 1807, Carton C²49.

52 Critics of Grouchy after Waterloo accused him of not being an able lieutenant or being able to operate as an independent commander. Indeed, he had served as an independent commander many times with great success before Waterloo.

53 Grouchy, *Memoires*, Tome 3, p. 331.

54 Ibid.

55 David Chandler, *The Campaigns of Napoléon*, p. 610.

56 Lunt, 'The Odd Man Out: Grouchy', p. 144.

57 Lunt, 'The Odd Man Out: Grouchy', p. 144.

58 David Markham, *Imperial Glory: The Bulletins of Napoléon's Grande Armeé, 1805–1814* (London: Greenhill, 2003), p. 208. For a second time, Grouchy demonstrated his talent for pursuing a defeated enemy.

59 Lunt, 'The Odd Man Out: Grouchy', p. 145.

60 Ibid.

61 Ibid.

62 T. M. Hunter. *Napoléon in Victory and Defeat* (Ottawa, Canada: Queen's Printer, 1964), p. 162.

63 Chandler, *The Campaigns of Napoléon*, p. 805. The Master of the Horse's brother.

64 Georges Blond, *La Grande Armée* (New York, NY: Sterling Publishing, 1997), p. 315.

65 Philippe-Paul Count de Ségur, *Napoléon's Russian Campaign* (Alexandria, VA: Time Life Books, 1980), p. 76.

66 Lunt, 'The Odd Man Out: Grouchy', p. 145. The most serious wound he would receive during his career, due to case shot.

67   Chandler, *The Campaign of Napoléon*, p. 805.

68   Ségur, *Napoléon's Russian Campaign*, p. 233.

69   Lunt, 'The Odd Man Out: Grouchy', p. 146.

70   Murat had abandoned Napoléon.

71   Ibid.

72   Owen Connelly, *Blundering to Glory* (Wilmington, DE: Scholarly Resources, 1987), p. 197.

73   *Le Moniteur*, 12 March 1814.

74   Grouchy to Louis XVIII, 11 September 1814, *Service historique de la Armée de Terre*, Dossier 6Yd 26a.

75   Grouchy, *Memoires*, Tome 3, p. 210.

76   Artois also thought that Grouchy betrayed his brother Louis XVI personally.

77   Duke de Berry was the Comte d'Artois' son.

78   Marmont was Napoléon's best friend until 1814. Napoléon and the army accused him of betraying Napoléon. This betrayal led to Napoléon's first abdication.

79   Diary entry Sir Neil Campbell, 2–10 July 1814. Sir Neil Campbell *Napoléon on Elba* (Welwyn Garden City, UK: Ravenhall Book, 2004), pp. 99–100.

80   Ibid.

81   Grouchy to Duchess Angoulême, 28 September 1814, *Service historique*, Dossier 6Yd 26a.

82   Her husband was fourth in line of succession. With the assassination of Duke de Berry in 1820, the Duke of Angoulême became heir and eventual Louis XIX (uncrowned). She was also the daughter of Louis XVI and Marie Antoinette.

83   Grouchy's confirmation to the Order of St Louis, 9 January 1815, *Service historique*, Dossier 6Yd 26a.

84   Ibid.

85   Guillaume Sauvigny, *The Bourbon Restoration* (Philadelphia: The University of Pennsylvania Press, 1966), p. 102.

86   Napoléon I, Correspondence of Napoléon, 22020. Napoléon to Prince Joseph. Dated at Avesnes, 14 June 1815, XXXI, p. 322.

87   For example, Napoléon's 1796 campaign and as recently as his 1814 campaign in France.

88   Napoléon I, Correspondence of Napoléon. 22055. Napoléon to Prince Joseph. Dated at Charleroi, 15 June at 9p.m., XXXI, p. 330.

89   Hyde Kelly, *The Battle of Wavre and Grouchy's Retreat*, (London: John Murray, 1905), p. 61.

90   Jacques Logie, *Waterloo: The Campaign of 1815* (Brussels: Racine, 2003), pp. 37–39.

91   These were elite light infantry of the French Army.

92   Napoléon I, *Correspondence of Napoléon*. 22061. Bulletin of the Armée; Battle of Ligny, near Fleurus, Dated at Laon, 20 June 1815. XXXI, p. 338.

93   David Howarth, *Waterloo: Day of Battle* (New York: Atheneum, 1968), p. 50–57.

94   Napoléon failed to think to send cavalry to the north in the direction of Wavre. He was convinced that the Prussians would retreat towards Namur and their lines of communication.

95   Peter Hofschröer, *Waterloo 1815: Wavre, Plancenoit and the Race to Paris* (East Yorkshire, UK: Pen and Sword Books, 2006), pp. 10–11. One of the great myths of the Waterloo campaign was that Gneisenau ordered a retreat towards their supply lines at Namur and that it was Blücher who countermanded his chief of staff. Sir Henry Hardinge, who was Wellington's representative at the Prussians headquarters, made these claims and his account made it into many official histories. However, there are many other sources that dispute Hardinge's claims.

96   Kelly, *The Battle of Wavre and Grouchy's Retreat*, p. 67.

97   Ibid., p. 84.

98   Emmanuel de Grouchy *Relation Succincte de La Campagne en Belgique* (Paris: Delanchy, 1843), p. 19. Pajol to Grouchy. 17 June 1815. Before Mazi (sic) at noon.

99   Hofschröer, *Waterloo 1815: Warvre, Plancenoit and the Race to Paris*, 11. This was very fortunate for the Prussians since it made an impression that the Prussian army was retreating towards Namur and away from Wellington's army.

100   Grouchy, *Relation Succincte de La Campagne en Belgique*, p. 22. Exelmans to Grouchy, 17 June 1815.

101   Ibid.p. 18. Grouchy to General Gerard, 17 June 1815.

102   The actual site of the Battle of Waterloo.

103   Grouchy, *Relation Succincte de La Campagne en Belgique*, p. 18. Napoléon to Grouchy, (dictated by Marshal Bertrand), 17 June at 3p.m.

104   Grouchy, *Relation Succincte de La Campagne en Belgique*, p. 20. Grouchy to Vandamme, 17 June, Gembloux.

105   Ibid. p. 20. Grouchy to Gerard, 17 June at 10p.m., Gembloux.

106   Detached from Lobau's VI Corps.

107   Grouchy, *Relation Succincte de La Campagne en Belgique*, p. 24. Vandamme to Grouchy, 17 June, Gembloux.

108   Ibid., p. 24. General Bonnemains to General Chastel. This letter was addressed to Grouchy, but it was later still found in the headquarters of General Chastel.

109   Ibid., p. 3. Grouchy to Napoléon, Campaigns, 17 June, Gembloux. Some historians have translated this as he was with all of his cavalry but in the original French is translates as a part of my cavalry. It was Exelmans's cavalry to be exact.

110   Ibid.

111   Ibid.

112   Ibid., p. 4–6. Grouchy to Napoléon, 18 June at 3a.m., Gembloux. This was fortunate for Grouchy later, since it gave his command an escape route back to France after receiving news of Waterloo. He also informed Napoléon that his command needed to be re-supplied.

113   Grouchy's letter, 17 June at 10p.m.

114 Grouchy, *Relation Succincte de La Campagne en Belgique*, p. 28. Headquarters to Grouchy, 18 June 1815 at 10a.m.

115 Grouchy, *Relation Succincte de La Campagne en Belgique*, p. 6. Grouchy to Napoléon, 18 June at 11a.m.

116 He had just finished the main course and had started on his dessert of strawberries. This scene was often depicted during the 19th and 20th century to demonstrate Grouchy's lack of vigorous pursuit of the Prussians.

117 It would actually have taken them longer to make the passages and would have further delayed them.

118 The Prussians outnumbered Grouchy's forces three to one. There was a real possibility that Blücher could have turned on Grouchy.

119 Peter Hofschröer, *1815 The Waterloo Campaign: The German Victory* (New York, NY: Greenhill Books, 1999), p. 93.

120 This was the order sent at 1p.m. to Grouchy from Napoléon via Soult.

121 This had already happened before the order was sent.

122 Grouchy, *Relation Succincte de La Campagne en Belgique*, p. 6. Grouchy to Napoléon via Soult. This letter was dispatched but never received or found afterwards and was assumed lost or captured.

123 Grouchy, *Relation Succincte de La Campagne en Belgique*, pp. 7–15. Grouchy to Napoléon, 20 June. This letter was started at 6a.m. and finished at 10p.m. Grouchy was writing while travelling.

124 The pursuit of the main army had already had its effect and the army had retreated beyond Charleroi at this point.

125 Grouchy, *Relation Succincte de La Campagne en Belgique*, pp. 7–15. Grouchy to Napoléon, 20 June.

126 Grouchy, *Relation Succincte de La Campagne en Belgique*, p. 14. Grouchy to Napoléon, 20 June. The enmity between Grouchy, Vandamme and Gerard only intensified over the years.

127 Ibid.

128 Emmanuel Grouchy. Mémoires Maréchal De Grouchy (Paris: Dentu, 1874), T.4, p. 301. This order was given at Philippeville on 19 June. Grouchy was already on the move back towards Paris at this time.

129 Ibid., p. 316.

130 Service historique, Dossier 6Yd 26a.

131 Emilio Ocampo. *The Emperors Last Campaign*, p. 51.

132 Ibid., p. 85.

133 Ibid., pp. 135–136.

134 Ibid., p. 86.

135 Records of Chateau Villette, Oise. Private archive of Olivia Hsu Decker, owner of Chateau Villette. The estate was designed by Le Notre and Marsart who also designed Versailles. It was also Grouchy's birthplace. The Chateau was also most famously featured in the book and movie *The Da Vinci Code*.

136 *Weekly Aurora*. Philadelphia. 'Battle of Waterloo', 21 September 1818.

137 Emmanuel Grouchy, *Observations sur la relation de la campagne de 1815, publiée par le général Gourgaud: et réfutation de quelques-unes des assertions d'autres écrits rélatifs à la bataille de Waterloo* (Philadelphia: Hurtel, 1818), p. 3.

138 Ibid.

139 Ibid, p. 5.

140 Ibid., pp. 5–6.

141 Ibid., p. 6.

142 Ibid.

143 Ibid., pp. 10–11.

144 Ibid., p. 11.

145 Ibid., p. 12.

146 Ibid. pp. 6–7.

147 Emmanuel Grouchy. *Observations sur la relation de la campagne de 1815, publiée par le général Gourgaud: et réfutation de quelques-unes des assertions d'autres écrits rélatifs à la bataille de Waterloo,* p. 17. At this time, the battle is *won* on the line of Waterloo.

148 Ibid., p. 20.

149 Ibid., p. 24.

150 Ibid., p. 25.

151 Ibid., pp. 28–31.

152 Ibid., pp. 30–33.

153 Ibid. p. 40.

154 Emmanuel Grouchy. *Observations sur la relation de la campagne de 1815, publiée par le général Gourgaud: et réfutation de quelques-unes des assertions d'autres écrits rélatifs à la bataille de Waterloo* (Paris: Chez Chaumerot, 1819), p. iii.

155 Ibid.

156 Étienne Gérard. *Quelques documens sur la bataille de Waterloo: propres a éclairer la question portée devant le public par M. le marquis de Grouchy* (Paris: Verdière, 1829), pp. 1–3. The marshal had remarried soon after the death of Cécile Doulcet de Pontécoulant, Grouchy's first wife, in 1827. This strained relations between Louis and the marshal.

157 Ibid., pp. 1.

158 Ibid., pp. 9–10, 12. He cited Colonel Simon Lorière, his temporary chief of staff on 18 June as a witness.

159 Ibid., pp. 30–35. See 'Retraction of Col. Grouchy', *Le Constitutionnel,* 21 January 1820.

160 Ibid., pp. 36–38.

161 Ibid., p. 1.

162 Emmanuel Grouchy, *Fragments historiques relatifs à la campagne de 1815 et à la bataille de Waterloo par le général Grouchy. De l'influence que peuvent avoir sur l'opinion les documents publiés par M. le comte Gérard* (Paris: Chez Firmin Didot, 1829), p. 14.

163 Ibid., pp. 17–18.

164 Ibid., p. 23.

165 Ibid., p. 8.

166 Ibid., pp. 23–24.

167 Ibid., p. 27.

168 Ibid., p. 32.

169 Ibid., p. 35.

170 Ibid., p. 37.

171 Barthélemy would be fined and jailed for printing the third volume of this series, *Le fils de l'homme, ou, Souvenirs de Vienne* (1829). The poem insulted Napoléon's son.

172 Auguste Méry and Joseph Barthélemy, *Waterloo: Au General Bourmont* (Paris: A.J. Denain, 1829), p. 6.

173 Ibid., p. 12.

174 Auguste Méry and Joseph Barthélemy, *Waterloo: Au General Bourmont*, p. 25. 'Que fais-tu donc si loin, Grouchy? Que te retard, /Exelmans, autrefois toujours à l'avant-garde? /Et Gérard, jamais sourd à l'apple du cannon? /Et Vandamme? Et vous tous de si puissant renom? /Sans doute qu'en voyant votre marche trompée,/Vous brisez dans vos mains votre inutile epée, /Et que vous convoitez, remplis, d'un saint courroux, /La plaine étincelante où l'on combat sans vous.'

175 Emmanuel Grouchy, *Fragments historiques relatifs a la campagne de 1815 et a la bataille de Waterloo: lettre a messieurs Méry et Barthélemy* (Paris: Chez Firmin Didot, 1829), pp. 19–20. See also *Waterloo: Au General Bourmont*, p. 56.

176 Ibid., pp. 21–22. Grouchy wrote to Napoléon four times within 24 hours.

177 Ibid., pp. 22–23.

178 Ibid., pp. 24–25.

179 Ibid. pp. 25–26.

180 Emmanuel Grouchy, *Refutation de quelques articles des mémoires de M. le Duc de Rovigo* (Paris: Chez Firmin Didot, 1829), pp. 1–2.

181 Published in 1828 by General Anne Jean Savary, Duc de Rovigo.

182 Emmanuel Grouchy, *Refutation de quelques articles des mémoires de M. le Duc de Rovigo*, p. 12.

183 Ibid., pp. 14–15.

184 Elting, *Swords Around a Throne*, p. 668.

185 Elting, *Swords Around a Throne*, p. 673.

186 Ibid.

187 After Waterloo, Marshal Grouchy was stripped of the rank of Marshal of France by King Louis XVIII. Now Gérard technically outranked Grouchy.

188 Philip J. Hayethornthwaite, *Napoléon the Final Verdict* (New York, NY: Sterling Publishing, 1996), p. 208.

189 In 2006, Michel De Grouchy and his daughter Sandrine De Grouchy wrote several articles defending the marshal. Family members have served in the French armed forces since 1815. They have nobly continued the tradition of military service. Colonel De Grouchy fought in World War I and was a member of the Resistance in World War II.

Chapter 4

1   *Traité des grandes opérations militaires in five volumes.*

2   John Shy, 'Jomini' in *Makers of Modern Strategy* (Princeton, NJ: Princeton University Press, 1986), p. 146.

3   *Histoire Critique et Militaire des Campagnes de la Revolution.*

4   Antoine Henri Jomini, *The Political and Military History of the Campaign of Waterloo*, trans. S. V. Benet (New York: Redfield Publishers, 1852), pp. 5–6. Translation of the original 1838 work by the same name. Stephen Vincent Benet was a West Point graduate, ordinance officer and West Point Professor of History. This book was a translation of Chapter 22 in Jomini's 1827 work, *Vie Politique et Militaire de Napoléon recontèe par lui-meme au Tribunal de Cèsar d'Alexandre et de Frederic.*

5   Ibid., p. 120.

6   Ibid., p. 123.

7   Ibid., p. 124.

8   Talleyrand's son Auguste-Charles-Joseph de Flahaut de La Billarderie, comte de Flahaut.

9   Ibid., p. 127.

10   Ibid., pp. 132–33.

11   Ibid., p. 133.

12   Ibid., pp. 133–34.

13   Ibid., p. 135.

14   Ibid., pp. 135–36.

15   Ibid., p. 145.

16   Ibid.

17   Ibid., p. 147.

18   Ibid., p. 148.

19   Ibid., p. 150.

20   Ibid., p. 149.

21   Ibid.

22   Ibid., p. 151.

23   Ibid., p. 153

24   Ibid., p. 154.

25   Ibid., p. 154.

26   Ibid., pp. 177–78.

27   Ibid.

28   Ibid., p. 179.

29   Ibid., p. 177.

30   Ibid., p. 155.

31   Ibid., p. 156.

32   Ibid., p. 158.

33   Ibid., p. 167.

34   Ibid.

35   Ibid., p. 170.
36   Shy, 'Jomini', p. 177.
37   Ibid., pp. 153–154.
38   Antione Jomini. *The Art of War*, trans. G. H. Mendell and W. P. Cragihill (Westport Connecticut: Greenwoood Press Publishers, 1862), p. 59. Originally titled *Précis de l'art de la guerre* printed in 1838.
39   Ibid., p. 67.
40   Ibid., pp. 78–79.
41   Ibid, p. 116.
42   Ibid., pp. 165–66.
43   Ibid., p. 166.
44   Ibid., p. 188.
45   Ibid., p. 279.
46   Ibid., p. 270.
47   Ibid., p. 317.
48   Ibid.
49   Ibid., pp. 324–25.
50   Michael Bonura. *Under the Shadow of Napoléon.* (New York: New York University Press, 2012), pp. 78–79. Denis Hart Mahan being one of them.
51   Shy, 'Jomini', pp. 180–81.
52   Peter Paret, 'Clausewitz' in *Makers of Modern Strategy* (Princeton, NJ: Princeton University Press, 1986), p. 188.
53   Ibid., p. 189. This was an article refuting the ideas of Heinrich von Bülow, the brother of Friedrich von Bülow.
54   Ibid., p. 191.
55   Ibid., p. 193.
56   Clausewitz, *On War.* p. 136.
57   Paret, 'Clausewitz', p. 197.
58   Ibid., p. 194.
59   Ibid., p. 195.
60   Hyde Kelly. *The Battle of Wavre and Grouchy's Retreat*, p. 55.
61   Ibid., p. 56.
62   Ibid., p. 106.
63   Ibid., p. 128.
64   *Vom Kriege.*
65   Paret, 'Clausewitz', p. 196.
66   Carl von Clausewitz. *On Wellington: A Critique of Waterloo*, trans. Peter Hofschröer (Norman, Oklahoma: Oklahoma University Press, 2010), p. 242.
67   Carl Müffling, *The Memoirs of Baron Müffling*, trans. Peter Hofschröer (London: Greenhill Books, 1997), p. 248. This was a posthumous work originally called Aus Meinem Leben published in 1851. Müffling was critical of Siborne in some aspects of his work but generally agreed that the allies were working together to defeat Napoléon.
68   Ibid., 250–251.

69   Clausewitz, *On Wellington*, p. 70.
70   Ibid., p. 82.
71   Ibid., pp. 92–93.
72   Ibid., p. 112.
73   Ibid., p. 117.
74   Ibid., p. 124.
75   Ibid., p. 144.
76   Ibid., p. 126.
77   Ibid., p. 128.
78   Clausewitz, *On War*, p. 75.
79   Carl von Clausewitz, *On War*, trans. Michael Howard and Peter Paret (Princeton, NJ: Princeton University Press, 1984), p. 519.
80   Clausewitz, *On War*, p. 136.
81   Ibid., p. 137.
82   Ibid. pp. 234–35.
83   Ibid., p. 265.
84   Ibid., p. 272.

Chapter 5

1   Particularly the Bonapartists.
2   Joseph Hugo, *Memoires du General Hugo* (Paris: Jadis et Naguere, 1934), p. 6. Hereafter, referred to as Joseph. See also, Georges Six, *Dictionnaire Biographique Des Generals et Amiraux Francis de La Revolution et de L'Empire* (Paris: Libraie Historique et Nobilaire, 1934), pp. 580–81.
3   Joseph Hugo, *Memoires*, pp. 14–15.
4   Joseph Hugo, *Memoires*, pp. 74–75. See also, Chapter 5 in *Les Misérables*. Marius (Victor Hugo's alter ego in the story) goes to see General Frision and General Jacques Bellavesne, commandant of Saint Cyr, to speak about his father during the Napoléonic Wars.
5   Louis Barbier, *Le General de la Horie 1766–1812* (Paris: Dujarric, 1904), pp. 19–21.
6   Since their service together in 1793, Lahorie had surpassed Joseph in advancement and was a full colonel while Joseph was still a captain. Joseph Hugo was a man who wanted promotions, but they were slow in coming. He certainly must have been frustrated by this fact while his friends and lesser men seemed to vault to general in little time.
7   Barbier, p. 25. Napoléon to Moreau.
8   Adele Hugo. *Victor Hugo, By A Witness To His Life*, trans. Charles Wilbour (New York: Carleton Publishers, 1864), p. 31. Joseph Hugo was a witness to this event being on Moreau's staff at the time. Lahorie embarrassed Leclerc in front of his men.
9   Barbier, pp. 30–35. One reason was that General Charles Leclerc (Napoléon's brother-in-law, husband of Pauline) had disobeyed an order of Moreau's by not advancing on

the Iser River when ordered. Lahorie held Leclerc responsible for not carrying out the order and it became a source of personal animosity between Lahorie and Napoléon.

10   Joseph Hugo, *Memoires du General Hugo* (Paris: Jadis et Naguere, 1934), p. 85.

11   Louis Barbier, *Le General de la Horie*, pp. 48–50. Upon agreeing, on the name, Hugo thanked his old friend.

12   Ibid., p. 94. He was also spared from going to Haiti.

13   His friendship with Firion had paid off.

14   Joseph Hugo, *Memoirs,* p. 101. Brother Devil. He was captured in a pharmacy.

15   Adele Hugo, p. 30.

16   Ibid., In the Faubourg St Jacques.

17   Guido Artom, *Napoléon is Dead in Russia*, trans. Muriel Grindrod (New York: Antheneum, 1970), pp. 30–31.

18   Ibid.

19   Six, *Dictionnaire Biographique Des Generals et Amiraux Francis de La Revolution et de L'Empire*, pp. 143–44.

20   General Lamotte would be referred to in *Les Misérables* as well as a maker of elixirs of gold or a charlatan, p. 509.

21   Barbier, pp. 186–87.

22   Six, *Dictionnaire Biographique Des Generals et Amiraux Francis de La Revolution et de L'Empire* (Paris: Libraie Historique et Nobilaire, 1934), p. 541.

23   Guido Artom, *Napoléon is Dead in Russia*, pp. 106–8. See also Everett Dauge, *Henri Clarke and the Malet Conspiracy.* (Tallahassee, Fl: Consortium on Revolutionary Europe, 1996), p. 280.

24   Ibid., pp. 286–88.

25   Everett Dauge, *Henri Clarke and the Malet Conspiracy*, pp. 282–83.

26   Joseph Hugo, *Memoires*, p. 310.

27   Michael Leggiere, *The Fall of Napoléon: The Allied Invasion of France 1813–1814.* (New York: Cambridge University Press, 2007), p. 347 and p. 397.

28   Joseph was continuing his extramarital affair with Catherine Thomas who he met while on Elba. After Sophie died, he a married Catherine.

29   The divorce was finalised in 1818 in which Sophie was awarded custody of the children.

30   Joseph Hugo, *Memoires du General Hugo* (Paris: Chez Ladvocat, 1823), Tome III.P, pp. 388–89.

31   Graham Robb, *Victor Hugo* (New York: W.W. Norton & Company, 1997), p. 45.

32   Joseph Hugo, *Memoires du General Hugo* (1823), p. 473. Letter signed by leading Jewish citizens, Mayer-Levi, Isreal, Hauem, Rosenwald, and Abraham-Levi. 11 November 1815.

33   Ibid., pp. 474–75. Signed by all of the officers defending the city of Thionville. 15 November 1815.

34   Victor despised his father at this time and was jubilant in his father's defeat as well.

35   Robb, *Victor Hugo*, p. 46.

36 Victor Hugo, *Poems of my Youth*. '*Le Corse a mordu la poussière /L'Europe a proclamé Louis, /L'Aigle perfide et meurtrière /Tombe devant les fleurs de Lys /Enfin ce maréchal perfide, /Ce Ney va marcher à la mort. /Tremblez, cohorte régicide; /Jacobins, voilà votre sort.*'

37 Robb, Victor Hugo. pp. 96–97.

38 Ibid.

39 The date was important since it was the anniversary of two of Napoléon's finest victories, Marengo and Friedland. However, the choice of Bourmont was ironic since many in the army blamed him for Napoléon's defeat at Waterloo for defecting to the Prussians on 15 June 1815.

40 George Barnett Smith, *Victor Hugo, His Life and Work* (London: Ward and Downey, 1885), p. 127.

41 John Porter Houston, *Victor Hugo* (NY: Twayne Publishers, 1988, p. 69.

42 Smith, *Victor Hugo, His Life and Work*, p. 94.

43 Victor Hugo, *Journal 1830–1848* (Brooklyn, NY: Greenwood Press, 1970), pp. 44–46. Originally published in Paris by Henri Guillemin.

44 Ibid., p. 56.

45 Ibid., p. 49. One who lies and cheats to have someone to make them do something.

46 Rafe Blaufarb, *Napoléon Symbol for an Age: A brief History with Documents* (New York: St Martin's Press, 2008), p. 211.

47 William Makepiece Thackeray, *The Second Funeral of Napoléon and Chonicle of the Drum*. https://www.gutenberg.org/files/2645/2645-h/2645-h.htm. Also printed undethe pen name M.A. Titmarsh. (London: Hugh Cunningham, 1841).

48 Ibid. The work refers to Saint Jerome's lament of the dancing girls of Rome. He was having a nightmare. It also symbolizes the judgment of God over man. Hugo would remark later that Waterloo was God's judgment on Napoléon.

49 Houston, *Victor Hugo*, pp. 71–73.

50 Louis-Napoléon, *Napoléonic Ideas*, trans. James A. Dorr (New York: Appleton & Company, 1859), pp. 16–18.

51 Ibid., pp. 25–26.

52 Ibid., pp. 29–33.

53 Ibid., pp. 44.

54 Smith, *Victor Hugo, His Life and Work*, p. 161.

55 Victor Hugo, *The Memoirs of Victor Hugo* (New York: G.W. Dillingham Co., 1899), p. 189.

56 Fred Shapiro and Joseph Epstein, *Yale Book of Quotations* (NY: Yale University Press: 2006), p. 327.

57 Victor Hugo. *Memoirs*, pp. 232–33.

58 Ibid, p. 253. The events of June 1848 and the political wrangling led many to look for order over democracy.

59 Son of Michael Ney. He was Napoléon Joseph Ney.

60 Ibid., pp. 314–15. 24 December 1848.

61 Ibid., pp. 327. 5 December 1850.

62   Smith, *Victor Hugo, His Life and Work*, p. 138.

63   Napoléon II, Duke of Reichstadt died in 1832 was Louis Cousin and son of Napoléon I.

64   The work, however, was not published until 1877.

65   Alphonse Grouchy (son of the marshal) was elected from the department of the Gironde in 1849 and was a member of the right wing of the legislative assembly of the second republic who sided with Louis-Napoléon. Alphonse was made a Senator of the empire on 31 December 1852. Hugo felt personally betrayed by former Napoléonic officers who he had admired but now detested. Despite the Waterloo controversy, the Grouchys were still Bonapartists!

66   Smith, *Victor Hugo, His Life and Work*, p. 144.

67   Jersey was ruled by the United Kingdom (but not part of it) and was off the coast of Normandy.

68   Victor Hugo, *Les Chatiments* (Brussels: H Samuel, 1853). Chapter II, trans. by author.

69   William VanderWolk, *Victor Hugo in Exile* (Cranbury, NJ: Associated University Press: 2006), p. 131.

70   Waterloo Museum of Waterloo, uncatalogued item, account left in margin, in *Livre D'Or* 1880–1884. Dated June.

71   For political reasons, the British government removed him from Jersey. Like Jersey, Guernsey was ruled by, but not part of, the United Kingdom and off of the Normandy coast.

72   The work was not finished until 1883. The work was published in three volumes: 1859, 1876 and 1883.

73   Kathryn Grossman, *Figuring Transcendence in Les Misérables: Hugo's Romantic Sublime* (Carbondale and Edwardsville, Illinois: Southern Illinois Press, 1994), p. 210.

74   Ironically made bishop by Napoléon.

75   Grossman, *Figuring Transcendence in Les Misérables*, p. 224.

76   Brombert. *Victor Hugo and the Visionary Novel* (Cambridge, Massachusetts: Harvard University Press, 1984), pp. 88–89. Bread stolen to feed his family.

77   Grossman, p. 192.

78   Andre Besson, *Victor Hugo: Vie d'un Geant* (Chaintreaux, France: Editions France-Empire Monde, 2010), pp. 405–7.

79   Jean Lacroix, *Victor Hugo, Mille Jour en Belgique* (Waterloo, Belgium: Ministry of Culture, 2002), pp. 72–73.

80   Hugo, *Les Misérables*, p. 1177.

81   Ibid., p. 1222. '*il dort. quoique le sort fût lui bien étrange. il vivait. il mourut quand il n'eut plus son ange. la chose simplement d'elle-même arriva, comme la nuit se fait lorsque le jour s'en va.*'

82   Kathryn Grossman, *Figuring Transcendence in Les Misérables,* p. 207.

83   Victor Hugo, *Les Misérables*, trans. Charles Wilbour (New York: The Modern Library, 1976), 520. Hereafter, Hugo, *Les Misérables*.

84   Ibid., p. 521. Many soldiers had their promotions annulled, most notably Marshal Grouchy who was stripped of his marshal's rank and returned to the rank of general under the second restoration.

85   Ibid., p. 532.

86   Ibid., p. 533.

87   Cosette was Marius' love interest in the novel. Cosette symbolized both love and liberty. Valjean symbolized virtue and personal honor.

88   Hugo did not yet know that Napoléon III really would have his own in 1870 at Sedan.

89   Victor Hugo, *Les Misérables*, p. 257.

90   Ibid., p. 280.

91   Hugo, *Les Misérables*, pp. 257–59. Also named Goumont. Whether or not Hugo knew that the last prison ship to land in Australia was also named *Huogoumont* is unknown.

92   Hugo, *Les Misérables*, p. 260.

93   Ibid., p. 263. 'All this in order that today a peasant may say to a tourist: Monsieur, give me three francs; if you like, I will explain to you the affair of Waterloo.'

94   Ibid., p. 265. This is particularly effective, since at once the reader is lulled into thinking that the author is not writing history but merely telling the truth. i.e., a history of the battle.

95   Hugo, *Les Misérables*, pp. 264–65.

96   They often are small paperback copies that were made to fit into pockets of travellers while sightseeing.

97   Ibid.

98   Ibid., p. 267.

99   Hugo, *Les Misérables*, pp. 277–79. This is the site of Pontmercy's fall. Also, the cavalry charge as described by Hugo is the subject of the Panorama of Waterloo. It supposedly represents the moment when France could have prevailed in the action.

100 In the story, a Napoléonic officer is trapped underneath a mass of corpses at the Battle of Eylau, like Pontmercy, in the sunken road near Ohain. When the Lion's Mound was built much of the earth surrounding the battlefield was disturbed and there has been controversy over its existence. For Hugo, it did not matter if it did or not; it was a story.

101 Grossman, *Figuring Transcendence in Les Misérables*, p. 210.

102 Hugo, *Les Misérables*, p. 276.

103 This sentiment was almost universally felt by the men that fought at Waterloo and the other men of the French army. Napoléon furthered this misinformation to cover his own fault of sending Grouchy away from him. He even told the army on the battlefield that Bülow's Prussians were actually Grouchy's men.

104 Ibid., p. 292.

105 Ibid., pp. 279–80.

106 Ibid., p. 280.

107 Ibid., p. 284. He felt that the most important of these was the arrival of the Prussians.

108 Hugo, *Les Misérables*, p. 289. The precise translation of shit is merde, but it also was meant to tell the enemy to 'go to hell'.

109 Robb, *Victor Hugo*, pp. 380–381. Hugo responded by saying 'To get a man the Legion of Honor, all I have to say is "Shit".'

110 However, the entire myth may be completely false. British accounts record General Cambronne as being captured before the square's destruction. Accordingly, he may have said nothing.

111 Hugo, *Les Misérables*, pp. 290–91. Hugo seems to also show his disdain for Europe of the 1860s by discounting honour and valour by finishing this section with the line 'at the spot where now (the spot of the last square), at four o'clock in the morning, whistling, and gaily whipping up his horse, Joseph passes, who drives the mail to Nivelles'.

112 Ibid., p. 292.

113 Hugo, *Les Misérables*, p. 298.

114 Hugo, *Les Misérables*, p. 295. Hugo had proposed a liberal one in 1849.

115 VanderWolk, *Victor Hugo in Exile*, p. 116.

116 Victor Hugo, *Les Misérables*, p. 296.

117 Hugo, *Les Misérables*, p. 271.

118 Ibid., p. 275. According to Hugo, he was killed by a landslide in 1783. This story demonstrated the type of stories told to Hugo by the local hoteliers.

119 No relation to General Drouet.

120 Juliette Drouet, *My Beloved Toto: Letters to Victor Hugo 1833–1882*, trans. Victoria Larson (Albany, NY: State University of New York, 2005), p. 189. Letter 137, Hugo to Auguste Vacquerie.

121 Lacroix, *Victor Hugo, Mille Jour en Belgique*, p. 86.

122 Victor Brombert. *Victor Hugo and the Visionary Novel*, p. 87.

123 From Molière's play, *Les Fourberies de Scapin*. Scapin lies and tricks everyone to do his bidding.

124 Hugo, *Les Misérables*, p. 527.

125 He was paid 5500 francs for completion of the work by the publishers Lacroix and Verboeckhoven.

126 Lacroix, *Victor Hugo, Mille Jour en Belgique*, p. 100. He also did an illustrated version of *The Three Musketeers* for Alexandre Dumas.

127 Ibid.

128 Robb, *Victor Hugo*, p. 377. Some censors objected to the use of 'merdre' or shit in the translations.

129 Houston, *Victor Hugo*, p. 150.

130 Lamarque had suppressed the Vendée rebels in 1815. Adolf Thiers cited the Vendée as a reason for losing Waterloo. Lamarque only had 10,000 men.

131 Smith, *Victor Hugo, His Life and Work*, p. 162. La Salle Corbell Pickett, *Pickett and his Men* (Atlanta: Foote and Davies, 1899), pp. 357–59. General George Edward

Pickett was sent a copy through the lines by an old friend, General Rufus Ingalls. Confederate editions were printed on 'sheep's wool paper'.

132 Ibid.

133 There were printings in Richmond and in New York in 1863.

134 Houston, *Victor Hugo*, pp. 153–5. This was also the first feature length movie made in the United States.

135 Ibid.

136 Robb, *Victor Hugo*, p. 525.

137 *Ceremonie de la pose de le premier piers du monument Victor Hugo a Waterloo 22 Septenber 1912* (Paris: Mynier et Brumeur, 1912), pp. 9–10.

138 Ibid.

139 Ibid., p. 23

140 Ibid., p. 25. He wanted his audience at the ceremony to think of them merely 'sleeping in the fields'.

141 Victor Hugo Monument inscription actual completion was 24 June 1956.

142 There is a small statue to Napoléon near the visitors' centre but nothing in scale compared to the Hugo monument.

Chapter 6

1 Geoffrey Treasure. *Who's Who in Late Hanoverian Britain 1789–1837* (Mechanicsburg, PA: Stackpole Books, 2002), p. 406.

2 Phillip Shaw, *Waterloo and the Romantic Imagination* (New York: Palgrave Macmillan, 2002), p. 44.

3 Harriet Wood, *Sir Walter Scott* (Devon, UK: Northcote House Publishers, 2006), p. x.

4 Shaw, *Waterloo*, p. 60.

5 Walter Scott to John Ballantine, Scottish National Library, 25 September 1815. Grierson, pp. 484–85.

6 Walter Scott to John Ballantine, Scottish National Library, 17 October 1815. Grierson, p. 487.

7 Walter Scott to John Ballantine, Scottish National Library, 30 April 1816. Grierson, p. 497.

8 Walter Scott, *The Field of Waterloo* (London: John Murray, 1815), p. 14.

9 Thomas Crawford, *Walter Scott* (Edinburgh: Scottish Academic Press, 1982), p. 11.

10 Walter Scott, *Paul's Letters to his Kinsfolk* (London: John Murray, 1816), p. 42.

11 Ibid., p. 111.

12 Ibid., pp. 117–18.

13 Ibid., p. 133.

14 Ibid., pp. 120–21.

15 Ibid., p. 135.

16 Ibid., p. 124.

17 Ibid., p. 126.
18 Ibid., p. 142.
19 Ibid.
20 Ibid., p. 162.
21 Ibid., pp. 155–56.
22 Ibid., p. 161.
23 Ibid., p. 164.
24 Ibid., p. 165.
25 Ibid., p. 169.
26 Ibid., pp. 171–72.
27 Ibid., p. 177.
28 Ibid., p. 180.
29 Ibid., p. 182.
30 Ibid., p. 185.
31 Ibid., p. 187.
32 Ibid., p. 189.
33 Ibid., p. 191.
34 William Deresiewicz, 'Persuasion: Widowhood and Waterloo', in *Jane Austen and the Romantic Poets* (New York: Chichester: Columbia University Press, 2004), pp. 147–48.
35 James Anderson, *Sir Walter Scott and History* (Edinburgh: The Edina Press, 1981), pp. 11–12.
36 Ibid.
37 Walter Scott, *The Life of Napoléon Bonaparte* (New York: Leavitt and Allen, 1858), p. 719. The entire work in one volume.
38 Ibid., p. 720.
39 Ibid.
40 Ibid., p. 721.
41 Ibid., pp. 721–22.
42 Ibid.
43 Ibid., p. 722.
44 Ibid., p. 726.
45 Ibid., pp. 722–24.
46 Treasure, *Late Hanoverian Britain*, p. 411.
47 Gillen D'Arcy Wood, *The Shock of the Real: Romanticism and the Visual Culture, 1760–1860* (London: Palgrave, 2001), p. 221.
48 Gillen D'Arcy Wood, *The Shock of the Real: Romanticism and the Visual Culture, 1760–1860*, p. 3.
49 Denise Oleksijczuk, 'The dynamics of spectatorship in the first panoramas: Vision, the body and British imperialism, 1787–1820' (University of British Columbia: Dissertation, 2001), p. 75.
50 Ibid., p. 98.

51 Ibid., p. 87.
52 Ibid., p. 90.
53 Wood, *The Shock of the Real*, p.100.
54 Ibid., p. 102.
55 Peter Harrington. *British Artists and War* (London: Greenhill Books, 1993), p. 94.
56 'Panorama Now Open', *The Times*, 25 March 1816.
57 Phillip Shaw. *Waterloo and the Romantic Imagination* (London: Palgrave Publishing, 2002), p. 83.
58 Henry Aston Barker, *Description of the field of battle, and disposition of the troops engaged in the action, fought on the 18th of June, 1815, near Waterloo; illustrative of the representation of that great event in the Panorama, Leicester-Square* (London: Adlard Publishing, 1816), p. 4.
59 Ibid.
60 Ibid.
61 Both Scott and Barker were from Scotland.
62 Barker, *Waterloo Panorama*, p. 10.
63 Ibid.
64 Ibid. Plan of the Panorama.
65 Ibid.
66 'Battle of Waterloo Panorama', *The Times*, 13 May 1816.
67 Hofschröer, *Wellington's Smallest Victory; The Duke, the Model Maker and the Secret of Waterloo* (London: Faber and Faber, 2004), p. 20.
68 Chris Williams, *A Companion to Nineteenth Century Britain*. (Malden: MA, 2004), p. 81.
69 Felix M'Donogh, *The Hermit in London; or, sketches of English manners* (London: Henry Colburn and Co., 1821), p. 123.
70 Ibid., p. 124.
71 Ibid. p. 125.
72 Ibid. pp. 125–27.
73 Ibid. pp. 128–30.
74 Wood, *The Shock of the Real*, p. 109.
75 Ibid., p. 115.
76 'Battle of Waterloo Exhibit to Close', *The Times*, 30 April 1818.
77 Shaw, *Waterloo and the Romantic Imagination*, p. 83.
78 Ibid., p. 84.
79 Hofschröer, *Wellington's Smallest Victory*, p. 21.
80 Shaw, *Waterloo and the Romantic Imagination*, p. 83.
81 'Panorama of the Battle of Waterloo', *The Times*, 22 March 1842.
82 Barker, *Waterloo Panorama*, plan of the Panorama.
83 'Panorama of the Battle of Waterloo', *The Times*, 22 March 1842.
84 'Harris' Panorama of Waterloo', *The Times*, 25 December 1889.
85 Harrington. *British Artists and War*, p. 107.
86 Ibid.

87 Katherine Kane, 'Robert Barker's Leicester Square Panorama: The Rotunda', http://regencyredingote.wordpress.com/2012/08/03/Robert-barkers-leicester-square-panorama-the-rotunda/ *The Regency Redingote*, Kalligraph, accessed 24 February 2013.

88 Peter Hofschröer. *Wellington's Smallest Victory*, p. 34.

89 Malcolm Balen, *A Model Victory* (London: Fourth Estate, 2005), pp. 12–13.

90 William added the 'e' to the end of his name.

91 Balen, *A Model Victory*, p. 5. The work was also to be funded by the government.

92 Ibid., pp. 13–14.

93 Ibid. p. 14.

94 Hofschröer. *Wellington's Smallest Victory*, p. 115.

95 Ibid., p. 97.

96 Balen, *A Model Victory*, 16.

97 Ibid., p. 17.

98 Ibid., pp. 22–23.

99 He spent nearly £1000 of his own money, which was a considerable sum in the 1830s. The money he put in building of the model could have been used to buy a captaincy. It took seven years to recoup his investment.

100 Balen, *A Model Victory*, pp. 23–24.

101 Ibid., p. 25.

102 Hofschröer. *Wellington's Smallest Victory*, p. 136.

103 Ibid.

104 Afterwards referred to as Wellington's *Dispatches*.

105 Hofschröer. *Wellington's Smallest Victory*, p. 124.

106 Ibid., pp. 53–54.

107 Ibid., p. 87.

108 Ibid., p. 151. 7 November, p. 1834.

109 Ibid., p. 186.

110 Hofschröer. *Wellington's Smallest Victory*, p. 131.

111 Balen, *A Model Victory* pp. 186–87.

112 Ibid., p. 207.

113 Hofschröer. *Wellington's Smallest Victory*, p. 75.

114 Ibid., p. 79.

115 Balen, *A Model Victory*, p. 208.

116 'Model of the Field of Waterloo', *The Times*, 6 March 1838.

117 Balen, *A Model Victory*, pp. 210–11.

118 'Plan of the Battle of Waterloo', *The Times*, 8 October 1838.

119 Hofschröer. *Wellington's Smallest Victory*, pp. 162–63.

120 Ibid., pp. 165–66.

121 Thierry Lentz, 'IV. La Prise des Voitures de Napoléon par les Prussiens au soir de Waterloo', *La Berlin De Napoléon: Le Mystere du Butin de Waterloo* (Paris: Editons Albin Michel, 2012), p. 65.

122 Balen, *A Model Victory*, p. 218.

123 Arthur Wellesley Duke of Wellington, *The dispatches of Field Marshal the Duke of Wellington, K. G. during his various campaigns in India, Denmark, Portugal, Spain, the Low Countries, and France. From 1799 to 1818.* Compiled from official and authentic documents, by Lieut. Colonel Gurwood. (London: John Murray, 1837–1839), pp. 146–49.

124 Ibid., p. 219. Letter to Lady Wilton, 23 April, p. 1840.

125 Ibid., p. 220.

126 Ibid., p. 229.

127 Ibid., p. 233.

128 Ibid., pp. 238–39.

129 'History of the Waterloo Campaign', *The Times*, 27 January 1845.

130 Ibid.

131 Siborne, *History of the Waterloo Campaign*, p. 191.

132 Ibid., p. 355.

133 Ibid.

134 Ibid., p. 374.

135 Balen, *A Model Victory*, pp. 235–36.

136 Hofschröer. *Wellington's Smallest Victory*, pp. 196–97.

137 'History of the Waterloo Campaign', *The Times*, 27 January1845.

138 George Gleig, *Story of the Battle of Waterloo* (London: John Murray, 1847), pp. i-iv.

139 Ibid.

140 Balen, *A Model Victory*, p. 241.

141 William Siborne, *History of the Waterloo Campaign* (London: Greenhill, 1990. Reprinting of London: T & W. Boone, 1848 edition), p. ix.

142 Hofschröer. *Wellington's Smallest Victory*, p. 227.

143 Siborne noted in his book on page 154 that the incident took place near 9p.m. in a drizzling rain. More amazing was the claim that Wellington saw Blücher fall from his horse at the end of the battle! Siborne also pointed out the physical impossibility of this occurring since from Quatre Bras the heights of Bry and Marbais are between the two positions.

144 Siborne, *History*, p. xiii.

145 Ibid., p. xiv.

146 Ibid., p. xxvii.

147 Balen, *A Model Victory*, pp. 243–44.

148 Ibid, p. 245.

149 Hofschröer, *Wellington's Smallest Victory*, p. 30.

150 Balen, *A Model Victory*, pp. 246–47.

151 Museum of Waterloo, uncatalogued item, account of Edward Jewett, in *Livre D'Or 1878–1879.* 9 July 1879.

152 Ibid., pp. 254–55.

153 Jacques Logie, *Waterloo: The Campaign of 1815* (Stroud, United Kingdom: Editions Racine, 2003), p. 201.

154 Ibid.

155 Ibid., p. 202.
156 Andrew Uffindell, *On the Fields of Glory: The Battlefields of the 1815 Campaign* (London: Greenhill Books, 1996), p. 33.
157 Ibid.
158 'Monument at Waterloo', *The Times*, 25 October 1825.
159 Uffindell, *On the Fields of Glory*, p. 34.
160 Tony Linck, *Napoléon's Generals: The Waterloo Campaign* (Chicago: The Emperor's Press, 1993), p. 118.
161 Logie, *Waterloo 1815*, p. 210.
162 Frank Huggett, *Modern Belgium* (New York, NY: Prager, 1969), p. 22.
163 Logie, *Waterloo 1815*, p. 210.
164 Emile Cammaerts, *The Keystone of Europe* (London: Peter Davies Ltd., 1939), p. 52.
165 Logie, *Waterloo 1815*, p. 210.
166 'Belgium', *New York Dailey Times*, 9 March 1852.
167 Logie, *Waterloo 1815*, p. 211.
168 Grace Greenwood, 'Notes from Over the Sea: Sights at Waterloo-Present condition of the Battlefield', *The New York Times*, 13 September 1875.
169 Don Russell, *The Lives and Legends of Buffalo Bill* (Norman, Oklahoma: University of Oklahoma Press, 1960), pp. 370–71.
170 Ibid.
171 John Burke, *Buffalo Bill: The Noblest Whiteskin.* (New York: G. P. Putnam's Sons, 1973), pp. 212–13.
172 Museum of Waterloo, uncatalogued item, '*Livre D'Or Hotel du Musee: 1888–1893*', Buffalo Bill (4 June 1891).
173 Joseph Rosa and Robin May, *Buffalo Bill and his Wild West* (Lawrence Kansas: University Press of Kansas, 1989), p. 154.

Chapter 7

1 Frederick Georges, *Images et Nostalgie Entre Bruxelles Waterloo, Braine-L'alleud* (Wavre, Belgium, Rail Memories, 2008), pp. 62–86.
2 George Speekaert, *Relics et Memorials of the Battles of 1815 in Belgium* (Brabant: ARC, 2000), p. 9.
3 Robin de Salle, 'Musees de Waterloo de 1815 it 1914', *Waterloorama*, No. 14 (Waterloo: Office of Tourism, 2008), p. 9.
4 Stephan Oettermann, *The Panorama: History of a Mass Medium* (New York: Zone Books, 1997), p. 51
5 Speekaert, *Relics and Memorials of the Battles of 1815 in Belgium*, p. 10.
6 Uffindell, *On the Fields of Glory*, p. 85.
7 Ibid.
8 Ibid.

9   Ibid., p. 88.
10   Oettermann, *The Panorama: History of a Mass Medium*, p. 49.
11   Ibid.
12   Brand Whitlock, *Belgium a Personal Narrative*, (New York, NY: Appleton, 1920), pp. 250–51.
13   Ibid., p. 247.
14   'March of the Second and Fourth Armies', *The Times*, 22 November 1918.
15   Brand Whitlock, *Belgium a Personal Narrative*, p. 98.
16   'Through German Eyes: Waterloo Celebrations in Brussels', *The Times*, 26 June 1915. Taken from German Newspapers.
17   'Waterloo', *The British Medical Journal*, 1, No. 2842 (1915), pp. 1050–52.
18   Yves Vander Cuysen. *Un Siecle d'histoires en Brabant Wallon* (Bruxelles: Editions Racine 2007), p. 53.
19   'Loi pour la preservation du champ de bataille de Waterloo', *Moniteur Belge*, 27 March 1914.
20   Ellen Furlough, 'Making Mass Vacations and Consumer Culture in France, 1930s to 1970s', *Comparative Studies in Society and History*, 40, No. 2 (1998), pp. 252–55.
21   Ibid.
22   Interview with Marie Therese Brassine.
23   Yves Vander Cruysen. *Recits de Guerre en Brabant et Wallon* (Bruxelles: Editions Racine 2004), p. 71.
24   Vander Cruysen. *Un Siecle d'histoires en Brabant Wallon*, p. 85.
25   http://www.longshoresoldiers.com/2013/07/on-leave-in-waterloo-1945.html, 'On Leave 1945', Longshore Soldiers, 27 July 2013, Andrew Broznya.
26   Livre D'Or. Waterloo Battlefield. Dated 1965.
27   Interview with Marie Therese Brassine.
28   Vander Cruysen. *Un Siecle d'histoires en Brabant Wallon*, pp. 144–145.
29   Ibid.
30   Alan Riding, 'The Second Battle of Waterloo', *New York Times,* 15 November 1998. http://search.ebscohost.com/login.aspx?direct=true&db=nfh&AN=1300256&site=ehost-live.
31   Brigitte Mahuzier, 'Forget Waterloo', *South Central Review*, 29, No. 3 (2012), pp. 5–19.
32   Neil Asher Silberman, 'Reshaping Waterloo', *Archaeology*, 60, No. 1 (2007), pp. 53–58.
33   Ibid.
34   https://www.independent.co.uk/travel/uk/battle-of-waterloo-how-the-french-em-peror-has-won-the-war-for-tourists-wallets-10324480.html, Gilbert Gauvin, 'Battle of Waterloo: How the French Emperor has won the war for tourists' wallets', 16 June 2015.
35   Kubula would be jailed for corruption in 2015.
36   Interview with Mark Schneider.

37   Jess Handsher and Olivier Roland, *Being Napoléon*, film (TM International: Bywater Films, 2017).

Conclusion

1   Although his brother-in-law has one called Rue de Condorcet.
2   Interview with Michael De Grouchy. Private family records.
3   http://www.bloomberg.com/apps/news?pid=newsarchive&sid=aBkB37NGricc, 'Yank Plays Napoléon, Wellington Is M. I. A. in Waterloo Rematch', Bloomberg Media, accessed 23 June 2013. James G. Neuger, 16 June 2009.
4   http://online.wsj.com/article/SB100014241278873241009045784004006609638 28.html, 'Complex Napoléon Rivalry Heads for Its Waterloo', *Wall Street Journal* online, accessed 30 September 2013, Max Colchester, 7 April 2013.
5   Grab, Alexander, *Napoléon and the Transformation of Europe* (New York: Palgrave Macmillan, 2003), p. 203.

References

Primary sources

Battle of Waterloo: Collected from Official Documents (New York: Jon Evans and Co., 1819)

Barker, Henry Aston. *Description of the field of battle, and disposition of the troops engaged in the action, fought on the 18th of June, 1815, near Waterloo; illustrative of the representation of that great event in the Panorama, Leicester-Square* (London: Adlard Publishing, 1816)

Ceremonie de la pose de le premier piers du monument Victor Hugo a Waterloo 22 September 1912 (Paris: Mynier et Brumeur, 1912)

Clausewitz, Carl von. *On War*, trans. by Michael Howard and Peter Paret (Princeton, NJ: Princeton University Press, 1984)

_____. *On Wellington: A Critique of Waterloo*, trans. by Peter Hofschröer (Norman, Oklahoma: Oklahoma University Press, 2010)

Drouet, Juliette. *My Beloved Toto: Letters to Victor Hugo 1833–1882*, trans. by Victoria Larson (Albany, NY: State University of New York, 2005)

Gérard, Étienne. *Quelques documens sur la bataille de Waterloo: propres a éclairer la question portée devant le public par M. le marquis de Grouchy* (Paris: Verdière, 1829)

Gleig, George. *Story of the Battle of Waterloo* (London: John Murray, 1847)

Gourgaud, Gaspard. *Campagne de dix-huit cent quinze, ou, Relation des operations militaires qui ont lieu en France et en Belgique pendant les cent jours* (London: Ridgeway, 1818)

_____. *Saint Helene: Journal inedit de 1815 a 1818* (Paris: Ernest Flammarion,1899)

_____. *Talks of Napoléon at Saint Helena*, trans. by Elizabeth Latimer (Chicago: AC McClurg, 1903)

Greenwood, Grace. 'Notes from Over the Sea: Sights at Waterloo-Present condition of the Battlefield', *The New York Times*, 13 September 1875.

Grouchy, Emmanuel. *Observations sur la relation de la campagne de 1815, publiée par le général Gourgaud: et réfutation de quelques-unes des assertions d'autres écrits rélatifs à la bataille de Waterloo* (Philadelphia: Hurtel, 1818)

_____. *Observations sur la relation de la campagne de 1815, publiée par le général Gourgaud: et réfutation de quelques-unes des assertions d'autres écrits rélatifs à la bataille de Waterloo* (Paris: Chez Chaumerot, 1819)

_____. *Fragments historiques relatifs à la campagne de 1815 et à la bataille de Waterloo par le général Grouchy. De l'influence que peuvent avoir sur l'opinion les documents publiés par M. le comte Gérard* (Paris: Chez Firmin Didot, 1829)

_____. *Refutation de quelques articles des mémoires de M. le Duc de Rovigo* (Paris: Chez Firmin Didot, 1829)

_____. *Fragments historiques relatifs a la campagne de 1815 et a la bataille de Waterloo: lettre a messieurs Méry et Barthélemy* (Paris: Chez Firmin Didot, 1829)

_____. *Relation Succincte de La Campagne en Belgique* (Paris: Delanchy, 1843)

_____. *Mémoires du Maréchal de Grouchy* (Paris: Dentu, 1874)

Hugo, Adele. *Victor Hugo, By A Witness To His Life*, trans. by Charles Wilbour (New York: Carleton Publishers, 1864)

Hugo, Joseph. *Memoires du General Hugo*, Tome III.P (Paris: Chez Ladvocat, 1823)

_____. *Memoires du General Hugo* (Paris: Jadis et Naguere, 1934)

Hugo, Victor. *Journal 1830–1848*, originally published in Paris by Henri Guillemin (Brooklyn, NY: Greenwood Press, 1970)

_____. *Les Chatiments*, Chapter II, trans. by author (Brussels: H Samuel, 1853)

_____. *Les Misérables*, trans. by Charles Wilbour (New York: The Modern Library, 1976)

_____. *The Memoirs of Victor Hugo* (New York: G.W. Dillingham Co., 1899)

Jomini, Antoine Henri, *The Art of War*, trans. by G. H. Mendell and W. P. originally titled *Précis de l'art de la guerre*, printed in 1838 (Cragihill Westport Connecticut: Greenwood Press Publishers, 1862)

_____. *The Political and Military History of the Campaign of Waterloo*, trans. by S. V. Benet (New York: Redfield Publishers, 1852)

Las Cases, Emmanuel. *Memorial de Saint Hélène*, journal of the private life and conversations of the Emperor Napoléon at Saint Helena (Boston: Wells and Lilly, 1823)

M'Donogh, Felix. *The Hermit in London; or, sketches of English manners* (London: Henry Colburn and Co., 1821)

Méry, Auguste and Joseph Barthélemy, *Waterloo: Au General Bourmont* (Paris: A. J. Denain, 1829)

Müffling, Carl. *The Memoirs of Baron Müffling*, trans. by Peter Hofschröer (London: Greenhill Books, 1997)

Napoléon Bonaparte. *Correspondence de Napoléon 1st* (Paris: Dentu, 1868)

Napoléon, Louis. *Napoléonic Ideas*, trans. by James A. Dorr (New York: Appleton & Company, 1859)

Pickett, La Salle Corbell. *Pickett and his Men* (Atlanta: Foote and Davies, 1899)

Regnault-Warin, Jean Joseph. *Mémoires Pour Servir à la Vie d'un Homme Célèbre* (Paris: Plancher, 1819)

Siborne, William. *History of the Waterloo Campaign*, reprinting of T. & W. Boone, London, 1848 edition. (London: Greenhill, 1990)

Scott, Walter. *The Field of Waterloo* (New York: Leavitt and Allen, 1858)

_____. *The Life of Napoléon Bonaparte* (London: John Murray, 1815)

_____. *Paul's Letters to his Kinsfolk* (London: John Murray, 1816)

Ségur, Philippe-Paul. Count de. *Napoléon's Russian Campaign* (Alexandria, VA: Time Life Books, 1980)

Soult, Napoléon Hector. *Mémoires du maréchal-général Soult*, pub. par son fils (Paris: Librairie d'Amyot, 1854)

Soult, Nicolas. *Memoirs Justicatif de Monsieur Le Marechal Soult Duc de Dalmatie* (Paris: Le Normant, 1815)

Thackeray, William Makepiece. *The Second Funeral of Napoléon and Chonicle of the Drum* (London: Hugh Cunningham, 1841)

Wellesley, Arthur, Duke of Wellington. *The dispatches of Field Marshal the Duke of Wellington, K. G. during his various campaigns in India, Denmark, Portugal, Spain, the Low Countries, and France. From 1799 to 1818. Compiled from official and authentic documents, by Lieut. Colonel Gurwood* (London: John Murray, 1837–1839)

Whitlock, Brand. *Belgium a Personal Narrative* (New York, NY: Appleton, 1920)

Archival sources

SHD or Service historique de la défense
Dossier 6Yd 26a
Series C^{2}49
Museum of Waterloo Archive
'Livre D'Or Hotel du Musee' 1878–1879
'Livre D'Or Hotel du Musee' 1880–1884
'Livre D'Or Hotel du Musee' 1888–1893
Private Archive of Records of Chateau Villette, Oise France
Records of Chateau Villette

Newspapers

Albany Advertiser
Le Constitutionnel
Le Moniteur Universal
Moniteur Belge
The New York Times
The New York Dailey Times
Niles Weekly Register
The Times
Weekly Aurora

Internet sources

Colchester, Max. '*Complex Napoléon Rivalry Heads for Its Waterloo*', http://online.wsj.com/article/SB10001424127887324100904578400400660963828.html, *Wall Street Journal* online, accessed 30 September 2013

Kane, Katherine. '*Robert Barker's Leicester Square Panorama: The Rotunda*', http://regencyredingote.wordpress.com/2012/08/03/Robert-barkers-leicester-squarepanorama-the-rotunda/ The Regency Redingote Kalligraph, accessed 24 February 2013

Neuger, James G. '*Yank Plays Napoléon, Wellington Is M.I.A. in Waterloo Rematch*', http://www.bloomberg.com/apps/news?pid=newsarchive&sid=aBkB37NGricc, Bloomberg Media, accessed 23 June 2013.

Secondary sources

Anderson, James. *Sir Walter Scott and History* (Edinburgh: The Edina Press, 1981)

Arnold, James. *Marengo and Hohenlinden* (South Yorkshire: UK: Pen and Sword, 2005)

Artom, Guido. *Napoléon is Dead in Russia*, trans. Muriel Grindrod (New York: Antheneum, 1970)

Balen, Malcolm. *A Model Victory*. London (London: Fourth Estate, 2005)

Barbier, Louis. *Le General de la Horie 1766–1812* (Paris: Dujarric, 1904)

Barnett, George Smith. *Victor Hugo, His Life and Work* (London: Ward and Downey, 1885)

Besson, Andre. *Victor Hugo: Vie d'un Geant* (Chaintreaux, France: Editions France-Empire Monde, 2010)

Blaufarb, Rafe. *Bonapartists in the Borderlands* (Tuscaloosa, Alabama: University of Alabama Press, 2005)

_____. *The French Army 1750–1820* (NY: Manchester University Press, 2002)

_____. *Napoléon Symbol for an Age: A brief History with Documents* (New York: St Martin's Press, 2008)

Blond, Georges. *La Grande Armée* (New York, NY: Sterling Publishing, 1997)

Bonura, Michael. *Under the Shadow of Napoléon* (New York: New York University Press, 2012)

Britt III, Albert Sidney. *The Wars of Napoléon* (Wayne, NJ: Avery Publishing, 1985)

Brombert, Victor. *Victor Hugo and the Visionary Novel* (Cambridge, Massachusetts: Harvard University Press, 1984)

Burke, John. *Buffalo Bill: The Noblest Whiteskin* (New York: G.P. Putnam's Sons, 1973)

Cammaerts, Emile. *The Keystone of Europe* (London: Peter Davies Ltd., 1939)

Campbell, Sir Neil. *Napoléon on Elba* (Welwyn Garden City, UK: Ravenhall Book, 2004)

Chandler, David. *The Campaigns of Napoléon* (New York, NY: Macmillan Publishing, 1966)

_____. *Napoléon's Marshals* (New York, NY: Macmillan Publishing, 1987)

_____. *Waterloo: The Hundred Days* (London: Osprey Publishing, 1980)

Charras, Jean Baptiste Adolphe. *Histoire de la campagne de 1815: Waterloo* (Bruxelles: 1863)

Colley, Linda. *Britons: Forging the Nation 1707–1837* (London: Vintage, 1996)

Connelly, Owen. *Blundering to Glory* (Wilmington, DE: Scholarly Resources, 1987)

Crawford, Thomas. *Walter Scott* (Edinburgh: Scottish Academic Press, 1982)

Dauge, Everett. *Henri Clarke and the Malet Conspiracy* (Tallahassee, Fl: Consortium on Revolutionary Europe, 1996)

Delderfield, R. F. *Napoléon's Marshals* (New York, NY: Cooper Square Press, 2002)

Deresiewicz, William. 'Persuasion: Widowhood and Waterloo', in *Jane Austen and the Romantic Poets* (New York: Chichester: Columbia University Press, 2004)

Dupuy, Trevor. The Harper Encyclopedia of Military Biography (Edison, NJ: Castle Books, 1992)

Elting, John. *Swords Around a Throne* (New York: The Free Press, 1988)

Furlough, Ellen, 'Making Mass Vacations and Consumer Culture in France, 1930s to 1970s', *Comparative Studies in Society and History*, 40, No. 2 (1998)

Georges, Frederick. *Images et Nostalgie Entre Bruxelles Waterloo, Braine-L'alleud* (Wavre, Belgium, Rail Memories, 2008).

Grab, Alexander. *Napoléon and the Transformation of Europe* (New York: Palgrave Macmillan, 2003)

Grossman, Kathryn. *Figuring Transcendence in Les Misérables: Hugo's Romantic Sublime* (Carbondale and Edwardsville, Illinois: Southern Illinois Press, 1994)

Handsher, Jess and Roland, Olivier. *Being Napoléon*. film (TM International: Bywater Films, 2017)

Harrington, Peter. *British Artists and War* (London: Greenhill Books, 1993)

Hayethornthwaite, Philip J. *Napoléon the Final Verdict* (New York, NY: Sterling Publishing, 1996)

Hazareesingh, Sudhir. *The Legend of Napoléon* (London: Granta Books, 2004)

Hofschöer, Peter. *1815 The Waterloo Campaign: The German Victory* (London: Greenhill Books, 1999)

_____. *Waterloo 1815: Wavre, Plancenoit and the Race to Paris* (East Yorkshire, UK: Pen and Sword Books, 2006)

_____. *Wellington's Smallest Victory: The Duke, the Model Maker and the Secret of Waterloo* (London: Faber and Faber, 2004)

Houssaye, Henry. *Waterloo: 1815*, 60th edition, first published 1889 (Paris: Perrin et cie, 1910)

Houston, John Porter. *Victor Hugo* (Boston: Twayne Publishers, 1988)

Howarth, David. *Waterloo: Day of Battle* (New York: Atheneum Books, 1968)

Huggett, Frank. *Modern Belgium* (New York, NY: Prager, 1969)

Hunter, T. M. *Napoléon in Victory and Defea.* (Ottawa, Canada: Queen's Printer, 1964)

Johnson, David. *The French Cavalry 1792–1815* (London: Belmont, 1989)

Kelly, Hyde. *The Battle of Wavre and Grouchy's Retreat* (London: John Murray, 1905)

Lacroix, Jean. *Victor Hugo, Mille Jour en Belgique* (Waterloo, Belgium: Ministry of Culture, 2002)

Leggiere, Michael. *The Fall of Napoléon: The Allied Invasion of France 1813–1814* (New York: Cambridge University Press, 2007)

Le Goff, Jacques. *History and Memory* (New York: Columbia University Press, 1992)

Lentz, Thierry, 'IV. La Prise des Voitures de Napoléon par les Prussiens au soir de Waterloo', *La Berlin De Napoléon: Le Mystere du Butin de Waterloo* (Paris: Editons Albin Michel, 2012)

Linck, Tony. *Napoléon's Generals: The Waterloo Campaign* (Chicago: The Emperor's Press, 1993)

Logie, Jacques. *Waterloo: The 1815 Campaign* (Stroud, United Kingdom: Racine, 2003)

Lunt, James D., 'The Odd Man Out: Grouchy' in David Chandler, editor, *Napoléon's Marshals* (New York, NY: Macmillan Publishing, 1987)

Mahuzier, Brigitte. 'Forget Waterloo', *South Central Review*, 29, No. 3 (2012)

Marchand, Louis-Joseph. *In Napoléon's Shadow*, trans. Proctor Jones (San Francisco, CA: Proctor Jones Publishing Company, 1998)

Markham, David. *Imperial Glory: The Bulletins of Napoléon's Grande Armée, 1805–1814* (London: Greenhill, 2003)

Nora, Pierre. *Rethinking France: The Sites of Memory* (Chicago: University of Chicago Press, 2001)

Ocampo, Emilio. *The Emperor's Last Campaign* (Tuscaloosa, AL: University of Alabama Press, 2009)

Oettermann, Stephan. *The Panorama: History of a Mass Medium* (New York: Zone Books, 1997)

Oleksijczuk, Denise. 'The dynamics of spectatorship in the first panoramas: Vision, the body and British imperialism, 1787–1820' (University of British Columbia: Dissertation, 2001)

Paret, Peter. 'Clausewitz' in *Makers of Modern Strategy* (Princeton, NJ: Princeton University Press, 1986)

Parker, Harold. *Three Napoléonic Battles* (Durham, NC: Duke University Press, 1983)

Reardon, Carol. *Pickett's Charge in History and Memory* (Chapel Hill, NC: University of North Carolina Press, 1997)

Riding, Alan. 'The Second Battle of Waterloo', *New York Times*, 15 November 1998

Robb, Graham. *Victor Hugo* (New York: W.W. Norton & Company, 1997)

Rosa, Joseph and Robin May. *Buffalo Bill and his Wild West* (Lawrence Kansas: University Press of Kansas, 1989)

Ross, Michael. *The Reluctant King* (New York: Mason/Charter Publishers, 1977)

Russell, Don. *The Lives and Legends of Buffalo Bill* (Norman, Oklahoma: University of Oklahoma Press, 1960)

Salle, Robin de. 'Musees de Waterloo de 1815 it 1914', *Waterloorama*, No. 14 (Waterloo: Office of Tourism, 2008)

Sauvigny, Guillaume. *The Bourbon Restoration* (Philadelphia: The University of Pennsylvania Press, 1966)

Shapiro, Fred and Joseph Epstein, *Yale Book of Quotations* (NY: Yale University Press: 2006)

Shaw, Phillip. *Waterloo and the Romantic Imagination* (London: Palgrave Publishing, 2002)

Shy, John. 'Jomini' in *Makers of Modern Strategy* (Princeton, NJ: Princeton University Press, 1986)

Silberman, Neil Asher. 'Reshaping Waterloo', *Archaeology*, 60, No. 1 (2007)

Six, Georges. *Dictionnaire Biographique Des Generals et Amiraux Francis de La Revolution et de L'Empire* (Paris: Libraie Historique et Nobilaire, 1934)

Speekaert, George. *Relics and Memorials of the Battles of 1815 in Belgium* (Brabant: ARC, 2000)

Treasure, Geoffrey. *Who's Who in Late Hanoverian Britain 1789–1837* (Mechanicsburg, PA: Stackpole Books, 2002)

Uffindell, Andrew. *On the Fields of Glory: The Battlefields of the 1815. Campaign* (London: Greenhill Books, 1996)

Vander Cruysen, Yves. *Recits de Guerre en Brabant et Wallon* (Bruxelles: Editions Racine 2004)

VanderWolk, William. *Victor Hugo in Exile* (Cranbury, NJ: Associated University Press: 2006)

White, Kelly Hyde. *The Battle of Wavre and Grouchy's Retreat* (London: John Murray, 1905)

Wieder, Ben. *Assassination at Saint Helena Revisited* (New York: John Wiley and Sons, Inc., 1995)

Williams, Chris. A Companion to Nineteenth Century Britain (Malden: MA, 2004, p. 81)

Winter, Jay. *Sites of Memory, Sites of Mourning* (New York: Cambridge University Press, 1995)

Wood, Gillen D'Arcy. *The Shock of the Real: Romanticism and the Visual Culture, 1760–1860* (London: Palgrave. 2001)

Wood, Harriet. *Sir Walter Scott* (Devon, UK: Northcote House Publishers, 2006)

Interviews

Michael De Grouchy

Marie Therese Brassine

Mark Schneider

Index